THE
ENTRUSTED
LEADER

THE
ENTRUSTED
LEADER

Developing Rock Solid Core Values

L. Hollis Jones, DMin

BCP

The ENTRUSTED Leader
Developing Rock Solid Core Values

All Scripture quotations, unless otherwise indicated, are taken from the
Holy Bible, New International Version®. *NIV*®. Copyright © 1973, 1978, 1984
by International Bible Society.

Scripture taken from the *New American Standard Bible,* © Copyright
© 1960, 1962, 1963, 1968, 1971, 1972, 1973, 1975, 1977, 1995 by The
Lockman Foundation.

Brown Christian Press
16200 North Dallas Parkway, Suite 170
Dallas, Texas 75248
www.brownbooks.com
(972) 381-0009

Serving with Excellence.

ISBN 978-1-934812-81-5
Library of Congress Control Number 2010938689
Printed in the United States.
10 9 8 7 6 5 4 3 2 1

For more information about Dr. L. Hollis Jones and
The Center for Entrusted Leadership, please visit EntrustedLeader.com.

This book is dedicated to followers from all walks of life—home, work,

church, civic, athletic, and academic—who long to be encouraged

and united by a leader whose decisions and actions proceed from core

values forged from the absolute truth of God's Word.

Contents

Acknowledgments

To Dawn, thanks for being my greatest source of encouragement, a reliable sounding board of ideas, standing shoulder-to-shoulder with me in all endeavors, and, most importantly, loving me unconditionally and faithfully praying for me. You truly are a wife of noble character whom I love more than words can express.

To every leader I have had the honor to follow who has invested wisdom, time, and energy to mentor me, I pledge to pass on to others what you have entrusted to me.

To every friend who has faithfully walked beside me, thanks for supporting, encouraging, counseling, and believing in me. I hope and pray I have been as faithful a friend to you as you have been to me.

To every person I have had the opportunity to lead, thank you for allowing me to serve, guide, and teach you. I hope our time together encouraged your heart.

AUTHOR'S NOTE:
What This Book Is About

The ENTRUSTED Leader seeks to help a leader establish a positive relational influence on followers. By encouraging the hearts of others, a leader can make good relationships better and even transform relationships mired in negativity into ones energized by undying loyalty. Healthier, more functional leader-to-follower relations grow when nurtured by the positive influence of encouragement. The leader who connects to followers in an uplifting manner stands to realize a strong sense of personal significance and satisfaction.

The first step a leader must take to develop more functional relationships with followers involves making a commitment to serve a calling higher than self. An Entrusted Leader's influence starts with a selfless heart that considers the needs of others first and foremost. Any leader will find it difficult to positively influence others if he or she consistently puts self-interests ahead of others and approaches relationships from the standpoint of self-centered core values.

Tragically, many otherwise skilled leaders fail to make any connection between their leadership actions (which originate within their core values) and the type of influence they exert on others—positive or otherwise! Consequently, leaders with underdeveloped or dysfunctional core values are left wondering why their leadership behavior fails to have a positive influence on followers. To become a different type of leader, an Entrusted Leader, one must look beyond just changing outward behaviors and inspire a person to allow biblical truth to transform one's inner core values.

So what is this book about? The ENTRUSTED Leader addresses every skilled leader's need to transform one's heart and develop biblically sound core values. This book is about developing core values that naturally produce leadership behaviors that in turn encourage the hearts of others and promote healthy leader-to-follower relationships.

INTRODUCTION:
A Leader's Journey toward Influence
and Significance

Leaders naturally seek to influence others. Most leaders want to know that their attempts at influence make a difference, are positively received, effect change, and get results. How a leader relates to followers ultimately determines the nature, receptivity, durability, and effectiveness of his or her influence.

Leaders also seek significance. Most leaders want to know that their attempts at influence bring purpose, meaning, authenticity, blessings, and an enduring legacy to their life. Real and lasting significance can come to the leader who uses all God has entrusted to serve a calling higher than self. The leader who selflessly encourages the hearts of others journeys a path toward an enduring legacy.

The opportunity to experience eternal purpose while having a temporal impact on followers lies within the reach of every leader's grasp. The leader who assumes the role of chief encourager of others will receive personal blessings that far exceed the love of money and the pursuit of silver and gold.

The relationship between the leader and the follower stands as the critical link between influence and significance. The quality of a leader's influence on followers can only be judged by evaluating the health of this relationship. At the same time, leaders who make healthy leader-to-follower relationships a priority typically experience meaning and purpose that transcends one's temporal existence.

Encouraging the hearts of others creates positive influence. Relationships flourish when fueled by encouragement. Discouragement, however, negatively impacts others and drains the life out of a relationship. Encouraging leaders find great satisfaction in positively influencing the lives of followers.

The author believes that deep down inside, most leaders desire the respect, admiration, and credibility of loyal followers. Few, if any, people set out to be the type of leader nobody wants to follow. Unfortunately for many leaders, the hunger for success eclipses their appetite for acceptance by followers, resulting in attitudes and actions that alienate others. Tragically the pinnacle of worldly leadership success is often occupied by lonely people who see no real purpose for their life and are loathed by those they have sought to control for selfish gains. A leader does not have to exist in this lonesome, meaningless, disrespected state.

The hope of finding significance through the positive influence on followers can become a reality for any leader. The journey to meaningful leadership involves uniting others in healthy relationships by encouraging their hearts and selflessly serving them. Human nature deceives a leader into believing that purpose in life comes from the acquisition of things, the consolidation of power, and the promotion of self-interests. The reality of life is, however, that purpose and significance can be found only by using all that God has entrusted to serve a calling higher than self for the benefit of others.

The choice to selflessly serve and encourage others springs from deep within a leader's heart. The inner core values of a leader, outwardly expressed as priorities, attitudes, and actions, have either a positive or a negative influence on others. Where a leader resides along the encouragement to discouragement continuum depends on the development and maturity of one's core values.

Many leaders fail to reach their potential influence and functionality not because they lack skills or abilities but as a result of dysfunctional core values. Sadly, many sincere and well-intentioned leaders never experience meaning, purpose, and significance because of a nagging void deep inside their heart that cannot be filled by any amount of worldly success. One of the goals of this book is to guide a leader down the path of developing one's core values in order to unlock the door to influence and significance.

> ## One of the goals of this book is to guide a leader down the path of developing one's core values in order to unlock the door to influence and significance.

The ENTRUSTED Leader features a series of lessons concerning seven core values of biblically sound leadership. These seven core values characterize the type of leader I believe God desires each individual to become. Every follower of Jesus Christ who has been, or will be, entrusted with the privilege of leading others at home, in the office, or in his or her community, represents the ideal audience.

The author is a businessman by education (BSBA and MBA) and by profession. His work history includes numerous executive leadership positions, and he is currently a self-employed investment manager. The lessons contained in this book stem from the combination of the author's time as a student at Dallas Theological Seminary (MABS, DMin), years of personal study on the topic of leadership, and his practical experiences as a marketplace leader. The absolute truth of God's inerrant Word provides the lens by which these leadership studies and experiences have come into focus.

The author recognizes the obstacles that make consistent participation a real challenge for a leader considering participating in a leadership development program. Pressures from a busy office schedule, travel, early morning meetings, and unexpected problems make regular attendance difficult. Add to these constraints a long list of family commitments and personal interests, and society has a leader with little or no capacity for anything else, much less personal leadership development. These realities characterize the culture in which we live. My hope is that the simple format of The ENTRUSTED Leader will help busy leaders find the time to partake in these lessons in spite of these obstacles and constraints.

The ENTRUSTED Leader exists to encourage the development of the core values of a leader. The behavior of a leader reveals his or her core values and provides evidence of the true condition of one's inner nature, or heart. Core values reflect what a person believes to be true about the world in which he or she leads. Behavior follows core values. To change one's long-term leadership behavior, there must first be a change of core values. This book seeks to encourage the transformation of a leader's core values in a manner consistent with biblical truth.

A leader who claims to be a follower of Jesus Christ defines the target audience of *The ENTRUSTED Leader*. The journey of following Christ involves a lifelong process of one's inner nature and outward behavior being changed in a manner consistent with how Jesus lived and led. Every follower of Jesus Christ moves along this path. It does not matter how far one has progressed toward the image that Christ lays before us. This book strives to encourage the development of seven core values that move one closer to the standard of leadership behavior set by our Lord Jesus Christ.

The reader should note that *The ENTRUSTED Leader* makes no attempt to advance the development of a leader's professional, management, or leadership skills. The author assumes the reader already has or is in the process of acquiring the appropriate skills and knowledge required for the profession he or she has chosen. The leadership values and practices taught in *The ENTRUSTED Leader* are designed to complement a leader's professional skills and knowledge, not replace them.

Before you read any further, I must share with you a word of warning. I regret that I have to start with such somber and perhaps sobering thoughts. After years of teaching on the subject of biblical leadership and how it applies to followers of Jesus Christ who lead others, I have found that I have to be very clear on the following warning:

The core values and principles taught in *The ENTRUSTED Leader* make no guarantee that a participant's career and life will be successful from a worldly point of view. This leader development book and program do not teach a prescribed path to material gain, prosperity, or greater leadership responsibility. The application of these core values and principles may result in persecution. This persecution may come in a variety of forms that are detrimental to a participant's life and leadership career. Possible rewards are limited to unspecified spiritual growth and enrichment. Such persecution was spoken of by our Lord and Savior Jesus Christ in John 15:20 and by the Apostle Paul in 2 Timothy 3:12. I encourage you to read these and other similar passages and to consider the potential costs of following Jesus publicly. As Paul told the Thessalonians in 1 Thessalonians 3:1–4, consider yourself warned!

Many people who claim to be followers of Jesus Christ approach their role as a leader unaware that their leadership attitudes and actions emanate from core values that will not stand up to the scrutiny of biblical truth. These leaders often wonder why followers respond to their leadership in a disloyal and dysfunctional manner. The reality of this distressing state of leadership among Christ followers inspired this author to write *The ENTRUSTED Leader*. Two motivations in particular fueled this effort.

The first motivation for writing comes from a sense of disappointment that too many followers of Christ use secular, authority-based models of leadership to pursue the American dream (myth) of temporal prosperity, material gain, happiness, success, and security. These leaders blindly waste their lives and God's entrusted talents on investments intended to ingratiate themselves instead of how God intended, i.e., making serving and encouraging others the top priority. Unfortunately, these misguided investments often find reinforcement because these leaders achieve some measure of worldly success and mistake material gains as an indication of God's blessing or endorsement. In defense of these misguided leaders, however, their pastors, teachers, and mentors have failed to teach them that how and why they seek to lead others may be contrary to biblical truth. The pace of this pursuit has left many leaders burned out, stressed out, and dysfunctional when relating to followers, family, and friends.

The second motivation for writing comes from a sense of sadness that so many followers of Christ fail to recognize the potential for eternal significance and purpose that resides in every opportunity to lead. Many of these leaders have a limited view that opportunities to serve God exist only for professional ministers or those who volunteer through a church or parachurch ministry. Nothing could be further from God's truth. God calls every follower of Christ to lead and minister to others. God calls only a few into the ministry vocationally or professionally, but He calls the rest of us to serve on the front lines of our everyday lives at home, in the office, or in the community. Every leader-to-follower relationship has the potential for eternal significance and purpose. The author does not believe in random chance meetings but contends that every person that crosses his path offers a divine appointment. Wherever you live right now, God has put you there to lead, encourage, and serve others as He intended and desires. This realization brings significance to every opportunity you have to influence others and to every leader-to-follower relationship in which you engage.

The path to real and lasting influence and significance starts with biblically sound core values that are expressed with a sense of encouragement in every leader-to-follower relationship.

By writing *The ENTRUSTED Leader*, the author hopes to inspire Christ followers who lead to faithfully serve the portfolio of investments entrusted to them by God. These investments include all the talents and opportunities one possesses for leading another person. This book does not target church leaders and professional ministers, although they too can find application of these core values. This book focuses on the laity of the church who consider themselves followers of Jesus Christ and desire to lead as God intends and desires. The author envisions mobilizing a generation of skilled leaders who will adhere to biblical core values, apply biblical practices of leadership at home, in the office, and in society at large, and leverage every opportunity of leadership to encourage healthy and functional relationships. The path to real and lasting influence and significance starts with biblically sound core values that are expressed with a sense of encouragement in every leader-to-follower relationship.

The Essence of Leadership:
RELATIONSHIPS

Proverbs 29:2

Leadership cannot be separated from relationships—in particular leader-to-follower relationships!

It does not matter how visionary, smart, knowledgeable, charismatic, or skilled you are, your leadership effectiveness depends on how well you relate to followers and they to you.

Relationships can make or break a leader! The health and functionality of a leader's relationships with followers often determine one's success or failure. Leadership moves from theory to practice only in the context of human relationships. If asked to characterize leadership in a word, I would have to say "Relationships." A person cannot be developed or evaluated as a leader apart from followers; for without followers, a person has no one to lead. The leader-to-follower relationship constitutes the essence of leadership.

Leadership cannot be separated from relationships—in particular leader-to-follower relationships!

The ENTRUSTED Leader promotes healthy and functional leader-to-follower relationships. The primary responsibility for creating and sustaining vigorous relationships resides with the leader. Followers naturally respond to how a leader approaches them. An Entrusted Leader views all relationships as opportunities to serve others, not to be served by others. The Entrusted Leader approach to leading presupposes that others will follow voluntarily as the leader seeks to serve, encourage, and guide them. The selfless attitudes and actions of an Entrusted Leader promote the growth of healthy leader-to-follower relationships. This book intends to help you develop healthy relationships wherever you lead.

Solomon clearly understood the wisdom of evaluating a ruler based on how people responded to that ruler's approach:

> [2] *When the righteous thrive, the people rejoice;*
> *when the wicked rule, the people groan. (Prov. 29:2)*

Do followers rejoice or groan in response to your approach to leadership?

The manner in which a follower responds to a leader's approach accurately characterizes the vigor and functionality of the leader-to-follower relationship. Rejoicing indicates healthy and functional relationships, while groaning indicates weak and dysfunctional relationships. An Entrusted Leader selflessly applies God's truth and wisdom to all circumstances, resulting in followers who rejoice. Conversely followers groan under the oppression of a leader who ignores God's Word, wields power and authority, and orchestrates all circumstances to benefit self. The evaluation of a leader's effectiveness cannot be separated from how would-be followers relate and respond. Relationships with would-be followers will make or break a leader!

God desires and intends to use every follower of Christ as a leader. Those who choose to follow the path of leadership blazed by Jesus Christ can rest assured that God wants to use them to positively influence the lives of others through healthy relationships. God calls every follower of Christ to the role of a leader. The leaders God intends to use come in a wide variety of guises: a parent leading a child, a corporate executive leading a multibillion dollar company, a teacher instructing a classroom of students, a coach developing a team, an elected official serving constituents, a pastor discipling a church, a friend encouraging a friend. God calls followers of Jesus Christ to lead others.

Furthermore, in His timing, God will entrust to a Christ follower all that is required to lead others according to the Lord's desires and intentions. God uniquely creates and specifically endows every follower of Christ with certain skills and abilities. Wise leaders recognize the presence of intelligent design in the makeup of their talents. One might argue that the single most important function of a leader involves faithfully investing God's entrusted talents in the lives of one's followers. The author coined the term "Entrusted Leader" in order to capture the essence of an approach to leadership available to anyone who recognizes God's entrusted talents and desires to faithfully invest them in the lives of other people.

A vast network of potential followers encircles every follower of Christ who leads others. This follower network provides a leader with a vast array of relational investment opportunities. Followers come in many forms. The most obvious include people for whom a leader has primary responsibility, such as a direct report at work, a child in a family, a student in a classroom, a player on a team, or the constituency of an elected official.

Sometimes, however, others not directly under a person's authority also choose to follow. For example, a superior may find that a wise course of action involves defaulting to a subordinate's lead in a given situation. In the same way, many circumstances arise where a friend chooses to follow a peer's leadership voluntarily. The potential network of followers extends beyond those under a leader's direct line of authority and proceeds outward in all directions to everyone with whom the leader has a direct and/or indirect relationship.

Every person in a leader's network of followers represents a potential "relational" investment opportunity. A financial investor balances variables such as available assets, risk, potential returns, and a mix of investment opportunities (such as stocks, bonds, precious metals, real estate) to build a financial portfolio. Most financial investors strive to achieve a maximum return on investment (ROI) within the bounds of such variables. Likewise a "relational" investor should strive to achieve a maximum ROI on the talents entrusted to their life by God. A leader can only realize a superior return by investing these talents in the lives of followers. While reading *The ENTRUSTED Leader*, consider how every truth and principle discussed might find an application within the context of a leader-to-follower relationship.

A leader has many talents available to invest in followers, such as time, energy, wisdom, compassion, experience, knowledge, and expertise. In order to calculate a "relational" ROI, one must consider how these invested talents benefit the follower(s), not the leader. Once relational investing becomes a leader's goal, the leader sees results in the form of loyal followers who feel empowered and enabled to reach their full potential. The leader who makes serving followers a top priority has taken the first step of creating the healthy leader-to-follower relationship necessary for others to grow, produce, thrive, and rejoice.

How and where a person chooses to invest God's entrusted talents starts with the orientation of one's heart. If a leader's heart orients on self, the leader will invariably use followers to selfishly gain personal fame, fortune, and power. If a leader's heart orients on God, then the leader will invest one's talents in opportunities consistent with God's will and invariably strive to serve and positively impact the lives of followers. Every leader has a choice of two diametrically opposed orientations of the heart: self or God/others.

The orientation of a person's heart shapes one's core values. In turn, these core values, which reside deep inside one's heart, invariably come to the surface of one's life in the form of actions and attitudes. Core values find expression in how a leader treats followers. A close examination of a person's core values will reveal the true orientation of one's heart and shed light on the motivation behind one's attitudes and actions. To change one's attitudes and actions as a leader, a person must be willing to honestly evaluate one's core values and realign the orientation of one's heart to God/others if necessary.

A leader can apply most if not every truth and principle found in the Bible to relationships. Scripture has much to say about a person's relationship with God and one's relationships with other people. The Bible truthfully reveals how the Creator desires and intends His creation to relate to Him. The Bible also truthfully reveals how God intends and desires His creatures to relate to each other. Sin has distorted our view of both our vertical relationship with God and our horizontal relationships with other people. Consequently only the Bible provides us a reliable source of information for how we should relate to God and others. When the truth of the Bible governs the leader-to-follower relationship, the followers rejoice!

Consider the Ten Commandments as an example. The first five commandments govern a man's relationship with God. The second five commandments govern a man's relationship with others. The leader who applies these commandments to one's life will relate well to God and others.

A Man's Relationship with God—Commandments 1–5:

[3] *You shall have no other gods before me.*

[4] *You shall not make for yourself an idol . . .*

[5] *You shall not bow down to them or worship them . . .*

[7] *You shall not misuse the name of the LORD your God . . .*

[8] *Remember the Sabbath day by keeping it holy.*

A Man's Relationship with Others—Commandments 6–10:

[12] *Honor your father and your mother . . .*

[13] *You shall not murder.*

[14] *You shall not commit adultery.*

[15] *You shall not steal.*

[16] *You shall not give false testimony against your neighbor.*

[17] *You shall not covet your neighbor's house . . . wife . . . manservant or maidservant, his ox or donkey, or anything that belongs to your neighbor.* (Ex. 20:3–17)

Leader-to-follower relationships constitute the essence of leadership. Investing in these relationships brings significance, meaning, and purpose to a leader. Although faithfully serving God's entrusted investments might make one a more effective temporal leader, the only lasting return on investment must be calculated in terms of eternal significance and purpose. Investing the talents of one's life can receive no greater return than to do so according to God's criteria for entrusting you with His valuables. For the leader striving to follow Christ, one's vast network of leader-to-follower relationships provides the marketplace for investing all God has entrusted.

Encouraging the hearts of others promotes healthy leader-to-follower relationships!

Heavenly treasures must become the goal of such investing, not earthly prosperity. Relationships will ultimately make you or break you as a leader, both on earth and in heaven. How you handle the relationships entrusted to you by God will stand as an indication of the orientation of your heart.

> [19] *"Do not store up for yourselves treasures on earth, where moth and rust destroy, and where thieves break in and steal.* [20] *But store up for yourselves treasures in heaven, where moth and rust do not destroy, and where thieves do not break in and steal.* [21] *For where your treasure is, there your heart will be also."*
> *(Matt. 6:19–21)*

> *Leadership cannot be separated from relationships—
> in particular the leader-to-follower relationship.*

> *Relationships constitute the essence of leadership. Wise leaders invest in temporal relationships and store up heavenly treasures.*

> *Encouraging the hearts of others promotes healthy
> leader-to-follower relationships!*

PERSONAL APPLICATION EXERCISE

Identify one leader-to-follower relationship (or set of relationships) you currently possess that affords you an opportunity to encourage the hearts of others. Describe and/or draw a picture of this relationship and kept it at hand as you progress through this book. You may find creating a reader's journal to combine your notes will be helpful.

2

The Higher Calling
of Leadership

Colossians 2:2–3

A sacred bond exists between God and a leader!

Every leader carries a higher calling to selflessly encourage the hearts of others.

The higher calling of leadership represents nothing less than an open invitation sent by the Lord God Almighty to every leader. This invitation beckons a leader to encourage and unite others based on God's unconditional love for all people.

This divine relationship and calling remains true for all of time for leaders who acknowledge God's presence in every leader-to-follower relationship, as well as those who do not. Leaders who encourage the hearts of others will reap healthy and functional relationships with followers and unite them in love.

Every leader carries a higher calling to selflessly encourage the hearts of others.

The Bible supports the concept of leadership. God's Word speaks positively in regard to one person leading another. The Apostle Paul encourages followers of Christ to recognize the legitimate authority of leaders because this leadership authority has been established by God (Rom.13:1). In his first letter to Timothy, Paul endorses leaders and encourages prayers for them (1 Tim. 2:1–4). Paul calls the job of a leader a fine work or a noble task (1 Tim. 3:1). Leadership is thus a biblically sound truth.

Influence defines a leader, not title, rank, or position. A title tells us what to call a person in a leadership position. Rank informs us how a leader stacks up in relation to others. Position delineates the scope of a leader's authority. Title, rank, and position most assuredly relate to a leader, but they cannot define one. Leaders must ultimately be evaluated based on the degree and nature of how they influence others.

In my experiences as a businessman, I have encountered many individuals who possessed an impressive title, rank, or position, yet their leadership influence on others was minimal or nonexistent. On the other hand, I have also observed people who held no official title, rank, or position, yet their leadership influence over others was significant.

Real leaders influence others with or without title, rank, or position. Without question, Jesus Christ stands as the most influential leader who ever lived. Even people who do not claim to follow him will agree with this judgment. Keep in mind that Jesus never held an officially recognized earthly title, rank, or position, yet his influence has endured for more than two thousand years. Influence defines a leader!

Leaders come in a variety of shapes and sizes. The question "Who is a leader?" invites a wide spectrum of answers. Some leaders hold a formal position as such, while for others the relationship with followers exists informally. The spectrum of leadership extends far and wide from a parent to a corporate executive, from a humanitarian worker to an elected politician, from a volunteer youth sports team coach to a university professor. Exerting leadership influence is not tied to a formal organizational chart. Informal leadership relationships with followers can be just as influential as formal ones. If you claim to follow Jesus Christ, you are a leader with potential for influence, whether you recognize it or not.

The role of the leader in a leader-to-follower relationship carries a higher calling. God considers every Christ follower a leader. Bond servants of Christ carry this higher calling to influence those they lead according to God's purposes. The Lord entrusts followers to a leader's care and expects a selfless discharge of this responsibility. Within the scope of His divine will, God stands ready to entrust anyone with all the talents required to flourish as a leader. God expects His Entrusted Leaders to heed a calling higher than self and to invest His assets serving others according to His will and purposes.

The higher calling of leadership involves encouraging the hearts of others in order that followers receive inspiration to become all God intended and form a bond of unity based on love. In his letter to the Colossians, the Apostle Paul indicates why he endures the struggles of leading:

> *² My purpose is that they may be encouraged in heart and united in love, so that they may have the full riches of complete understanding, in order that they may know the mystery of God, namely, Christ, ³ in whom are hidden all the treasures of wisdom and knowledge. (Col. 2:2–3)*

Paul states his twofold purpose for leading in terms of encouraging others and uniting them in love. His ultimate goal involves seeing his followers come to a complete understanding of Christ. These purposes and goal apply to any and every leader-to-follower relationship.

Every leader desires the respect and admiration of loyal followers. Healthy and functional leader-to-follower relationships yield positive results for any organization. From a parent raising a child to a corporate executive managing a team of associates, the challenges of leadership remain the same—how can the leader:

- Connect to followers in a more meaningful way?
- Attract loyal supporters who follow because of love and admiration?
- Empower others to develop their full potential as an individual?
- Gain the trust and respect of superiors, subordinates, and peers?
- Forge an authentic bond of unity with and among followers?
- Motivate others to give 110 percent effort?
- Give hope and courage to the downtrodden?
- Ensure justice for the oppressed and defend the weak?
- Provide a vision worthy of personal sacrifice?

- Help others see and believe what is possible?
- Encourage the hearts of others?

Encouragement holds the key to unlocking answers to these and many other leadership questions. The leader who masters the art of encouraging the hearts of others wins the respect and admiration of loyal followers. Leader-to-follower relationships cemented with courage grow in health and functionality.

Encouragement is not simple flattery. Lavishing insincere words of praise on a follower provides no benefits for a leader. Excessive adulation will not produce healthy leader-to-follower relationships. The adage "Flattery will get you nowhere" rings true when speaking of leadership.

The leader who masters the art of encouraging the hearts of others wins the respect and admiration of loyal followers.

The term "encourage" has two primary parts that relate to its meaning: "en" means to give or supply something to someone, and "courage" refers to one's inner strength or confidence to withstand adversity. Consider *Merriam-Webster's* definition of "courage": "mental or moral strength to venture, persevere, and withstand danger, fear, or difficulty."[1] Therefore, the leader who encourages the hearts of others is the leader whose words and actions serve to give courage to followers regardless of the difficulty of a situation.

Giving others courage involves much more than words. Wise leaders learn that followers gain in confidence when they accomplish assignments designed to stretch but not break their skills and knowledge. A good example would be a parent teaching a child to ride a bike. A normal progression of gaining confidence to ride a bike would start with a tricycle, move on to a bike with training wheels, and finally progress to a two-wheeler. Each step is designed to instill courage and confidence along the way.

Becoming a source of encouragement requires understanding the real needs and struggles of others. A wise leader learns the strengths and weaknesses of those who follow and responds accordingly. Knowing the fears and stresses of followers helps a leader choose the right words and actions when dealing with others. Leaders who relate well to others do so from a base of understanding his or her followers' thinking and emotions.

Fear holds a follower back. Insecurity causes a person to pause. Doubt creates passivity among workers. Anxiety often leads to dysfunctional actions and decisions. Stress diminishes the effectiveness of one's efforts. Influential leaders provide followers with the courage necessary to offset these and many other negative detractors to productivity. Providing courage builds healthy and functional leader-to-follower relationships.

God resides at the apex of a biblically sound hierarchy of leadership. This hierarchy has God at the vertical top with the leader and followers inhabiting a common horizontal plane. Within this hierarchical arrangement, God entrusts the leader with certain responsibilities and authorities in regard to followers; however, the leader and the follower each maintain independent relationships with God.

God

Leader-to-Follower

Figure 2.1: The Hierarchy of Leadership

The Lord expects leaders to positively influence followers and create healthy and functional relationships. The degree of health and functionality of a leader's horizontal human relationships depends on the health and functionality of his or her vertical relationship with God. No leader can exert biblically sound influence on followers without first embracing a personal relationship with God through Jesus Christ, which starts the transformation of a leader's heart (core values).

The ENTRUSTED Leader presents a biblical perspective of seven core values which enhance a leader's efforts to encourage the hearts of others. Core values dictate the attitudes, priorities, and actions a leader brings to a relationship. The choices a leader makes in respect to heart, mission, approach, stability, lifestyle, fortitude, and worldview ultimately determine how one relates to others and contribute to forging a lasting bond of unity among followers. The development of an authentic voice of influence and encouragement among followers begins with a leader's core values. The seven core values discussed in *The ENTRUSTED Leader* are the following:

1. A HEART willing to do all God asks.
2. A MISSION for leading characterized by a faithful commitment to multiplying followers of Jesus Christ that supersedes all other endeavors.
3. An APPROACH to leadership characterized by denial of self and serving others.
4. The STABILITY for leading created by applying a balance of skills, character, and compassion.
5. A LIFESTYLE that is beyond reproach and publicly demonstrates faith, hope, and love.
6. The FORTITUDE for leading built on faith in the love and sovereignty of God and the discipline of prayer.
7. A WORLDVIEW founded on absolute truth and the words of Jesus Christ.

These seven core values directly impact every leader-to-follower relationship. A leader should begin to think about how each core value might influence his or her followers. Relationships constitute the essence of leadership with the leader-to-follower relationship forming the primary connection. The role of the leader in any leader-to-follower relationship includes providing encouragement and positive influence. A leader's core values have a dramatic impact on whether his or her influence is encouraging or discouraging to followers.

The ENTRUSTED Leader strives to enable every type of leader— from a parent to a corporate executive—to positively influence his or her followers with encouragement. Regardless of one's title, rank, or position, anyone can become a CEO—Chief *Encouragement* Officer! Anyone can make a difference and positively influence the life of others.

The corporate executive who lavishes associates with encouragement empowers them. The parent who constantly encourages his or her child builds within them a healthy self-esteem. Become a source of encouragement to others, and people will respond positively to your influence.

A sacred bond exists between God and a leader.

Every leader carries a higher calling selflessly to encourage the hearts of others.

The higher calling of leadership involves encouraging the hearts of others and creating a bond of unity based on love.

PERSONAL APPLICATION EXERCISE

Describe your vertical relationship with God and how this relationship impacts the leader-to-follower relationship you identified in the previous chapter. List two or three things you can do to improve the health of your vertical relationship with God that will positively impact your relationships with followers.

3

The Entrusted Leader

Matthew 25:14–30

God stands ready to entrust all you need to lead according to his purposes!

Every person who influences others does so with a portfolio of talents entrusted to them by God. The skills and abilities you rely on to lead followers ultimately find their origin in God. The Lord has entrusted His property to you according to His purposes for your life and the lives of those who follow you.

God desires and intends to use you as a leader. God has already begun preparing you to lead others in His own unique manner. Furthermore, according to His timing, God will entrust to you all you need to lead according to His desires and intentions. Becoming the type of leader God desires you to be requires faithful service to God's investments in your life!

My definition of a leader focuses on actions that positively influence followers. Leading others requires a combination of appropriately developed skills and biblically sound core values. A leader's core values that have been shaped by God's Word generate leadership attitudes and behaviors that positively influence followers.

In addition to the link between a person's core values and leadership behavior, my definition of a leader also contemplates the concept of being "entrusted." The purpose of this chapter is to explain in more detail why I use this term in regard to a leader who claims to be a follower of Jesus Christ. Hopefully when you have finished this chapter you will understand why I have chosen the term "Entrusted Leader."

Below you will find my definition of an Entrusted Leader. Take some time to read it slowly and carefully. Consider the different terms I use, for they have been thoughtfully selected for a reason. Future lessons in *The ENTRUSTED Leader* will reference this definition periodically.

An Entrusted Leader is a person of vision who faithfully serves the investment God has "entrusted" in one's life by using skills, character, and compassion to encourage others toward a common goal while upholding an Entrusted Leader's core values.

I believe an entrusted relationship exists between God and a leader. God entrusts a leader with valuable assets that enable one to lead others. God expects a leader to faithfully serve this investment. The privilege and opportunity to lead others involve a sacred bond of trust between God, the leader, and the followers. God created and loves every follower and entrusts followers into the care of a leader. God raises up leaders to serve His plans and purposes in every arena of human endeavor. A leader has the opportunity to positively or negatively influence the lives of followers. A wise leader approaches the responsibility of these relationships with a humble and selfless attitude.

I believe an entrusted relationship exists between God and a leader.

The ENTRUSTED Leader targets followers of Jesus Christ who lead in every walk of life. My concept of an Entrusted Leader can be applied to a broad audience. I believe the definition of an Entrusted Leader stated above applies to any and every relationship where one individual influences another. The breadth of the leader-follower relationship knows no end and spans from a parent informally volunteering to coach a child's athletic team to a corporate executive formally overseeing the activities of a global organization. This definition of a leader, an Entrusted Leader, speaks to all family, marketplace, social, neighborhood, and volunteer relationships.

Whether or not you recognize it, numerous assets designed to aid your leading of others currently reside at your disposal. The vault of your life already holds many deposits that serve to enable you as a leader. The reservoir of your life continually receives a flow of valuable possessions intended to prepare you as a leader. God always entrusts, in accordance to his desires and intentions, everything a person needs to lead. You may not think of the assets of your life this way, but God does.

To fully appreciate the privilege and responsibility of being entrusted, a leader must recognize the difference between a possession entrusted and a present given. When a person gives a present to another, he or she does not expect the gift to be given back at some time in the future. The receiver takes possession of the present, and ownership of the gift transfers from one to another. The one receiving a gift stands free to do whatever he or she desires with it. Typically the giver of the present does not tell the receiver what he or she wants done with the gift. The receiver has no responsibility to report back to the giver what one did with the gift.

Entrusted possessions differ from a present given in a number of significant regards. When a person entrusts a possession to a trustee, the owner fully expects the asset to be returned at some time in the future. Ownership of the entrusted asset does not transfer to the trustee even though possession does. The owner typically conveys instructions along with the transfer of the possession and expects the asset to be used accordingly by the trustee. Normally, an owner expects the asset to be used to generate an increase or return while in the possession of the trustee. The owner reserves the right to repossess the asset and entrust it to another if the trustee does not follow the instructions or generate the owner's desired return on the investment. A wise trustee keeps in mind that the owner expects an accounting of how one invests and manages an asset while in his or her possession.

So you may be thinking, *What does the difference between a gift and an entrusted possession have to do with being a leader?* Consider the implications of Romans 13:1 in the context of being a leader: "Everyone must submit himself to the governing authorities, for there is no authority except that which God has established. The authorities that exist have been established by God." If you possess leadership authority, then recognize that God established this authority and "entrusted" His possession to you for His purposes. God did not "gift" this asset to you to be used as you see fit. You do not own the leadership authority you possess; God does.

God rises up leaders in every arena of human endeavor and entrusts to them leadership authority. Every leader received his or her opportunity to lead others from a being greater than themselves. All authority and opportunity to lead find their origin in God. The sovereign ruler of the universe entrusts and recalls the authority to lead according to His purposes. Consider the case of Saul, the first king of Israel. In 1 Samuel 15:23, Samuel says of Saul: ". . . Because you have rejected the word of the LORD, he has rejected you as king." Saul knew the purposes and limitations that came with being entrusted the authority to lead Israel. Saul foolishly chose to ignore these limitations and use the authority entrusted to him by God for self-centered reasons. Saul did not faithfully serve God's intentions and desires. Consequently, God repossessed the leadership authority entrusted to Saul and entrusted it to another: David.

Jesus told his followers a story about a master who entrusted his possessions to three servants. This story, commonly called the "Parable of the Talents," can be found in Matthew 25:14–30. This parable resides within teachings of Jesus that are often referred to as the Olivet Discourse, which spans all of Matthew 24 and 25. Read Matthew 24:1–25:13 to set the context of studying Matthew 25:14–30.

> [14] *"Again, it will be like a man going on a journey, who called his servants and entrusted his property to them.* [15] *To one he gave five talents of money, to another two talents, and to another one talent, each according to his ability. Then he went on his journey.* [16] *The man who had received the five talents went at once and put his money to work and gained five more.* [17] *So also, the one with the two talents gained two more.* [18] *But the man who had received the one talent went off, dug a hole in the ground and hid his master's money.*

¹⁹ *"After a long time the master of those servants returned and settled accounts with them.* ²⁰ *The man who had received the five talents brought the other five. 'Master,' he said, 'you entrusted me with five talents. See, I have gained five more.'*

²¹ *"His master replied, 'Well done, good and faithful servant! You have been faithful with a few things; I will put you in charge of many things. Come and share your master's happiness!'*

²² *"The man with the two talents also came. 'Master,' he said, 'you entrusted me with two talents; see, I have gained two more.'*

²³ *"His master replied, 'Well done, good and faithful servant! You have been faithful with a few things; I will put you in charge of many things. Come and share your master's happiness!'*

²⁴ *"Then the man who had received the one talent came. 'Master,' he said, 'I knew that you are a hard man, harvesting where you have not sown and gathering where you have not scattered seed.* ²⁵ *So I was afraid and went out and hid your talent in the ground. See, here is what belongs to you.'*

²⁶ *"His master replied, 'You wicked, lazy servant! So you knew that I harvest where I have not sown and gather where I have not scattered seed?* ²⁷ *Well then, you should have put my money on deposit with the bankers, so that when I returned I would have received it back with interest.*

²⁸ *"'Take the talent from him and give it to the one who has the ten talents.* ²⁹ *For everyone who has will be given more, and he will have an abundance. Whoever does not have, even what he has will be taken from him.* ³⁰ *And throw that worthless servant outside, into the darkness, where there will be weeping and gnashing of teeth.'"(Matt. 25:14–30)*

Faithfulness captures the central theme of the Parable of the Talents. This story underscores a servant's responsibility to faithfully use entrusted possessions. In particular, Jesus taught this lesson to His disciples to prepare them for faithful service in the age between His first and second comings.

To fully appreciate the force of Jesus' teaching, one must remember that the Parable of the Talents is part of the Olivet Discourse (Matt. 24 and 25). The Olivet Discourse contains a lengthy teaching by Jesus on the events surrounding end times and His second coming. The disciples asked the question "When?" Jesus changed the question to "What?" What should a disciple be doing during the absence of the master?

This discourse contains two parables. First we find the Parable of the Ten Virgins (Matt. 25:1–13). Readiness summarizes the central theme of this parable. A disciple should be ready—attentive and prepared—for the master's arrival. Second we find the Parable of the Talents, which has a central theme of faithfulness. A disciple should faithfully serve the instructions associated with property entrusted by the master when he departed.

As the story goes, a man left on a long journey. Before his departure, he called three of his servants and entrusted his property to them. To one servant the man gave five talents, to another he gave two, and to the third he gave one. The servants with five and two talents put their master's money to work immediately and doubled his investment. The servant with one talent, however, went away, hid his master's money, and the asset earned nothing.

The Greek term for "entrusted" found in Matthew 25:14 is the third-person singular form of the verb *paradidomi*. In his enhanced lexicon, Strong defines *paradidomi* as follows: "1 to give into the hands (of another). 2 to give over into (one's) power or use. 2A to deliver to one something to keep, use, take care of, manage."[1] In the New Testament, the term "entrusted" carries the idea of being given something of great value to take care of or to use in accordance with the giver's purposes. Entrusted possessions are not gifts. An entrusted asset is not a loan that can be freely used as long as it is returned intact and according to the loan provisions. Something entrusted is still owned by the giver and is to be used specifically according to the instructions of the owner.

In the Parable of the Talents, the master eventually returned from his long journey. He called his three servants together and asked for an accounting of the property he had entrusted to them. The servants with five and two talents reported their results. The master replied: "Well done, good and faithful servant! You have been faithful with a few things; I will put you in charge of many things. Come and share your master's happiness!" (Matt. 25:21, 23).

The servant with one talent reported to his master that because of fear he had not put the entrusted talent to work as his master intended. This servant confessed that he hid the entrusted possessions in the ground for safekeeping, thereby earning no return. The master replied: "You wicked, lazy servant! . . . you should have put my money on deposit with the bankers, so that when I returned I would have received it back with interest. Take the talent from him and give it to the one who has the ten talents" (Matt. 25:26–28).

The obvious moral of the Parable of the Talents can be summed up in one word: faithfulness. A master expects his servants to faithfully use the possessions entrusted to them according to the owner's desires and intentions during his absence. The spiritual moral of the Parable of the Talents is less obvious but can be summed up in the same word: faithfulness. Jesus left on a long journey when He ascended into heaven. Jesus expects His followers to faithfully use the possessions entrusted to them according to God's desires and intentions during His absence. This biblical truth has a very practical leadership application. As modern-day followers of Christ who lead, we must faithfully serve what God has entrusted to us, which enables us to encourage and influence others.

God will entrust all you need to lead according to His desires and intentions. This you can count on! Becoming the type of leader God desires and intends you to be requires your faithful service to His investments. A fair question at this point is How does a leader faithfully serve what God has entrusted? I believe there are three steps one should consider in this regard.

The first step involves recognizing God's entrusted investments in your life. Some of these possessions you may think of as yours when in reality they actually belong to God. The next step focuses on discovering what God desires and intends for you to do with the possessions entrusted to your care and keeping. The third step can be summed up with Ephesians 4:1 where the Apostle Paul urges us to ". . . live a life worthy of the calling you have received." The leadership behavior that emanates from the seven core values of an Entrusted Leader is a starting point for approaching your leader-to-follower relationships in a manner worthy of your calling as a follower of Jesus Christ.

STEP ONE:
Recognize what God has entrusted to you.

The Bible reveals many of God's valuable possessions entrusted to a born-again leader. It is our responsibility to recognize them as such. Many leaders take some or all of these possessions for granted or view them as gifts. Some prideful leaders go so far as to take credit for what has been entrusted to them by grace. Other busy leaders fail to recognize the assets already at their disposal. God entrusts us so we can lead as He intends and desires. An Entrusted Leader recognizes that God has invested His property in his or her life and orders the priorities of his or her leadership behavior accordingly. Consider the value of the following in regard to leading others.

Psalm 139:13–14 tells us that God created each person uniquely and distinctly. Ephesians 2:10 says: "For we are God's workmanship, created in Christ Jesus to do good works, which God prepared in advance for us to do." God carefully crafted you with a purpose that He contemplated in advance. God brought you into this world exactly as He desired so you could serve Him in a manner that no other human ever created could. Your opportunity to influence and lead others stands unprecedented and unparalleled in all of creation. As funny as it sounds, God has entrusted all He created you to be—to you!

God has endowed your life with natural skills and abilities. Passages such as Exodus 31:1–11 illustrate how God distributes skills to each individual He creates to serve His purposes: "Then the LORD said to Moses, 'See, I have chosen Bezalel . . . and I have filled him with the Spirit of God, with skill, ability and knowledge in all kinds of crafts . . . Also I have given skill to all the craftsmen to make everything I have commanded you. . . . They are to make them just as I commanded you." Before God commanded Moses to build the tabernacle and its furnishings, He entrusted the skill and ability to fashion them to individual craftsmen. God expected these craftsmen to faithfully serve His purposes when the opportunity arose. Whatever you are good at can be attributed to God's provision in your life. God desires and intends for you to use the skill, ability, and knowledge He has entrusted to you as you lead others. A wise leader takes careful stock of one's life in order to clearly recognize those assets entrusted by God.

STEP TWO:
Discover what God desires and intends you to do with his assets.

God has a universal plan for the redemption of mankind that includes every Christian in the body of Christ. The Bible says God has an individual plan for every born-again follower of Jesus Christ (Eph. 2:10, Jer. 29:11). These individual plans work together to accomplish God's broader universal plan.

Discovering what God desires and intends for you to do as an individual starts with a clear understanding of God's universal plan. The Bible stands alone as a Christian's only reliable and authoritative source for gaining this understanding. As we begin to understand God's broad universal plan, we can more clearly see how God desires and intends to use what He has entrusted to us as individuals to accomplish this plan.

Consider for a moment how one aspect of God's universal plan of the redemption of mankind impacts us as an individual leader. Jude 1:3 tells us that "the faith" has been "entrusted" to "the saints." The Greek word in Jude 1:3 for "entrusted" is *paradidomi,* the same Greek word used in Matthew 25:14. Every leader who claims to be a follower of Jesus Christ has been entrusted with the good news of Jesus Christ. This investment extends to the lives of all the saints, not just professional ministers. The accomplishment of God's universal plan has been placed in the hands of all the saints. Unlike the servant who hid his master's valuable possession because he was afraid, God expects us to invest His property in the lives of those we lead and produce a return.

Think of the limitless opportunities you have as a leader to extend the love and grace of the gospel to those you lead. Every leader-to-follower relationship you possess has this potential. Have you ever considered the possibility that God has entrusted to you an opportunity to lead where you work and to be His ambassador? Have you ever considered that there are people you lead who have no other connection to the good news of Jesus Christ other than you? Many of these people will never go into a church or entertain a pastor. They will, however, listen to you. They will watch how you lead others.

God's Word reveals His universal plan. God's Word reveals many of the assets He has entrusted to the saints that enable them to accomplish this plan. The process of discovering God's individual plan for one's life starts with the Bible. Discovering what God desires and intends you to do as a leader with his entrusted assets requires study of God's Word.

STEP THREE:
Lead others in a manner worthy of your calling.

The lessons contained in *The ENTRUSTED Leader* center on teaching a leader the seven core values that produce biblically sound leadership behavior. The goal stands to encourage a leader to take ownership of these core values and apply them to his or her life as a leader. Once these core values are adopted and applied, a leader is well on the way toward leading in a manner worthy of the calling of Christ and faithfully serving what God has entrusted. The body of this book provides an explanation of how a leader might apply the seven core values previously mentioned:

1. HEART willing to do all God asks.
2. A MISSION for leading characterized by a faithful commitment to multiplying followers of Jesus Christ that supersedes all other endeavors.
3. An APPROACH to leadership characterized by denial of self and serving others.
4. STABILITY for leading created by applying a balance of skills, character, and compassion.
5. A LIFESTYLE that is beyond reproach and publicly demonstrates faith, hope, and love.
6. The FORTITUDE for leading built on faith in the love and sovereignty of God and the discipline of prayer.

7. A WORLDVIEW founded on absolute truth and the words of Jesus Christ.

God will entrust all you need to lead according to His desires and intentions. I use the term "entrusted" to define a leader because I truly believe each follower of Jesus Christ who leads others has been entrusted by God with everything he or she needs to fulfill God's purpose for one's life. Becoming the type of leader God desires and intends you to be requires faithful service to God's investment in your life.

God will entrust all you need to lead according to His desires and intentions.

Each leader must stop and ask questions such as: Am I using opportunities associated with my position of leadership as God intended? Am I faithfully serving God's desires and intentions? What am I investing my life in? God allows each of us to decide where, when, and how we invest the valuable assets He entrusts to us. We will, however, have to give an accounting to where, when, and how we invested God's assets. My goal is to hear the Master say to me, "Well done, my good and faithful servant."

Discussion Questions based on the Parable of the Talents (Matt. 25:14–30)

1. A trusting relationship exists between the master and his servants. Describe and characterize your relationship with God.
2. The master initiated a new dynamic to how he related to his servants when he entrusted his property (talents) to them. What "talents" has God entrusted to you that can be used to lead and encourage others?
3. The master gave instructions to his servants relating to how he wanted his property invested. What "instructions" has God attached to the talents He has entrusted to you? How did you discover/understand these instructions?
4. Reread Matthew 25:21. What is the central theme of this parable? Describe how you think you are doing as a servant invest-

ing what your master has entrusted. Are you faithfully generating the return on investment God expects?

5. The third servant received a very different response from the master than did the first two based on how he invested the master's talents. Which of the servants do you identify with most closely? What steps can you take going forward that will result in God saying to you, "Well done, my good and faithful servant"?

The higher calling of leadership involves investing in your leader-to-follower relationships all that God has entrusted to you!

PERSONAL APPLICATION EXERCISE

Perhaps in your reader's journal, describe some assets God has entrusted to you that you can invest in the leader-to-follower relationship previously identified. Discuss how this investment might encourage and influence others.

4

How God
Develops a Leader

Acts 7:20–36

God develops a leader differently than how the world does! God seeks to transform a leader's inner nature and core values as a spiritual complement to God-given ability. Humanity settles for developing leadership skills and knowledge as a complement to outward appearances.

God's purposes, timing, focus, and methods for preparing a leader differ from how the world prepares leaders. To recognize clearly God's hand of development in your life, you must view the process from God's perspective.

God's preparation of a leader involves eternal purposes. His timing typically lasts longer than we perceive necessary. God's focus of preparation centers on our inner nature, or heart, resulting in core values that produce biblically sound leadership behavior. God's method includes and even utilizes our failures, disappointments, and brokenness.

God seeks to transform a leader's inner nature and core values as a spiritual complement to God-given ability.

Humanity tends to prepare a leader to maximize earthly/temporal success. We want the process to be as short as possible. Humans focus on preparing the outward appearances of skills and knowledge. The world's method avoids circumstances that allow emotional pain and seeks experiences that enrich the intellect.

God selects a leader differently than man does. Man looks at outward appearances such as physical stature, personality, drive, skills, intelligence, knowledge, experience, and past positions of authority. The wise man acknowledges that God entrusted these, and many other leadership assets, to him or her in the first place. God looks beyond these outward appearances to what resides inside a leader. The Bible calls this inner nature of man the heart. Because He selects a leader differently than man, God also prepares a leader differently than man does. Becoming the type of leader God desires you to be requires viewing your preparation from God's perspective.

God desires and intends to use you as a leader. God wants to use you to positively influence and encourage the lives of the people you lead. God uniquely created you with specific leadership opportunities in mind. From the moment of your birth to this very second, God has orchestrated the circumstances of your life to prepare you to lead.

The Bible contains many examples of how God prepares a leader. As we study the lives of these leaders, we can gain perspective into how God might be preparing us as leaders today. To illustrate how God prepares a leader, we will look at the life of Moses. In particular, I want you to look for differences between how we might view leadership preparation and what God actually did to prepare Moses to lead the Israelites. I think you will see that God's purpose for raising Moses up as a leader was part of His eternal plan for His people; His timing was twice as long as Moses thought it should be (eighty years versus forty years); God's preparation included the development of Moses' heart and core values, as well as his skills; and God allowed failure, brokenness, and time in the desert as part of this process. The end result was the type of leader God desired Moses to be and intended to use.

The entire story of the life of Moses can be found in the Old Testament. The New Testament, however, records a summary of Moses' life in Acts 7:20–36.

²⁰ *"At that time Moses was born, and he was no ordinary child. For three months he was cared for in his father's house. ²¹ When he was placed outside, Pharaoh's daughter took him and brought him up as her own son. ²² Moses was educated in all the wisdom of the Egyptians and was powerful in speech and action.*

²³ *"When Moses was forty years old, he decided to visit his fellow Israelites. ²⁴ He saw one of them being mistreated by an Egyptian, so he went to his defense and avenged him by killing the Egyptian. ²⁵ Moses thought that his own people would realize that God was using him to rescue them, but they did not. ²⁶ The next day Moses came upon two Israelites who were fighting. He tried to reconcile them by saying, 'Men, you are brothers; why do you want to hurt each other?'*

²⁷ *"But the man who was mistreating the other pushed Moses aside and said, 'Who made you ruler and judge over us? ²⁸ Do you want to kill me as you killed the Egyptian yesterday?' ²⁹ When Moses heard this, he fled to Midian, where he settled as a foreigner and had two sons.*

³⁰ *"After forty years had passed, an angel appeared to Moses in the flames of a burning bush in the desert near Mount Sinai. ³¹ When he saw this, he was amazed at the sight. As he went over to look more closely, he heard the Lord's voice: ³² 'I am the God of your fathers, the God of Abraham, Isaac and Jacob.' Moses trembled with fear and did not dare to look.*

³³ *"Then the Lord said to him, 'Take off your sandals; the place where you are standing is holy ground. ³⁴ I have indeed seen the oppression of my people in Egypt. I have heard their groaning and have come down to set them free. Now come, I will send you back to Egypt.'*

³⁵ *"This is the same Moses whom they had rejected with the words, 'Who made you ruler and judge?' He was sent to be their ruler*

and deliverer by God himself, through the angel who appeared
to him in the bush. [36] *He led them out of Egypt and did wonders*
and miraculous signs in Egypt, at the Red Sea and for forty years
in the desert." (Acts 7:20–36)

Moses' childhood can be described as nothing short of miraculous, as God's sovereign hand protected him from day one. The Lord orchestrated every circumstance of Moses' life to prepare him to lead the Israelites according to God's purpose and timing. Moses' birth brought with it a death sentence. The king of Egypt had made a proclamation that forced Hebrew parents to throw out their newborn babies so they would die. Moses' parents placed him outside, leaving him to die, when he reached the age of three months. Pharaoh's daughter found Moses and raised him as her own son. Moses grew up in the adopted home of Pharaoh, king of Egypt, the same king who supported a death sentence on Hebrew babies.

Moses lived the first forty years of his life in Egypt. His education included all the wisdom of the Egyptians, and he grew up to be powerful in speech and action. By all human measures, Moses stood fully prepared to lead by the age of forty. Moses' education, words, behavior, and royal position empowered him to lead however he saw fit. As far as Moses knew, his development as a leader was complete. Moses thought he was ready to do something for God and his people.

Unbeknown to Moses, the most difficult stage of his development as a leader still lay in front of him. Moses was strong in leadership skills and knowledge, but his inner nature was underdeveloped and weak. Moses' core values would not produce leadership behavior consistent with God's intentions and desires, and he was not ready to lead others according to God's desires and intentions.

At the age of forty, Moses decided to visit his fellow Israelites. His Hebrew brothers and sisters suffered under the heavy hand of Egyptian oppression. During this fateful visit, Moses witnessed an Egyptian mistreating an Israelite. Moses came to the defense of his Hebrew brother and rescued him from the attack. But Moses did not stop here. According to Acts 7:24, Moses "avenged him," taking the law into his own hands and deciding that the Egyptian deserved capital punishment.

Moses killed the man abusing his fellow Israelite. Although he was a powerful royal leader, Moses had no right to do this.

Evidently Moses had an appreciation that the God of Israel desired and intended to use him to deliver his people from the oppression of the Egyptians. It must have made logical sense to Moses that the royal power and authority he possessed would be the means by which God would act through him. It was obvious in Moses' mind that this is why God saved him from sure death as an infant and placed him in the royal family. Unfortunately neither the Israelites nor the Egyptians recognized Moses as a leader of the Hebrews at this time.

To recognize clearly God's hand of development in your life, you must view the process from God's perspective.

This lack of leadership recognition was confirmed the very next day. Moses was out among his people once more and witnessed two of his fellow Israelites fighting. Moses interceded and tried to reconcile them. The aggressor in this argument pushed Moses aside and said: "Who made you ruler and judge over us? Do you want to kill me as you killed the Egyptian yesterday?" (Acts 7:27–28). Evidently Moses believed that his ungodly act of murder would be overlooked by the Egyptians and would endear him to the Israelites. Neither of these results would prove to be true. Moses fled to Midian a fallen and failed leader where he settled as a foreigner.

In a sense, Moses had good intentions and a "godly" motivation that led him to the error in judgment that brought about his downfall as a leader. Moses acted on the power and authority of his royal position of leadership, relying on his own power and authority as a leader instead of God's. Moses' inner nature and core values were primarily shaped by his education, experience, and Egyptian culture. By the age of forty, Moses evidently knew of the God of Israel; however, Moses had not encountered the Lord in such a way as to fashion his inner nature and core values. This phase of his development as a leader was still ahead of him.

Think about Moses as a foreigner in the desert, estranged from his adopted royal family and his own oppressed people. While the Bible does not tell us so, it is not hard to imagine that Moses must have had moments of regret for the actions that had cost him so dearly. Surely Moses would have liked to undo what was done. Certainly he had plenty of time alone to replay in his mind the events of that day and speculate what life would be like if he had not acted so irrationally. Thoughts like this are only natural when a leader makes a mistake that costs someone his or her position of leadership. Moses may have thought he failed God as the deliverer of the Hebrews.

Perhaps Moses blamed himself for his circumstances, or maybe he blamed God. Whatever the case may be, Moses must have felt all alone and humiliated. Surely feelings of sadness, anxiety, confusion, fear, doubt, and insecurity raced through his thoughts.

Moses undoubtedly felt like a failure as a leader. He probably viewed his life as a leader to be over at age forty. Moses knew he would never lead the Egyptians again from a position of royal power. I doubt he harbored thoughts of leading or rescuing his fellow Israelites ever again. Think about the hopelessness Moses must have felt in the desert. Moses did eventually find another family, get married, and have two children. He put the past behind him and settled into a completely different life in the desert.

When we think of the story of Moses, we concentrate on the last phase of the story where at age eighty Moses triumphantly returns to Egypt after forty years of banishment in the desert to lead his fellow Israelites out of the oppression of the Egyptians and to the promised land. In our minds, we quickly jump from age forty to age eighty, mainly because that is what the biblical text does. We know Moses left Egypt in disgrace at age forty, and we know Moses encountered the Lord God Almighty in a burning bush at age eighty. We know very little of the particulars in between. We can speculate, however, that he did a lot of soul searching in that forty-year period. Most likely, Moses did not have visions of grandeur that he would encounter the Lord at age eighty and return to lead the Israelites.

After forty years in the desert, Moses observed a burning bush. Upon closer inspection, Moses heard the Lord's voice. The God of Abraham, Isaac, and Jacob spoke directly to Moses. His first reaction was one of fear and the impulse to turn away. The Lord instructed Moses to respect the holiness of being in God's presence by removing his sandals. God informed Moses that He indeed saw the oppression of the Israelites at the hands of the Egyptians. The God of Abraham told Moses that the time had come to set them free, and the Lord invited Moses to come, for God intended and desired to send Moses back to Egypt. Moses, who forty years earlier had fled Egypt for his life and had failed to lead his own people, was being sent back to deliver them, this time by God's power and authority, not his own.

Now eighty years old, Moses was finally prepared to lead as God desired and intended. During his forty years in the desert, it is hard to imagine that Moses' education in the wisdom of Egypt had expanded. There is no reason to believe that Moses had become more powerful in speech or action while he was away. Certainly Moses no longer possessed any royal position, authority, or influence. We must ask ourselves: If Moses' education, skills, and authority diminished his outward appearance as a leader, what changed? How was Moses different at eighty compared to forty that God deemed him ready to lead His people? I would suggest to you that the change was internal. Moses had personally encountered the God of the universe, coming face-to-face with the Lord's holiness. He had learned to respect and listen to God and came to understand that God would work through him as a leader to free His people as opposed to Moses using the lofty influence of his royal position to do something for God and His people. The change in Moses involved his inner nature, or heart. This change involved a new set of core values based on God's will and intentions. This change inside Moses was evidenced over the next forty years as he led the Israelites out of Egypt and to the brink of the Promised Land, just as God intended and desired.

Now that we have studied the life of Moses, we must ask ourselves: What can we learn from the story of this leader? What can we apply to our life as a leader in the third millennium? How can the story of a man who lived fifteen hundred years before Christ inspire us today?

The primary element of the story I want you to concentrate on is how God prepared Moses as a leader. God's eternal purpose for preparing Moses involved delivering the Israelites from bondage. The timing of God's preparation was twice as long as Moses thought it should be.

The central focus was the preparation of Moses' inner nature and core values that produced godly leadership behavior. God's method included Moses' failure, brokenness, and time alone in the desert. Do you recognize God's hand working to prepare you as a leader in any of these four ways?

1. God's purpose for preparing you as a leader contemplates His eternal plan for mankind. Every position of leadership you hold can be viewed in light of this truth. God raising you up to lead will always be according to His purposes. Have you ever considered that in your leadership capacity there are lives you can impact for the cause of Christ that no other follower of Jesus Christ can touch? Have you ever thought of developing an eternal perspective of how and why you lead?

2. God's preparation of you as a leader is on God's timetable. It took God eighty years to get Moses prepared to lead. Most likely, God is still working in your life even at this very minute. Pray that God opens the eyes of your mind so you can see His hand working to prepare you to be the leader He desires you to be. Do you see evidence of such activity in your life at this time? Have you ever thought of where you might be on God's timetable to prepare you as a leader?

3. God's preparation of a leader is not complete until God has dealt with a leader's inner nature, or heart. No leader can serve according to God's desires and intentions until He has dealt with the leader's heart. The leader who develops only the functional aspects of leading is not yet ready to lead others as God intends. At the age of forty, Moses had the functional aspect of education, skills, and position of authority mastered, but his inner nature was not prepared. I believe God spent the first forty years of Moses' life in Egypt preparing his leadership skills and the second forty years in the desert preparing his inner nature and core values. It may very well be that God has allowed for your skills to develop first as He did Moses and is now working on your inner nature and core values. In what ways do you think development of your inner nature and core values will complement the leadership skills you already have? What do your lead-

ership core values and behavior indicate about the development of your heart/inner nature?

4. God uses our failures and disappointments in His process of developing us as a leader. In His infinite wisdom, God allows pain and suffering to touch our lives in order to prepare us to lead in a manner that might not be otherwise possible. As humans we do not particularly like this necessary aspect of how God works. Maybe you have failed as a leader in the past. I want you to keep in mind that this does not make you a failure in God's eyes. God allows pain and suffering and uses them to get our attention and prepare us to lead. Does knowing that God allows difficult circumstances as part of how He prepares a leader put into perspective some of your past disappointments?

God prepares a leader differently than man. Man concentrates on the outward appearances of leadership knowledge, skills, and positions of authority. God concentrates His preparation of a leader on a leader's inner nature and core values. Becoming the leader God desires and intends you to be requires you to shift your preparation from man's perspective to God's.

God's purposes, timing, focus, and methods for preparing a leader differ from how men prepare leaders. How does God prepare a leader? By allowing difficult circumstances that shape a leader's inner nature and core values according to His timing and eternal purposes! To clearly recognize God's hand of preparation in your life, you must view the process from God's perspective.

Discussion Questions based on the life of Moses (Acts 7:20–36)
1. The Bible records that by the age of forty Moses might have relied on three personal assets to lead others:
   • Education (knowledge)
   • Powerful speech (skills and abilities)
   • Royal position

   What personal assets do you rely on to lead others?

2. At the age of forty, do you think Moses was fully prepared to lead others according to God's desires and intentions? Why or why not?

   Are you fully prepared to lead others according to God's desires and intentions? Why or why not? What keeps you from leading others as God desires and intends?

3. Think about Moses as an exile and a foreigner in the desert, estranged from his adopted family and separated from his own people.

   Do you think Moses might have:
   - Regretted his actions that cost him everything he had in Egypt?
   - Felt like a failure as a leader?
   - Viewed his life as a leader over by age forty?
   - Blamed himself, or even God, for his circumstances?
   - Thought he failed God?
   - Felt all alone, humiliated, sad, anxious, depressed, angry, bitter, or confused?
   - Felt paralyzed by fear, doubt, or insecurity?
   - Missed the wealth, power, and authority he possessed as royalty in Egypt?

   Do you think at age forty, forty-five, sixty, or even seventy-nine, Moses was entertaining thoughts of:
   - Returning to Egypt to rescue his people?
   - Returning to Egypt to reclaim his power, authority, and royal position?
   - Being used by God as a leader?
   - How God might use his failure for a greater good?
   - How God was using his brokenness to develop his inner nature and core values?

   Brokenness and failure are part of the process God uses to develop leaders. Briefly describe a time when God used disappointment, failure, and/or brokenness to shape your inner nature and core values.

4. Moses' leadership knowledge (education) and skills did not increase after the age of forty. He no longer held a position of royal leadership authority. What do you think might have changed about Moses during his forty years in the desert that led God to deem him prepared to lead his people? How might this same transformation apply to your life and impact how you lead others?

God seeks to transform your inner nature and core values as a spiritual complement to your God-given ability!

PERSONAL APPLICATION EXERCISE

Identify and describe two or three areas of your inner nature that God is presently transforming that will impact your core values and how you lead others.

5

Heart
CORE VALUE: A HEART willing to do all God asks.

How God Selects a Leader
1 Samuel 10:1–16:7

When selecting a leader, God looks at the heart!

God's primary selection criterion for a leader is the human heart . . . a heart fixed on serving others and willing to do all God asks.

God selects a leader based on the inner orientation of his or her heart, not the outward beauty of one's physical appearance. "But the LORD said to Samuel, 'Do not consider his appearance or his height, for I have rejected him. The LORD does not look at the things man looks at. Man looks at the outward appearance, but the LORD looks at the heart'" (1 Sam. 16:7). In God's administration, the primary criterion for the selection of a leader consists of attributes of the heart. Becoming the type of leader God desires you to be requires the development of your inner nature, or heart. God looks for leaders who in the core of their inner nature value a heart willing to do all God asks of them.

God examines the orientation of a person's heart when looking for a potential leader, not one's physical appearance, charisma, knowledge, or skill level. While necessary, the functional aspects of leading pale in comparison to the condition of the leader's heart. The development of one's heart, a person's inner nature, unlocks the door to becoming the type of leader God desires and intends to use. Make no mistake about it: When it comes to leadership development, the condition of the individual's heart ultimately determines what kind of leader a person will become.

We live in a society that places a premium on a person's physical appearance and discounts a person's core values when selecting a leader. Our culture reveres the outward or functional aspects of a leader such as beauty, charisma, knowledge, and skills. The world often develops, selects, promotes, and rewards leaders based on these qualities. The world ignores the shortcomings of a leader in regard to his or her heart as long as the job gets done. The world has the priority for developing leaders backward. Following the world's formula may result in a measure of temporal success, but this approach will not qualify one to be selected and used by God in the administration of His will on earth.

God takes a different approach than the world does when selecting a leader. God examines a person's heart and looks for a heart willing to do all He asks. God properly values the functional aspects of leading as we will see in later lessons. Skills and a person's core values exist as two sides of the leadership coin. You cannot lead others as God desires without both. In fact, God reigns as the one who creates and entrusts a person's leadership skills, knowledge, and authority. What God understands and man fails to recognize is that regardless of the skill level, if a person's heart is not willing to obey all God asks, then that leader is of no use to God.

In 1 Samuel 16:7, God tells Samuel that He selects a leader differently than mankind does. To fully appreciate why God revealed this truth, a leader must first go back and examine the leadership of Saul, the first king of Israel. Saul refused to obey all God asked of him and displayed leadership behavior that originated from a prideful, self-centered, and rebellious heart. God ultimately rejected Saul as king of Israel and selected another based on a different set of criteria. The following passages from the Old Testament book of 1 Samuel illustrates that Saul may have had the skills and outward appearance of a leader, but he failed as a leader and was rejected by God because of a dysfunctional heart.

God's instructions to newly anointed King Saul (1 Sam. 10:1, 8)

> [1] Then Samuel took a flask of oil and poured it on Saul's head and kissed him, saying, "Has not the LORD anointed you leader over his inheritance? . . . [8] Go down ahead of me to Gilgal. I will surely come down to you to sacrifice burnt offerings and fellowship offerings, but you must wait seven days until I come to you and tell you what you are to do."

Saul's disobedience and God's rejection of him as king (1 Sam. 13:7–14)

> [7] . . . Saul remained at Gilgal, and all the troops with him were quaking with fear. [8] He waited seven days, the time set by Samuel; but Samuel did not come to Gilgal, and Saul's men began to scatter. [9] So he said, "Bring me the burnt offering and the fellowship offerings." And Saul offered up the burnt offering. [10] Just as he finished making the offering, Samuel arrived, and Saul went out to greet him.

> [11] "What have you done?" asked Samuel. Saul replied, "When I saw that the men were scattering, and that you did not come at the set time, and that the Philistines were assembling at Micmash, [12] I thought, 'Now the Philistines will come down against me at Gilgal, and I have not sought the LORD's favor.' So I felt compelled to offer the burnt offering."

> [13] "You acted foolishly," Samuel said. "You have not kept the command the LORD your God gave you; if you had, he would have established your kingdom over Israel for all time. [14] But now your kingdom will not endure; the LORD has sought out a man after his own heart and appointed him leader of his people, because you have not kept the LORD's command."

Saul disobeys God's instructions in regard to the Amalekites (1 Sam. 15:24–29)

> *24 Then Saul said to Samuel, "I have sinned. I violated the LORD's command and your instructions. I was afraid of the people and so I gave in to them. 25 Now I beg you, forgive my sin and come back with me, so that I may worship the LORD."*
>
> *26 But Samuel said to him, "I will not go back with you. You have rejected the word of the LORD, and the LORD has rejected you as king over Israel!"*
>
> *27 As Samuel turned to leave, Saul caught hold of the hem of his robe, and it tore. 28 Samuel said to him, "The LORD has torn the kingdom of Israel from you today and has given it to one of your neighbors—to one better than you. 29 He who is the Glory of Israel does not lie or change his mind; for he is not a man, that he should change his mind."*

Most leaders who fail do so as a result of matters of the heart, not from a lack of skill or knowledge. Consider the collapse of Saul, the first king of Israel. He possessed all the outward qualities, knowledge, skills, and authority to lead God's people. Yet Saul failed as a leader in God's administration. The Bible clearly reveals why God replaced Saul as king of Israel. Although he still held the office, God had rejected Saul as king of Israel: "But now your kingdom shall not endure. The LORD has sought out for Himself a man after His own heart, and the LORD has appointed him as ruler over His people, because you have not kept what the LORD commanded you" (1 Sam. 13:14 NASB).

God ultimately rejected Saul because of his unwillingness to obey God's commands. This violation on Saul's part originated in his heart, not from a lack of knowledge or leadership skills. Saul's development as a leader was exposed as incomplete because he was unwilling to align his heart with God's will and relinquish his own selfish will. God entrusted the leadership of the nation of Israel to Saul, but Saul was unwilling to use what God had invested in him according to His divine desires and will.

Two separate incidents demonstrate Saul's unwillingness to obey God's commands. The first occurred at Gilgal when Saul felt compelled to make an offering to the Lord (1 Sam. 10:1, 8, 13:7–10). Samuel the priest anointed Saul as king of Israel. He instructed Saul to go to Gilgal and wait seven days for him. Upon his arrival, Samuel promised to make a sacrifice to the Lord and then tell Saul what he was to do next. Saul grew impatient and offered the sacrifice himself before Samuel arrived.

Saul was a political/military leader but not the spiritual leader of Israel. Saul may have been the king but as prophet and priest Samuel's responsibilities entailed representing God to the people of Israel. Saul had no authority to make a sacrifice before the Lord. He knew this limitation of his power and authority as king, but he chose in his heart to ignore God's restriction in this regard. Saul allowed the difficult circumstances of Samuel's delay, scattering men, and the enemy's pending attack to cloud his judgment. Saul's willful disobedience formed the basis for his rejection as a leader fit for God's purposes. Consider Samuel's judgment of Saul when he learned of Saul's disobedience: "'You acted foolishly,' Samuel said. 'You have not kept the command the LORD your God gave you . . .'" (1 Sam. 13:13). This willful disobedience was born in Saul's heart, not from a void of leadership skills.

In 1 Samuel 15, we find a second incident in which Saul failed to obey God's commands. God sent Saul on a mission to destroy the Amalekites. God explained to Saul the reason for this judgment and told Saul exactly how He wanted the mission executed: "Now go, attack the Amalekites and totally destroy everything that belongs to them. Do not spare them; put to death men and women, children and infants, cattle and sheep, camels and donkeys" (1 Sam. 15:3). The instructions from the Lord were clearly communicated to Saul.

Saul went on the mission as assigned. Unfortunately, he decided that partial obedience to how God wanted the mission executed was good enough. Saul spared the life of Agag, the king of the Amalekites, and the best of the livestock. Saul was unwilling to destroy everything as God commanded. Saul's willful disobedience grieved God. "Then the word of the LORD came to Samuel: 'I am grieved that I have made Saul king, because he has turned away from me and has not carried out my instructions . . .'" (1 Sam. 15:10–11).

Saul tried to blame his men, but Samuel laid the responsibility at the feet of Saul and informed him that God had rejected him as king. Saul collapsed as a leader because he decided to follow his own selfish desires instead of obeying God's Word. This decision reflected a heart that was not willing to do all God asked of him.

Saul failed as king of Israel and a leader in God's administration because of matters of his heart. Outwardly, Saul possessed a physical appearance that had no rival among his fellow Israelites. Despite displaying the outward image of a leader, he failed. God rejected Saul because of his willful disobedience. Saul knew what God had commanded; however, he chose in his heart to disobey. Saul was unwilling to do what God asked of him.

The Selection Criterion of King David (1 Sam. 16:1–7)

> [1] *The LORD said to Samuel, "How long will you mourn for Saul, since I have rejected him as king over Israel? Fill your horn with oil and be on your way; I am sending you to Jesse of Bethlehem. I have chosen one of his sons to be king."* . . . [6] *When they arrived, Samuel saw Eliab and thought, "Surely the LORD's anointed stands here before the LORD."* [7] *But the LORD said to Samuel, "Do not consider his appearance or his height, for I have rejected him. The LORD does not look at the things man looks at. Man looks at the outward appearance, but the LORD looks at the heart."*

God wanted a different man to lead Israel. Specifically God wanted a different type of man to lead Israel. In the same breath that God spoke of the rejection of Saul, He characterized the type of man He desires as a leader: "But now your kingdom shall not endure. The LORD has sought out for Himself a man after His own heart . . ." (1 Sam. 13:14 NASB).

God dispatched Samuel to identify, select, and anoint the next king of Israel, a king that God had already said would be a man after His own heart. The selection criterion for the second king would be the heart, or inner nature. Following his own selfish heart instead of God's will characterized Saul's kingship. God rejected Saul and unveiled His plan for a different type of king to rule over the people of Israel. Back then and still today, God's will for a leader in His administration of the world contemplated a person after God's own heart. The selection criterion remained clear. God told Samuel the key attribute He desired in a king. In I Samuel 16, the Bible records the events that surrounded Samuel, beginning with the process of implementing God's instructions for identifying and anointing the next king. Unfortunately, Samuel did not seem to fully understand the heart criterion God described to him for selecting a leader.

God directed Samuel to go to Bethlehem, in particular to the house of Jesse. God had not revealed to Samuel the exact identity of the man after His own heart but told Samuel that upon arrival in Bethlehem he would be shown whom God had chosen as king. God had, however, made the decision clear to Samuel that the criterion used to select Saul would not be used again. The new standard for a leader would focus on a person's heart, not one's outward appearance.

Unfortunately, even Samuel failed to comprehend the full implication of God's selection criterion. Samuel obediently went to the house of Jesse. The first son of Jesse whom he considered was Eliab. When Samuel first saw Eliab, he thought: ". . .'Surely the LORD'S anointed is before Him'" (1 Sam. 16:6 NASB). Samuel fell into the trap of selecting a leader based on human values. Eliab, the oldest of the sons, appeared physically impressive, and his seniority and outward appearance led Samuel to incorrectly conclude that God had chosen Eliab. Samuel had applied the wrong standard for selecting a king. The error repeated here originated with the attributes used to select Saul, which concentrated on his physical superiority over other leaders.

God immediately rejected Eliab and reminded Samuel that His selection criterion had no relevance to a man's physical appearance: "But the LORD said to Samuel, 'Do not look at his appearance or at the height of his stature, because I have rejected him; for God sees not as man sees . . .'" (1 Sam. 16:7 NASB). Obediently, Samuel passed over Eliab and moved on to the next son of Jesse.

God also rejected Jesse's next son, Abinadab. This process occurred seven times until God had rejected all of the sons of Jesse present that day. Samuel asked Jesse if there were other sons to consider: "Thus Jesse made seven of his sons pass before Samuel. But Samuel said to Jesse, 'The LORD has not chosen these.' And Samuel said to Jesse, 'Are these all the children?' And he said, 'There remains yet the youngest, and behold, he is tending the sheep.' Then Samuel said to Jesse, 'Send and bring him; for we will not sit down until he comes here'" (1 Sam. 16:10–11 NASB).

Finally in 1 Samuel 16:12, God revealed the man after His own heart and next king. God had selected David, Jesse's youngest son, as king of Israel. God rejected Saul because of matters of his heart. God disqualified David's seven older brothers because they lacked the heart God desired in a leader. David was the man; the basis of His selection considered the heart. Consider 1 Samuel 16:7 again in its entirety: "But the LORD said to Samuel, 'Do not look at his appearance or at the height of his stature, because I have rejected him; for God sees not as man sees, for man looks at the outward appearance, but the LORD looks at the heart'" (1 Sam. 16:7 NASB). From the rejection of Saul to the selection of David, God announced that His selection criterion for a leader started with the heart.

The next section in *The ENTRUSTED Leader* will examine a biblical definition of the human heart and reveal how this definition might apply to leaders. For now, the one truth to be mindful of is that when selecting a leader, God looks at the heart! This stands true for all leaders. A leader's inner nature takes priority over one's outward appearances including all functional aspects of leading. Regardless of skill level, God will not use a leader with a heart unwilling to do all He asks. This applies to all walks of life.

We live in a culture steeped in dualism—the idea that the spiritual world and material world exist in two distinct realms that do not overlap or mix. Philosophically, most leaders who claim to be a follower of Jesus Christ would reject dualism. Unfortunately, these same leaders often live compartmentalized lives characterized by an invisible wall of separation between the things of God (spiritual) and the things of men (material). Such leaders fail to realize any connection between God's Word and will and how they lead others in the compartment of everyday life. Their Sunday world appears white-washed with what is religiously expected; however, from Monday to Saturday they lead others from the decaying tomb of a heart unaware or unwilling to do all God asks.

As we continue our study of the human heart, keep in mind that what the Bible has to say applies directly to where and how you lead at home, at work, and in your community at large. Remember that Saul was not a "religious leader"; Samuel was. Saul reigned primarily as a political/military leader, and his leadership impacted the average citizen of his day. God did, however, hold Saul, the political/military leader of Israel, to the same standard of obedience that he did Samuel, the religious leader of Israel.

When selecting a leader, God looks at the heart! A leader must recognize the priority of developing one's heart in the process of becoming the type of leader God desires to use. A heart willing to do all God asks summarizes the goal of this process. A leader with a heart willing to do all God asks will be guided by core values that result in biblically sound leadership behavior.

Discussion Questions based on the rejection of Saul and the selection of David

1. God communicated His commands to Saul through the prophet Samuel. God has communicated His instructions to modern-day leaders through the authors of the Bible. Discuss your responsibility as a leader to understand and obey what God has communicated.

2. God looks at a person's heart when selecting a leader, not one's outward appearance. Briefly describe what this means to you.

3. Why do you think a heart willing to obey is more important to God than a leader's outward appearance and skills?

4. Briefly discuss your understanding of what God desires of you as a leader, based on the Bible, and your willingness to do all God asks.

When selecting a leader, God looks at the heart!
God selects a leader based on the inner orientation of his or
her heart, not the outward beauty of one's physical appearance.

PERSONAL APPLICATION EXERCISE

Describe some steps you can take that can more closely align the orientation of your heart with how God expects a person to lead others.

A Heart Like David's

1 Samuel 13:14, Acts 13:22, Psalm 40:8

David was not perfect; however, he was willing to do all God asked of him.

God does not expect you to be perfect; however, God does expect you to be willing to do all He asks, everywhere you lead others.

What worldwide crisis concerns the average Christian the most? What looms as the greatest crisis facing the world today? If asked, would you pick one of the following: terrorism, AIDS, poverty, world hunger, global warming, discrimination, proliferation of nuclear weapons, a shortage of oil, or the moral decay of American culture? Maybe another problem should be at the top of the list!

Dr. Howard Hendricks has said: "The greatest crisis in the world today is a crisis of leadership. And the greatest crisis of leadership is a crisis of character."[1] I believe Dr. Hendricks has accurately characterized today's leadership environment. Furthermore, I would suggest that this "crisis of character" that has produced a "crisis of leadership" can trace its origin to the dysfunctional hearts of otherwise functionally skilled leaders.

The number of books published on the topic of leadership appears to have grown exponentially in the past few years. This flood of literature provides all the evidence one needs to conclude that people recognize this crisis of leadership. Leaders and followers alike hunger for a solution to this problem. Unfortunately most writers fail to see the connection between this crisis of leadership and a leader's character and heart. Consequently most writers offer solutions to this crisis that ignore the root problem of a leader's dysfunctional heart.

This crisis appears to be worldwide. I only intend, however, to address the crisis of leadership in the United States. In particular, I hope to speak to what I perceive as a crisis of leadership among American leaders who claim to be followers of Jesus Christ. I will not address secular leaders who make no pretense in regard to following Jesus Christ, nor will I address religious leaders who focus on church leadership issues. The lessons included in this book target followers of Jesus Christ who lead at home, in the marketplace, and in American society at large. The goal is to inspire them to lead no matter where one influences and leads others with a heart willing to do all God asks, a heart like David's.

God does not expect you to be perfect; however, God does expect you to be willing to do all He asks, everywhere you lead others.

Some people might question whether or not a connection exists between this crisis of leadership and a leader's heart and character. Take a moment to think of a person who failed as a leader or failed to reach his or her full potential as a leader. Recent and ancient history contain many examples of such individuals. Perhaps someone you know personally failed as a leader. Maybe a leader comes to mind whose story made the newspaper or a history book. Now ask this question: Why did this individual fail as a leader? Stop and think about this question a moment: Why did this individual fail?

Typically the answer to this question involves a matter of the person's heart, not a lack of leadership knowledge, skill, or ability. Many leaders have forfeited their position of leadership because of a poor moral or ethical choice. Other leaders falter because of a failure to act decisively or courageously. These are all matters of a leader's heart. Years of observation suggests to me that many leaders who claim to be a follower of Jesus Christ fall short of their usefulness to God. Sadly, these leaders end up ineffective or unproductive or collapse altogether because of matters of the heart, not from a lack of leadership knowledge or skills.

The majority of leaders who fail do so because of a dysfunctional heart. I have no statistical data to prove this point, but experience and observation have led me to this conclusion. Incredibly, most leadership development programs ignore this reality altogether. Such programs focus on developing leadership skills and knowledge, not a leader's inner nature. Unfortunately, most "Christian" leadership development programs commit this oversight as well. Most leadership development programs that claim to be "Christian" in nature relate little more than Management 101 concepts repackaged in religious language.

From God's perspective, when the discussion comes to developing a leader, the "issue" is the heart! Any leadership development effort that fails to address a leader's need for development of the heart is more likely to produce a leader like Saul than a leader like David. God looks for leaders willing to do all He asks. God looks for leaders with a heart like David's. As a leader begins to question what it means to have a heart like David's, there are three passages of Scripture one must first consider: 1 Samuel 13:14, 1 Samuel 16:7, and Acts 13:22.

> *[14] But now your kingdom will not endure; the LORD has sought out a man after his own heart and appointed him leader of his people, because you have not kept the LORD's command."*
> *(1 Sam. 13:14)*

> *[7] But the LORD said to Samuel, "Do not consider his appearance or his height, for I have rejected him. The LORD does not look at the things man looks at. Man looks at the outward appearance, but the LORD looks at the heart." (1 Sam. 16:7)*

> *[22] "After removing Saul, he made David their king. He testified concerning him: 'I have found David son of Jesse a man after my own heart; he will do everything I want him to do.'" (Acts 13:22)*

A Biblical Definition of a Leader's Heart

God looks at a person's heart when selecting a leader. God made this criterion clear with the rejection of Saul and the selection of David. Every follower of Jesus Christ who leads others should strive to emulate David. To be useful to God, a leader must develop a heart like David's. This process begins with the formation of a clear understanding of a biblical definition of the term "heart."

If a person becomes interested in learning about the type of leader for whom God looks, he or she must consider the question: What does God look for in a leader in regard to his or her heart? A word study of the term "heart" provides an answer to this question. A close examination of both the Old Testament Hebrew and New Testament Greek meanings of the term "heart" reveals a clear picture of a leader after God's own heart.

The following word study will show that the biblical usage of the term "heart" in relation to a leader focuses on the orientation of the leader's will. The Bible clearly reveals that only two points of orientation exist. A leader must choose between the polar opposite orientations of God's will or self-will. No middle ground exists in regard to the alignment of a person's heart: The compass of a leader's heart points to either God's will or self-will. The direction the leader travels profoundly impacts the type of leader one becomes. Ultimately, the orientation of a person's heart dictates the attitudes and actions one takes as a leader. This idea of heart orientation will be the primary focus of the next lesson, "The Choices of Jonah and Jesus."

The Definition of Heart in the Old Testament

The Hebrew terms translated as "heart" in 1 Samuel 13:14 and 1 Samuel 16:7 come from the same root word: לבב (lebab). Strong defines lebab as follows: "[lebab /lay·bawb/] . . . inner man, mind, will, heart, soul, understanding."[2]

The characteristics Strong uses to define the term "heart" clearly contrast with a definition of heart that might center on the physical aspects of a blood-pumping organ. Consequently one can conclude that when God looks for a man after His own heart, He inspects the inner attitudes of the man's heart, not the physical strength of the man's heart. In the *Theological Wordbook of the Old Testament*, Harris, Archer, and Waltke describe the biblical distinction of the physical and abstract meanings of the Old Testament concept of heart by concluding that the most common usage centers on the abstract or a person's inner nature.

> *Concrete meanings of lēb referred to the internal organ and to analogous physical locations. However, in its abstract meanings, "heart" became the richest biblical term for the totality of man's inner or immaterial nature. In biblical literature it is the most frequently used term for man's immaterial personality functions as well as the most inclusive term for them since, in the Bible, virtually every immaterial function of man is attributed to the "heart."*[3]

Harris, Archer, and Waltke also observe that the abstract or attitudinal nature of a person's heart refers to the three personality functions of man: emotion, thought, and will. "By far the majority of the usages of *lēb* refer either to the inner or immaterial nature in general or to one of the three traditional personality functions of man; emotion, thought, or will."[4] When we consider this threefold view (thought, emotion, will) of man's heart in the context of the rejection of Saul and the selection of David, our focus of what God is looking for in a leader centers on one's inner nature.

God rejected Saul because he made a willful choice to disobey a command from God that he clearly understood. The rejection did not result from an improper thought on Saul's part. Saul's impatience and desire for power hastened his poor choice, but these emotions did not lead God to reject Saul. God rejected Saul because the orientation of his will on himself led to a choice to disobey God. Saul's rejection occurred because he oriented his will on his own selfish nature and not on God's will.

The Old Testament term for "heart" refers to the inner nature (thought, emotion, and will) of a person. When the Old Testament uses the term "heart" in the context of selecting a leader, the person's will becomes the focal point. The determining factor concerning a leader's heart hinges on the orientation of his or her will. Two possible alignments exist: God's will or the person's sinful nature. The alignment of a leader's will (heart) ultimately determines one's usefulness to God.

The Definition of Heart in the New Testament

To understand more fully the role of a person's will in the discernment of a leader's heart, one must consider the life of David once more. God selected David because God viewed David as a man after His own heart. In the New Testament, this selection criterion appears again in the book of Acts: "After He had removed him, He raised up David to be their king, concerning whom He also testified and said, 'I HAVE FOUND DAVID the son of Jesse, A MAN AFTER MY HEART, who will do all My will'" (Acts 13:22 NASB).

In Acts 13:22, the Greek term translated as "heart" is from the root word καρδία (*kardia*). This term is used essentially the same

way *lebab* is used in the Old Testament. Strong defines *kardia* as fo
lows:

> "[kardia /kar·dee·ah/] 1 the heart . . . 2B the centre and seat of
> spiritual life. 2B1 the soul or mind, as it is the fountain and seat
> of the thoughts, passions, desires, appetites, affections, purposes,
> endeavours. 2B2 of the understanding, the faculty and seat of th
> intelligence. 2B3 of the will and character. 2B4 of the soul so far
> as it is affected and stirred in a bad way or good, or of the soul a
> the seat of the sensibilities, affections, emotions, desires, appetite
> passions."[5]

Kittel, Friedrich, and Bromiley suggest that the New Testament
of the term "heart" refers to the same three functions of persona
(emotion, thought, and will) previously discussed in relation to the
Testament usage: "There is in the NT a rich usage of kardía for a.
seat of feelings, desires, and passions . . . b. the seat of thought and
derstanding . . . c. the seat of the will. . . ."[6]

The heart of each leader contains the capacity to make a choic
the will. The Bible cites numerous examples of the will being the pro
nent attribute of a person's heart. One finds 2 Corinthians 9:7 of
ticular interest concerning the role of heart in the selection of a lea
This verse substantiates that people have the capacity in their hea
choose a course of action: "Each one must do just as he has purpose
his heart . . ." (2 Cor. 9:7 NASB). The New Testament's use of the
"heart" involves a choice of the will. When used in the context of se
ing a leader, a person's capacity to decide between following God's "
or one's own "will" comes into question.

The previous discussions of the Old Testament term *lebab* an
New Testament term *kardia* lead one to conclude that the two t
have essentially the same meaning and become interchangeable. A
er finds further evidence of this truth in Matthew 13:15 where
quotes Isaiah 6:10. Both of these passages refer to the hearts of p
becoming insensitive or dull. In Isaiah, the term for heart is *lebab*,
in Matthew the term is *kardia*.

The Role of the Leader's Will in Defining Heart

In addition to the Old Testament revelation that God looks for a leader after His own heart, Acts 13:22 provides a qualifier that helps us understand more specifically what this means. God considers David a man after His own heart because David is a man ". . .who will do all My will" (Acts 13:22 NASB). A man after God's own heart is a man who will do all of God's will, all that God asks him to do. For the selection of a leader, God's evaluating measure is the person's willingness to embrace all of God's will. A person's will moves ahead of the other personality attributes of emotion and thought when God selects a leader. The attitudes and actions of a leader's heart reveal the true orientation of his or her heart more than what the person thinks or feels.

Acts 13:22 proclaims that David would enact all of God's will. The Greek term for "will" is θελήματά from the root θέλημα (*thelema*). Strong defines this word as: "θέλημα [*thelema* /thel·ay·mah/] . . . 1 what one wishes or has determined shall be done. 1A of the purpose of God to bless mankind through Christ. 1B of what God wishes to be done by us. 1B1 commands, precepts. 2 will, choice, inclination, desire, pleasure."[7] When a student of the New Testament considers the use of *thelema* in conjunction with heart, one must conclude that choice, action, and doing are in the forefront as opposed to thought or emotion.

The picture drawn from the New Testament use of the word *thelema* leads one to conclude that the primary sense of the term involves a choice. *Thelema* conveys the idea of obedience or disobedience to another's will. In particular, the majority of New Testament uses of *thelema* reference man's opportunity to choose to obey God's will.

Acts 13:22 uses *thelema* as a descriptor of why God judged David a man after His own heart. David was a person on whom God could count to choose to do His will whenever presented the choice. Knowing and/or desiring God's will alone do not qualify a person to lead in God's administration. The true test that distinguished David from others involved the orientation of the will of his heart to choose to do God's will at all times. God could count on David to obey.

David was not perfect, yet God considered him a man after His own heart. David was willing to do all God asked of him. To fully appreciate what it means to have a heart like David, there are two other attributes

one must consider. David was not perfect, but he possessed a repentant heart. When confronted with his own sin, David was quick to confess his transgression to God and turn away from the wrongful behavior. David also understood that there was a connection between his internalization of God's Word and his desire to do God's will. Any leader can apply the lessons learned from David's heart. A leader can start the application process with three initiatives: 1. Assess his or her attitude toward sin, 2. Evaluate one's commitment to know God's Word, and 3. Examine the extent to which one is willing to do God's will.

David was not perfect as evidenced by his many transgressions: committing adultery, fathering an illegitimate child, and conspiring to commit murder. David's affair with Bathsheba resulted in her becoming pregnant. To cover his sin, David recalled Uriah from his military post, then sent him to the front lines where he knew Uriah would be killed. Yet God considered David a man after His own heart. How can this be? Leading with a heart like David's does not require perfection, but possessing a heart like David's does require repentance for sin.

Don't misunderstand; God does not treat sin lightly. David's sin did have painful consequences, including the death of his infant son. God did, however, forgive David and restore him. When the prophet Nathan confronted David with his sins of adultery and murder, David admitted his guilt and asked God to forgive him. In Psalm 51, David clearly communicates his cry for grace, mercy, and forgiveness. God desires to use every follower of Christ as a leader. God does not require perfection, but He does require repentance of sin.

The first point of application in regard to developing a heart like David's involves confession of sin and a cleansing of one's heart. If past sins are hindering the development of your heart, then make Psalm 51 the focus of your prayer to God in regard to your particular circumstances. The first two verses of this psalm clearly communicate the sincerity of David's heart in regard to his sin.

> *¹ Have mercy on me, O God,*
> *according to your unfailing love;*
> *according to your great compassion*
> *blot out my transgressions.*

> *² Wash away all my iniquity*
>   *and cleanse me from my sin.*
> *(Ps. 51:1–2)*

Also keep in mind that when Christians do confess their sin to God, He has promised to forgive and cleanse them from all unrighteousness. John has said: "If we confess our sins, he is faithful and just and will forgive us our sins and purify us from all unrighteousness" (1 John 1:9).

David was not perfect, but he dealt honestly and openly with God about his sin. Additionally, he was perfectly willing to do all God asked of him. In an earlier psalm, David states this desire clearly and then gives some insight into how this attitude developed in his heart. From Psalm 40:8, a leader can glean a second point of application for this lesson: "I desire to do your will, O my God; your law is within my heart." In this psalm, David states a connection between his desire to do God's will and the retention of God's Word in his heart. The more a follower of Christ takes in God's Word, the more a desire to do all God asks will develop in one's heart.

The more a follower of Christ takes in God's Word, the more a desire to do all God asks will develop in one's heart.

This is the second of three lessons on the first core value: *A HEART willing to do all God asks.* In the previous lesson, leaders learned that God selects a leader based on one's heart, not his or her outward appearance. This lesson focused on a biblical definition of heart to emphasize that the key issue with a leader's heart is the will. The last lesson on this core value will explore a leader's choice of orienting the will of one's heart on God as opposed to self.

Developing a "heart like David's" will help a person become the type of leader God desires a follower of Christ to be. Achieving this goal requires a repentant attitude toward sin, a commitment to know God's Word, and a willingness to do all God asks.

Discussion Questions based on "A Heart Like David's"

1. When the Bible refers to the human heart, what three aspects of a person's inner nature come into view? Which of the three does God examine most closely when selecting a leader?
2. Describe the only two possible orientations of a leader's heart or will.
3. How was David's heart different from Saul's?
4. What connections exist between being a man after God's own heart and having a willingness to do all God asks?
5. Based on passages such as Psalm 51, 1 John 1:9, and Psalm 40:8, describe some ways you can develop a heart more like David's.

God does not expect you to be perfect; however,
God does expect you to be willing to all He asks, just like David!

PERSONAL APPLICATION EXERCISE

Identify an area of your life in which your will may be more oriented on "self-will" than God's will. Describe some steps you can take to reorient your heart.

The Choices of Jonah and Jesus
Jonah and Matthew 26:36–46

Every leader faces this choice of the heart: Do I orient the will of my heart on God or self?

Pleasing God as a leader requires one to orient his or her heart toward God's will.

God selects a leader based on the inner orientation of his or her heart. A leader's heart, or inner nature, encompasses a person's intellect, emotion, and will. The central question that determines a leader's usefulness to God centers on the orientation of the leader's will, and every individual faces this choice.

A self-oriented leader faces the possibility that God will intervene to get his or her attention. A leader who follows self-centered desires may find that God sends a "big fish" to redirect his or her course. A leader with a self-centered heart needs further development as preparation for God's service.

A follower of Jesus Christ who leads others publicly may face some very difficult choices in regard to orienting one's heart on God's will. Just the very thought of choosing God's will might overwhelm a leader with sorrow and anxiety. God patiently allows a person's internal struggle as he or she comes to grips with what God asks of those who claim to follow His Son. God looks for leaders who resolutely strive to understand and pursue His will.

Moses required forty years in the desert to prepare his heart to lead as God desired. Saul clearly understood God's will, but his self-oriented heart enticed him to disobey. God considered David a man after His own heart because David was willing to do all of God's will. This lesson examines two other individuals who faced the choice of will orientation. Jonah chose to run from the Word of the Lord. Consequently God intervened with a storm and a "big fish" to redirect his path. Even Jesus struggled emotionally in the Garden of Gethsemane when faced with the prospect of drinking the cup of God's will in the form of a cross.

The ENTRUSTED Leader strives to encourage the development of seven core values that move a leader closer to the standard of leadership behavior set by our Lord Jesus Christ. This lesson, "The Choices of Jonah and Jesus," along with the previous two, focuses on the first core value: *A HEART willing to do all God asks.* This core value lays the foundation for the other six. The leader who is willing to do all God asks may struggle emotionally with the personal costs but will ultimately embrace the other six core values as one's own. On the other hand, a self-oriented leader will resist and maybe even run from them. Each one of the seven core values of an Entrusted Leader conveys a unique facet of a leader with a heart oriented on God's will.

1. A HEART willing to do all God asks.

2. A MISSION for leading characterized by a faithful commitment to multiplying followers of Jesus Christ that supersedes all other endeavors.
3. An APPROACH to leadership characterized by denial of self and serving others.
4. The STABILITY for leading created by applying a balance of skills, character, and compassion.
5. A LIFESTYLE that is beyond reproach and publicly demonstrates faith, hope, and love.
6. The FORTITUDE for leading built upon faith in the love and sovereignty of God and the discipline of prayer.
7. A WORLDVIEW founded on absolute truth and the words of Jesus Christ.

This lesson, "The Choices of Jonah and Jesus," examines two examples of an individual who faced the choice of heart orientation. Example one covers the life of Jonah. Every person faces the choice to orient the will of his or her heart on God's will or one's own selfish will. Take some time and read the entire book of Jonah and keep this truth in mind. Below are some of the key passages from the story of Jonah.

The Choice of Jonah

¹ The word of the LORD came to Jonah son of Amittai: ² "Go to the great city of Nineveh and preach against it, because its wickedness has come up before me."

³ But Jonah ran away from the LORD and headed for Tarshish. He went down to Joppa, where he found a ship bound for that port. After paying the fare, he went aboard and sailed for Tarshish to flee from the LORD.

⁴ Then the LORD sent a great wind on the sea, and such a violent storm arose that the ship threatened to break up. ⁵ All the sailors were afraid and each cried out to his own god. And they threw *the cargo into the sea to lighten the ship. . . . ¹⁵ Then they took Jonah and threw him overboard, and the raging sea grew calm. ¹⁶ At this the men greatly feared the LORD, and they offered a sacrifice to the LORD and made vows to him.*

¹⁷ But the LORD provided a great fish to swallow Jonah, and Jonah was inside the fish three days and three nights. (Jon. 1:1–5, 15–17)

¹ From inside the fish Jonah prayed to the LORD his God. . . . ¹⁰ And the LORD commanded the fish, and it vomited Jonah onto dry land. (Jon. 2:1, 10)

¹ Then the word of the LORD came to Jonah a second time: ² "Go to the great city of Nineveh and proclaim to it the message I give you."

³ Jonah obeyed the word of the LORD and went to Nineveh. (Jon. 3:1–3)

The Lord sent His Word to Jonah. The commands that followed did not originate within Jonah but from the sovereign ruler of the universe. God instructed Jonah to take two actions. He told Jonah to go to Nineveh. Once in Nineveh, God desired Jonah to preach a message of judgment and repentance to the people of this great city. God clearly communicated His will to His servant. Jonah had a heart orientation choice to make. He could orient his will with God's will and go to Nineveh, or he could pursue his own self-centered agenda and not go to Nineveh.

Jonah chose to disobey. Ideally, he might have simply ignored God's command and continued on with his life in Israel as if nothing had ever happened. Perhaps he felt the conviction of the Holy Spirit, for Jonah did not just disregard the Lord's commands; he fled from the Lord's presence. Jonah ran as far away from God's will as he could. God commanded Jonah to travel east from Israel to Nineveh. Jonah chose to run west through the seaport of Joppa to Tarshish. Have you ever noticed that people who volitionally resist God's will tend to flee from God's presence? Have you ever noticed that people who run from God's will and presence often shy away from people who do embrace God's will?

Jonah ran from God's will and presence in a geographical manner. Perhaps his conscience bothered him for he confided with the sailors that he was running away from the Lord. Jonah clearly knew God's will and volitionally chose to orient the will of his heart on his own agenda. This misalignment of his will led Jonah to take actions diametrically opposed to God's desires and intentions for him as a leader.

Later in the story, readers learn why Jonah ran from the Lord's will. The relevant point to any study of leadership stems from the reality that Jonah understood God's will but did not agree with it. Jonah harbored his own agenda for the Ninevites. Jonah thought he knew better than God how to handle this situation. Jonah wanted to see the Ninevites punished for their wickedness. Jonah knew that if he went to Nineveh and preached against them, the citizens would repent and God would forgive them.

As followers of Christ who lead, we must be careful not to make the same mistake Jonah did. Perhaps the word of the Lord has come to you recently. Maybe God has opened your eyes to a new chapter of His will for your life that runs counter to all you have envisioned up to now. Let me encourage every leader who follows Christ not to ignore these leadings of the Holy Spirit or run from the presence of the Lord as Jonah did.

The lessons in *The ENTRUSTED Leader* present God's will to followers of Jesus Christ as revealed in God's Word. Some of the principles gleaned from this study may be new to some leaders or may run counter to what they have been told. Please do not accept them to be true just because I have said so. I encourage the reader to look at the passages and ask the Lord to reveal His Word and to show how it applies to one's life as a leader.

God initiated two actions intended to interrupt and intercept Jonah's flight from His will. First, the Lord sent a great wind to halt the progress of the ship, and Jonah, to the west. This storm was so violent that the ship and its crew were in peril. Once the connection between the storm and Jonah's running from God was established, the sailors threw him overboard.

Perhaps you have steered a course in the opposite direction of God's will. Have you ever been frustrated with circumstances that seem to impede the progress of your life's agenda? Have storms seemingly popped up out of nowhere? Keep in mind that this may very well be the hand of God lovingly trying to get your attention. You may view the great winds that threaten to break up your ship as bad, when in reality they blow from God's grace as He patiently works to alter your voyage.

The second action God initiated included a great fish that reoriented the direction of Jonah's trip. Jonah and the sailors assumed Jonah would perish once thrown into the stormy seas, but God had another plan for the passenger thrown overboard. God sent a great fish to swallow Jonah, and Jonah lived in the fish's belly for three days.

Jonah cried out to the Lord from deep inside the fish. He had finally sunk low enough into his self-centered agenda that he was willing to let go of his will and orient his life according to God's will. Jonah was finally ready to go to Nineveh to preach God's message of grace. Jonah described his circumstances as dire and hopeless, yet he called on the Lord to restore him. Jonah recognized that the storm and the fish were instruments of God's grace intended to draw him back to God's will. Jonah did turn the orientation of his heart back to God's will and vowed to extend to his enemies, the Ninevites, God's message of salvation by grace.

Sometimes when followers of Christ head in the wrong direction, God sends a storm to impede one's misdirected journey. Other times God intervenes in a more pronounced way and sends a "big fish" to literally redirect one's path. Maybe you find yourself in the belly of a "big fish" at this very moment. Perhaps the course of your life has been altered 180 degrees. While life in the belly of a fish appears cold, damp, smelly, lonely, and uncomfortable at best, in the long run such circumstances can be good for a person. Once a leader lets go of his or her self-oriented will and begins to follow God's will, he or she may very well find themselves regurgitated onto a warm, dry, aromatic, crowded, and comfortable beach as Jonah did.

By grace, God sent His Word to Jonah a second time. The command contained the same two instructions: Go to Nineveh and proclaim

God's message. This time Jonah obeyed; he oriented his will onto God's will, not his own. Jonah went to Nineveh and warned the citizens of God's imminent judgment. As Jonah suspected, the Ninevites repented and God forgave them.

The Word of the Lord came to Jonah. He clearly understood God's message. Jonah had the opportunity to orient the will of his heart on God's will or his own self-centered will. Jonah initially chose to run from the Lord and follow his own agenda. God sent a storm and a fish to impede his flight and redirect his journey. Once Jonah's heart was like David's, willing to do all God asked of him, God used Jonah to bring a great salvation to Nineveh.

As a leader, you will face the choice of whose will to follow. God's plan for your life may include storms and a "big fish." Let me encourage you to view God's interruption of your personal agenda as part of your preparation as a leader. If you are in a storm or the belly of a fish, seek God's favor and ask Him to restore your path according to His will.

The Choice of Jesus

Jesus is fully divine and fully human. Within His humanity, Jesus possesses a will. Accordingly, Jesus faced the same choice to follow the will of the Father or His own will that Jonah did. The devil tempted Jesus in the desert to choose a path other than God's will (Matt. 4:1–11). Jesus' response to the devil's suggestion included quoting Scripture that revealed the will of the Father. One must assume that the possibility did exist that Jesus might choose His will over the Father's. Without two possible choices, the devil's temptation had no potential for thwarting God's plan of salvation for mankind. The story of Jesus being tempted by Satan presumes Jesus faced the choice of whose will to follow.

Jesus was without sin in part because at no time was His will not oriented on God's will. Consequently Jesus' actions were always in line with God's commands. Within His humanity, Jesus had the capacity to choose His own will over the Father's. Perhaps there is no better illustration of the tension between Jesus' human will and the divine will of the Father than is captured by Matthew in his description of Jesus in the Garden of Gethsemane.

[36] Then Jesus went with his disciples to a place called Gethsemane, and he said to them, "Sit here while I go over there and pray." [37] He took Peter and the two sons of Zebedee along with him, and he began to be sorrowful and troubled. [38] Then he said to them, "My soul is overwhelmed with sorrow to the point of death. Stay here and keep watch with me."

[39] Going a little farther, he fell with his face to the ground and prayed, "My Father, if it is possible, may this cup be taken from me. Yet not as I will, but as you will."

[40] Then he returned to his disciples and found them sleeping. "Could you men not keep watch with me for one hour?" he asked Peter. [41] "Watch and pray so that you will not fall into temptation. The spirit is willing, but the body is weak."

[42] He went away a second time and prayed, "My Father, if it is not possible for this cup to be taken away unless I drink it, may your will be done."

[43] When he came back, he again found them sleeping, because their eyes were heavy. [44] So he left them and went away once more and prayed the third time, saying the same thing.

[45] Then he returned to the disciples and said to them, "Are you still sleeping and resting? Look, the hour is near, and the Son of Man is betrayed into the hands of sinners. [46] Rise, let us go! Here comes my betrayer!" (Matt. 26:36–46)

The will of the Father for Jesus included the cup of suffering and death on a cross. This instrument of punishment provided the means whereby God's perfect lamb would pay the penalty required for man's sin and purchase our salvation. Jesus asked the Father if there was another way. Three times Jesus left His disciples to make this request of the Father, and three times He returned without the answer for which He hoped. Finally seeing that God's plan was already in motion, Jesus told His disciples to rise, for His time to submit to the cup of God's will had come.

Before He left with His captors, Jesus struggled mightily with the personal price God's will was going to extract from Him. Matthew described Jesus as sorrowful and troubled. Jesus Himself said, "My soul is overwhelmed with sorrow to the point of death" (Matt. 26:38). In His humanity, Jesus struggled with the choice of God's will over His own will. Fortunately for mankind, Jesus chose to orient the will of His heart on the Father's will, even though much pain and suffering resulted.

The reality of what God is asking of you may bring you to your own Garden of Gethsemane experience. A follower of Christ may become sorrowful and troubled when one considers the implications of God's will on his or her life as a leader. I for one am encouraged that Jesus struggled emotionally with the choice of God's will over His own will. As a follower of Jesus Christ, I find comfort in knowing that I can do as Jesus did and go to the Father in prayer when faced with the prospect of sacrificially obeying God's commands. If you are facing such circumstances, I encourage you to pour your heart out to God in prayer.

Every leader has a choice to orient the will of his or her heart on God's will or one's own selfish will. Becoming the leader God desires requires one to orient his or her will toward God's will. Jonah initially chose to follow his own will and ran from the Lord. God sent a storm to impede his flight and a fish to redirect his path. God gave Jonah a second chance to obey His commands. Once Jonah aligned his heart with God's, the Lord used Jonah to carry out His will in Nineveh. Jesus struggled with the personal price of orienting His will with the will of the Father. Jesus asked God for another way while affirming His commitment to do God's will when the time arrived.

The choices of Jonah and Jesus illustrate why God looks for a leader willing to do all He asks. This criterion used by God to select leaders summarizes the first core value of an Entrusted Leader: *A HEART willing to do all God asks.* Each follower of Jesus Christ who leads others must honestly ask: Am I willing to do all God asks of me? The implications of applying the second core value of an Entrusted Leader (*A MISSION for leading characterized by a faithful commitment to multiplying followers of Jesus Christ that supersedes all other endeavors*) will quickly expose the limits to which a leader will follow through and actually do all God asks!

Discussion Questions based on "The Choices of Jonah and Jesus"

1. The stories of Jonah and Jesus are different in that Jonah initially oriented his heart on self and disobeyed God, while Jesus always kept His heart oriented on God's will and obeyed it to the point of death. Which can you more closely relate to and why?

2. God used a storm, a fish, and even the sailors to get Jonah's attention. What has God used in your life to get your attention on His will? Did you listen? How did you react?

3. Jonah was literally alone in the belly of the fish. Jesus was essentially alone in the garden. Both cried out to God in anguish. Have you ever found yourself in a similar situation—alone before God in anguish? Describe the circumstances and outcome.

4. What steps can you take in your life that will better align your heart with God's will?

God selects a leader based on the inner orientation of his or her heart. Every leader faces this choice: Do I orient the will of my heart on God or self? Pleasing God as a leader requires one to orient his or her heart toward God's will.

PERSONAL APPLICATION EXERCISE

Briefly describe a circumstance when you faced a choice of your heart's will just as Jonah and Jesus did. Be sure to include the choice you made and how it turned out. If you cannot recall such a personal circumstance, write a brief summary of how you think you might react if faced with this choice.

6

Mission

CORE VALUE: A MISSION for leading characterized by a faithful commitment to multiplying followers of Jesus Christ that supersedes all other endeavors.

The Mission of Making Disciples
Matthew 28:16–20

Every position of leadership provides a platform for a leader to engage in the mission of multiplying disciples of Jesus Christ.

Jesus Christ pronounced the mission: ". . . go and make disciples. . . ." He desires leaders in all walks of life to engage in this process by first becoming His disciple and then a disciple maker. Leaders find significance and meaning when this mission transcends all others. To become the leader God desires, you must adopt this mission as the top priority of your life everywhere you lead others.

Have you ever asked yourself these questions: Why do I do what I do? Why do I work in a particular profession? Why do I volunteer my time with a certain charity? Why do I associate with this group or that? Answers to these types of questions might be: To provide financially for my family. I love my job. I want to give back to the community. I enjoy socializing with this group or that group.

Many people never get beyond these obvious answers. I want the reader to dig deeper for an answer that goes to the core of his or her existence. Ask yourself: What is the point of what I do? Does what I strive to accomplish have enduring value? Can you say your efforts bring meaning and significance to your life? Will the results of what you do carry on into eternity?

Let me ask you a related question: What mission shapes your life? Whether you realize it or not, your life exists conjoined to some agenda. How you choose to invest your life will generate some sense of importance to your existence. Deep down inside, we all want to know that our life has an enduring value. This need drives a person to choose a life mission to pursue. How are you investing your life? Is the return on the investment of your life significant, enduring, and eternal?

What priorities dominate your schedule? The mission in which you choose to invest your life will dictate your priorities. Once a person chooses a mission, he or she typically orders the time and energy of his or her life accordingly to accomplish the objective. Your calendar reflects your mission. Look back over the past few years and calculate where you have invested the majority of your waking hours, and you will develop a good picture of the mission or agenda to which your life is conjoined.

Every leader strives to accomplish a mission. People adopt their mission through a variety of means. The wise leader, guided by a heart willing to do all God asks, selects a mission through prayer, the study of God's Word, and the counsel of others. The foolish leader allows circumstances, culture, and the desires of a dysfunctional heart to guide the choice of a life mission. How did you select a mission in which to invest your life?

Commonly pursued missions are the following: pleasure, money, fame, influence, and power. These "things of men" ultimately prove to be meaningless. A leader will not find security or significance from these earthly endeavors. A leader will not acquire an enduring or eternal return on the investment of his or her life no matter how much worldly success one experiences pursuing these missions. Have you ever calculated a return on investment for your life?

Jesus Christ has already designated the mission for the church. Jesus expects His followers to invest their lives in pursuit of this mission. This mission returns eternal significance and purpose. No greater return on the investment of your life exists than serving this mission. One's priorities will quickly come into alignment with God's will once he or she allows the mission of Jesus to supersede all other endeavors. Jesus commanded His followers to go into the world and make disciples of all nations (Matt. 28:16–20). This mission extends to every opportunity a leader has to lead. God looks for leaders who are willing to leverage their leadership opportunities to make disciples.

A misconception exists in the church today in regard to the mission of making disciples. Many followers of Jesus assume that this mission relates only to professional ministers, not the laity. Let us be clear: Jesus has called every one of His followers to personally participate in the mission of making disciples. Simply contributing money to professional ministry efforts does not fully satisfy this call. God expects every follower of Jesus Christ to participate in the mission of making disciples within his or her sphere of influence. No exclusions from this effort exist.

Ask yourself the following question and think about it for a few minutes.

Is a "born-again" Christian free to invest the "talents" of his or her life in any "mission" he or she desires, as long as the pursuit is done in a "godly" fashion and does not directly violate God's Word?

On the surface, it seems that an affirmative answer to this question would be God-honoring and biblical, doesn't it? Unfortunately, it's not! A "born-again" Christian does not possess the freedom to invest the "talents" of one's life however he or she sees fit. Here's the problem with this statement: You did not just choose to follow Jesus; He purchased your life for His purpose. The Apostle Paul said, ". . . You are not your own; you were bought at a price. Therefore honor God with your body" (1 Cor. 6:19–20). Do you know the purchase price paid by God for our life? Consider the words of the Apostle John as he describes Jesus in Revelation 5:9–10: "You are worthy to take the scroll and to open its seals, because you were slain, and with your blood you purchased men for God from every tribe and language and people and nation. You have made them to be a kingdom and priests to serve our God, and they will reign on the earth." Jesus purchased you with His blood to serve God's mission on earth. Consequently, Jesus owns the rights to your life, and He has assigned you to serve His agenda. To become the leader God desires, you must adopt this mission as the top priority of your life everywhere you lead others—home, work, and your community at large.

I am on a mission to mobilize a generation of skilled leaders who will uphold the seven core values of an Entrusted Leader and leverage every opportunity for leadership to multiply followers of Jesus Christ. I believe this mission is consistent with God's calling to make disciples. This life mission brings eternal meaning and purpose to my life. This quest determines the priorities of my life and guides the investment of my time and energy. The genesis of this mission can be traced directly to a desire to obey Jesus' command to go forth and make disciples of all nations. I view the return on investment of my life strictly from an eternal perspective. I hold out the hope to someday hear my master say, ". . . Well done, good and faithful servant! . . . Come and share your master's happiness!" (Matt. 25:21).

Scholars commonly refer to this mission of Jesus for His followers as the Great Commission. Matthew recorded the words of Jesus' final instructions to His disciples in Matthew 28:16–20. To fully appreciate the urgency of this mission entrusted by the Master to His servants, one must understand the broader context within which Jesus spoke these words.

Two passages of Scripture, Matthew 27:32–28:10 and Acts 1:1–11, set the historical context within which Jesus spoke the words of the Great Commission recorded in Matthew 28:16–20. Matthew records for us the key events that precede Jesus assigning the Great Commission to His followers. In the book of Acts, Luke records the key events that surround and follow Jesus' command to make disciples.

We pick up the story of Jesus' final days on earth in Matthew 27. The rulers of Israel decided Jesus had to die. They turned him over to the Roman governor, Pontius Pilate, and requested Jesus' execution. The soldiers took Jesus to the praetorium. They stripped, mocked, spat upon, and beat God's only Son. Next, at a place named Golgotha, Jesus was crucified. Crucifixion, nailing someone to a cross, was a common method of execution by the Romans in the first century.

Shortly after the ninth hour, Jesus died. A man by the name of Joseph asked Pilate if he could take charge of Jesus' body. Pilate agreed, so Joseph took the Lord's body, wrapped it in linen, placed it in a tomb, and rolled a big rock in front of the entrance. Fearing that His disciples might try to steal Jesus' body, the rulers of Israel asked Pilate to secure the tomb. Pilate ordered the tomb be secured by putting a seal outside the entrance and posting a guard.

Early on the day following the Sabbath, Mary Magdalene and Mary went to visit the tomb. Shockingly these women found the tomb empty. An angel told Mary Magdalene and Mary that Jesus had risen from the dead. The angel told the women to go to Galilee, where they would see Jesus alive.

Luke begins his account of the Acts of the Apostles with Jesus' resurrection, which is where Matthew concludes his gospel. Luke records that after Jesus rose from the dead, He appeared to His disciples over a forty-day period. During this time, Jesus gave many convincing proofs that He was really alive and spoke about the kingdom of heaven. At the end of this forty-day period, Jesus ascended into heaven. Suddenly, two men dressed in white appeared to Jesus' disciples and promised them that Jesus would return to earth someday just as He had departed.

Jesus spoke the Great Commission (Matt. 28:16–20) during this forty-day period between His resurrection and ascension. This brief time period establishes the historical context within which Jesus instructed His followers to go and make disciples. The communication of the mission of Jesus for His followers stands apart from the many lessons He taught during the three-year public ministry that preceded His death. Jesus spoke these words literally during His final hours on earth. No time remained for small talk; Jesus only had time to communicate the most important of instructions to His followers. The context of Jesus' pending departure should suggest to His followers a sense of urgency and importance to the mission of making disciples.

During this forty-day period, Jesus also promised His disciples that He would return. Just as the master in the Parable of the Talents expected his servants to faithfully serve what had been entrusted to them while he was on a long journey, so also I believe Jesus expects each of His followers to faithfully serve His instruction to go and make disciples until He returns. The promise of Jesus' second coming suggests to His followers a sense of stewardship and accountability to one's service to the mission of making disciples during His absence.

Perhaps more than any other passage of Scripture you will study in *The ENTRUSTED Leader*, Matthew 28:16–20 requires a thorough understanding of the key terms and grammatical construction of the sentences. As a leader, you must acquire an accurate interpretation of these verses if you hope to develop an appreciation of how this mission applies where you lead others. The Great Commission contains five key terms relevant to our study: authority, go, make disciples, baptizing, and teaching. We will begin by considering the original Greek term and its meaning for each of these words.

The English word "authority" comes from the Greek term *exousia*. The risen Lord Jesus tells His disciples that He possesses all "authority." Does He? Do you believe Jesus possesses all authority in heaven and on earth? How you answer this question will dramatically impact the approach you take to making disciples. The original group of disciples believed Jesus possessed all authority. These followers of Jesus endured hardship and persecution and sacrificed everything they had to accomplish this mission, in part because these disciples truly believed they were acting on behalf of the sovereign ruler of heaven and earth.

Jesus claims to have authority—the power to choose and act however He saw fit. He exercised this right to set the agenda for His followers based on this unlimited authority. Jesus professed the power to rule, and He expected His will and commands to be obeyed. This absolute authority provides the basis upon which Jesus assigned the Great Commission to His followers. Consider Strong's definition of authority:

> 1849 ἐξουσία [exousia /ex·oo·see·ah/] . . . 1 power of choice, liberty of doing as one pleases. . . . 3 the power of authority (influence) and of right (privilege). 4 the power of rule or government (the power of him whose will and commands must be submitted to by others and obeyed). . . .[1]

Jesus' claim of authority seems out of place, bold, and unexpected. The events surrounding Jesus' capture, trial, and execution might suggest that Jesus lacked the power or authority to defend and control what was happening to Him. Nothing could be further from the reality of the situation. Jesus voluntarily submitted to humiliation and suffering to pay the penalty our sin deserves and to purchase us for God. Jesus assured His followers that regardless of how recent events may look He possessed authority over all of heaven and earth. Nothing escapes Jesus' rule. The truth of Jesus' authority becomes significant to His followers for two reasons. First of all, Jesus' authority establishes His right to entrust the mission of making disciples to His followers for all of time. Secondly, Jesus' followers have the implied authority to move into the world and make disciples because believers act on Jesus' authority.

Jesus still possesses all authority today. Jesus currently sits at the right hand of the Father, awaiting the command to return to earth. The mission entrusted to His followers during His absence has not changed. Modern-day followers of Jesus Christ can pursue the mission of making disciples with the peace of mind that one acts on the basis of Jesus' authority, not just human authority.

After Jesus established the scope and reality of His authority, He immediately exercised His control by telling His followers what He wanted them to do once He had departed. The term "therefore" stands as the key connection between Jesus' authority and the Great Commission. Jesus told His disciples that He had the right to rule as He saw fit in heaven and earth, and based on this authority, He told his followers to go and make disciples. Matthew 28:16–20 contains Jesus' final marching orders for His disciples.

Jesus instructed his followers to "go and make disciples." To fully appreciate the force of this command, one must understand the construction of the original Greek grammar. If one only considers the English translation, a temptation exists to place an emphasis on the word "go." One could easily assume that obedience to the Great Commission requires moving geographically from our present location to another and then making disciples. Such an emphasis on the verb "go" leads to an improper interpretation and application. The word "go" in the Greek exists as a participle functioning as the secondary verb in the sentence. I believe the force of this sentence conveys the instruction, "As you are 'going' about the normal course of your life, I want you to accomplish something." The something involves "making disciples."

The primary verb of this sentence is "make disciples." This action carries the force of what Jesus is saying in this passage. The Greek word for "make disciples" is an imperative. Jesus is giving His followers a command or an order. Making disciples is not a suggestion or a nice thing to do if we have time. Based on His authority as ruler over all heaven and earth, Jesus commands that His followers produce other followers wherever they might be going in life. There is no room for ignoring or disobeying this command. This order extends to all followers of Jesus Christ for all of time until His second coming. This command extends to every facet of life, even as one leads at home, in the marketplace, and in the community. The mission Jesus assigned suggests to modern-day leaders that as a Christ follower goes about the normal course of leading, he or she should use every opportunity and circumstance to make disciples. Leaders who desire to follow Christ must view every relationship from the perspective of the potential of engaging in the process of disciple making.

Leaders who desire to follow Christ must view every relationship from the perspective of the potential of engaging in the process of disciple making.

An obvious question arises at this point: If all Christ followers stand responsible to "make disciples," then how does one make disciples? What defines a disciple? How does a leader proceed to make one? What process or steps are involved? Jesus helps answer this question with two key terms that describe the process. Jesus tells us to "baptize" and "teach." The idea of baptizing addresses the act of conversion or justification. The process of making disciples starts with evangelism. Believers must be quick and ready to share their faith and the truth of the gospel with those who do not know the Lord Jesus as their personal savior. The idea of teaching addresses a believer's lifelong journey of spiritual growth and maturing, sanctification, that starts at the moment of conversion and continues for the rest of one's time on earth. The primary emphasis involves teaching a new convert God's Word and encouraging him or her to apply and obey all Jesus taught. The process of disciple making is discussed in more detail in the next lesson.

Jesus commanded all His followers to go and make disciples. Believers should view this mission as an unbelievable opportunity, not an obligation. Incredibly, the ruler of heaven and earth has included the efforts of Christ followers in His mission of building His kingdom on earth. Go back and reconsider the opening questions of this lesson in light of the opportunity to make disciples. Why do I do what I do? Why do I work in a particular profession? Why do I volunteer my time with a certain charity? Why do I associate with this group or that? The opportunity to make disciples brings an eternal perspective and enduring meaning to the answer to every one of these questions. For example: I work in a particular profession because God intends to use me as His ambassador among those I lead.

God does not expect a believer to "go" somewhere different to apply this mission. If you truly believe it is God's will for you to lead wherever it is you lead, then you are already positioned where God wants you to make disciples. Consider Jesus' words as recorded in John 4:35: "Do you not say, 'Four months more and then the harvest'? I tell you, open your eyes and look at the fields! They are ripe for harvest." As a modern-day follower of Jesus Christ who leads others, you already labor in a mission field that stands ripe for making disciples. Obedience to serving the mission of making disciples probably does not require you to change leadership positions or resign your job to enter the professional ministry. God wants to use you right now, right where you are. Think of it this way: There are lives you can touch for the cause of Christ where you currently lead that no other follower of Jesus Christ can reach.

Those who know me well know that I am not a fan of "water-cooler" evangelism. I do not believe God has called us to stand by the company coffeepot handing out religious tracts for Jesus. Making disciples involves much more than simply testifying vocally the gospel to one's work associates. As a leader, I believe a better approach involves building trusting and authentic relationships with those we lead. The public demonstration of our faith as seen by others in our actions and decisions—in how we lead—ultimately earns us the right to vocalize our faith at the appropriate time. Conversely, if our actions and decisions as a leader do not mirror our faith, then by default our words will fall on the deaf ears of those we lead and our perception will be one of a hypocrite. The next lesson will look more specifically into how a leader can develop and implement a plan to make disciples where one leads others.

Every follower of Jesus Christ is called to personally participate in the church's mission of making disciples. To become the leader God desires, you must adopt this mission as the top priority of your life everywhere you lead others. God instructs each Entrusted Leader to look for opportunities to make disciples wherever he or she leads others. This instruction exists as part of God's will for every believer.

One great aspect of God's call to make disciples suggests that in most cases a leader who follows Christ does not have to go anywhere to faithfully serve the Lord's will. God desires and intends to use you right where you are. Your family, neighborhood, and workplace constitute fields ripe for the harvest. God has already entrusted all you need to lead and make disciples. The question of faithfulness resides with you. You have the choice to orient your will on God's will and view your world from the vantage point of disciple-making opportunities.

The first core value of an Entrusted Leader is: *A HEART willing to do all God asks.* This lesson introduced us to the second core value: *A MISSION for leading characterized by a faithful commitment to multiplying followers of Jesus Christ that supersedes all other endeavors.* Core value one provides the standard by which the other six are measured. We cannot say we are willing to enact all God asks unless we are willing to adopt as our top priority the mission of making disciples where we lead others. Now that we have studied this decision point in regard to serving God's will, go before God in the power of the Holy Spirit and ask Him to reveal to you the truth of these passages and how they may apply to your particular situation as a leader. This lesson introduced the "what" of God's mission for a follower of Jesus Christ, which focuses on disciple making. The next lesson will begin to answer the question of how one sets about making disciples as he or she goes about leading others.

Discussion Questions based on "The Mission of Making Disciples"

1. Given His authority and the context within which Jesus spoke, describe your personal responsibility to engage in the mission of making disciples.

2. How can making disciples bring meaning and purpose everywhere you lead?

3. What does it mean to you to "go"? (Remember the earlier discussion of translating this word as "going" or "as you are going about the normal course of your life.")

4. What mission has dominated how you have invested the assets (time, skills, opportunities, and relationships) of your life up to know? (Be honest!) What actions (changing priorities, schedules, activities, etc.) can you take to be sure the mission of making disciples takes precedence over all others?

> *Jesus Christ pronounced the mission:*
> *". . . go and make disciples. . . ." Leaders find significance and*
> *meaning when this mission transcends all others. To become the*
> *leader God desires, you must adopt this mission as the top priority*
> *for every leader-to-follower relationship.*

PERSONAL APPLICATION EXERCISE

In your reader's journal, write or draw a depiction of how the mission of making disciples might bring added meaning and significance to one of your leader-to-follower relationships.

The Strategy of Multiplication
2 Timothy 2:2

Jesus Christ pronounced the mission: ". . . go and make disciples. . . ." The Apostle Paul defined the strategy: ". . . entrust to reliable men. . . ." Disciple making begins with and cannot be divorced from a life-on-life relationship whereby a spiritually mature follower of Jesus Christ personally entrusts spiritual truth to another. Every opportunity to lead involves leader-to-follower relationships that hold the potential for a disciple-making exchange of spiritual truth.

Jesus assigned a mission to His followers: Make disciples. Jesus' original followers did not have to ask what He meant or how to approach this mission. The apostles understood Jesus' command. They knew what actions to initiate. First-century disciples, as have many since then, faithfully served the mission of making disciples above all other endeavors.

As modern-day followers of Jesus Christ, the mission has not changed. An unbroken chain of disciple making exists between twenty-first-century believers and first-century disciples. We owe our status as followers of Jesus Christ in large part to disciple makers who have faithfully served this mission for two thousand plus years. Our generation of followers of Jesus Christ stands as a link to future disciples and disciple makers. Modern-day followers of Christ must ask if they truly understand the Master's command and what actions to initiate. Leaders who follow Christ must honestly assess whether making disciples ranks as the top priority in all their endeavors. The future of the church literally hinges on how twenty-first-century disciples answer these questions.

Every successful mission comes to life through a practical strategic plan. Jesus gave His followers the mission: Make disciples! The Apostle Paul gave followers of Jesus a practical strategic plan. Disciple making begins with a life-on-life relationship whereby a spiritually mature disciple personally entrusts to others spiritual truth. Paul's relationship with Timothy provides a model of a life-on-life disciple-making relationship. Paul summarizes his strategy for making disciples in 2 Timothy 2:2. This passage provides a practical strategic plan that addresses the actions leaders can take today to faithfully serve Jesus' command to make disciples.

Before we look at the practicality of Paul's strategy for making disciples, we must define a "disciple." After all, we cannot make that which we do not clearly understand. The most common Greek term found in the New Testament that translates to the English word "disciple" is *mathetes*. This Greek term generally refers to someone described as a pupil or learner. Strong defines *mathetes* as follows: "μαθητής [*mathetes* /math·ay·tes/] n m. . . . 269 occurrences; . . . 1 a learner, pupil, disciple."[2]

In the context of the first-century Christian Church, a "disciple" meant much more than a student engaged in an academic exercise of pursuing knowledge. The term *mathetes* refers to a person who fully devoted his or her existence to a transforming way of life, who adhered to all the teachings of Jesus Christ, and who personally participated in the mission of making disciples. This concept of a disciple has not changed in two thousand years. To "make a disciple" means to produce a follower of Jesus Christ who commits to living a transformed life, obeys the Word of God, and makes the mission of disciple making his or her top priority.

Making a disciple requires a spiritual growth process. Discipleship describes the process that produces a disciple. Thus a disciple maker engages in the process of discipleship to make another disciple. I like to think of discipleship as a three-step process.

The first step in the discipleship process focuses on conversion. A person must come to know Jesus Christ as his or her personal Lord and Savior before one can experience life transformation. Consider John 3:3: "In reply Jesus declared, 'I tell you the truth, no one can see the kingdom of God unless he is born again.'" In this passage, Jesus answers Nicodemus' question about what a person must do to be saved. A disciple maker's primary focus in this regard involves evangelism. A person must be born spiritually before he or she can begin to mature spiritually.

The second step in the discipleship process spans a lifetime of spiritual growth. Learning the Word of God and embracing spiritual disciplines, such as prayer, fellowship, worship, and service, lead a babe in Christ toward spiritual maturity. Peter's sermon recorded in Acts 2:14–40 resulted in the conversion of three thousand disciples. Luke tells us in Acts 2:42 what happened next: "They devoted themselves to the apostles' teaching and to the fellowship, to the breaking of bread and to prayer." This passage provides a good blueprint for the spiritual growth of a new disciple.

The third step in the process involves becoming a disciple maker. The Apostle Paul provided a strategy that leaders who follow Christ can still pursue today. Read 2 Timothy 2:2 and consider Paul's charge to Timothy. In fact, I want to go one step further and challenge you to memorize this verse and to make multiplying followers of Jesus Christ the priority in your life that supersedes all other endeavors.

> *²And the things you have heard me say in the presence of many witnesses entrust to reliable men who will also be qualified to teach others. (2 Tim. 2:2)*

In prison and nearing the end of his ministry, Paul addressed his final New Testament epistle to Timothy. Paul wrote 2 Timothy to encourage his protégé in his ministerial efforts. Among the many words of wisdom passed from Paul to Timothy is a one-sentence summary of Paul's strategy for making disciples. Jesus gave the mission: Make disciples! Paul provided a strategy: "Entrust reliable men." Many describe Paul's strategy as a strategy of multiplication.

Timothy lived in Lystra when Paul visited there during his second missionary journey. Paul invited Timothy to join him as he traveled. Paul and Timothy co-labored in an effort to make disciples. In many respects, Paul became a spiritual father to Timothy. Paul fostered Timothy's spiritual growth as a disciple and led him to become a disciple maker himself.

Paul and Timothy worked closely together for many years in faithful service to the mission of making disciples. Paul reminds Timothy of all the statements he had heard Paul say in the presence of many witnesses. Paul and Timothy separated at times, but there is little doubt that Timothy heard Paul teach all the essential truths related to following Jesus Christ.

Paul directs Timothy to "entrust" all he had heard to others. This concept of "entrusting" parallels the lessons learned from the Parable of the Talents. Please refer to chapter 3, "The Entrusted Leader," for an explanation of the biblical concept of entrusting valuable assets to another. Paul's statement to entrust reveals an imperative. Paul commands Timothy to "entrust" all he had heard Paul say to others. Paul charged Timothy with the responsibility of passing on the fundamental teachings of the faith to others.

Paul uses a word and a phrase to describe the type of individual to whom Timothy should "entrust" his words. Paul encourages Timothy to target "reliable" individuals who can become "qualified to teach." Think of "reliability" as a prerequisite to the act of "entrusting" and "qualified to teach" as the end product of the "entrusting" process.

The advice to target "reliable" individuals remains fundamental to a strategy of multiplying disciples. Without trustworthy people who will carry on, the process of multiplying disciples will break down. No wise investor would entrust one's money to an "unreliable" financial institution. Similarly, a wise disciple maker quickly learns that entrusting time, energy, and God's Word to "unreliable" individuals often results in a low return on investment. Paul instructs Timothy to look for individuals with proven track records of reliability evidenced by the actions and priorities of their lives.

The Greek word used by the Apostle Paul is *pistos.* This term conveys the characteristic of being a faithful and trustworthy individual. "Reliable" people can be counted on to do what they say they are going to do. "Reliable" people follow orders, handle responsibility, and discharge their duties without having to be checked on. Strong defines the Greek term *pistos* as follows: "πιστός [*pistos* /pis·tos/] . . . 1 trusty, faithful. 1A of persons who show themselves faithful in the transaction of business, the execution of commands, or the discharge of official duties. 1B one who kept his plighted faith, worthy of trust. 1C that can be relied on.[3]

Paul also uses the phrase "qualified to teach" to describe the type of individual to whom Timothy should entrust the truths and disciplines of the faith. Paul wisely looked beyond Timothy to the others who would have to be counted on to continue the disciple-making process once he and Timothy were no longer around. Timothy demonstrated "reliability" and "qualifications to teach" in his life. Paul witnessed Timothy's "reliability" and knew he could count on him. Timothy stood "qualified to teach" in large part because Paul had trained him. The time had come for Timothy to carry the torch of disciple making to the next generation of disciple makers.

Paul expected that the entrusting of his teachings to "reliable" people would produce "qualified" individuals who would in turn continue the process. Paul's goal went beyond producing disciples to include producing disciple makers. This multiplication of disciples would be the highest return for the investment Paul made in Timothy. Similarly, continuation of this process would be the highest return Timothy could expect for what he entrusted to reliable men.

Two key Greek words make up the phrase "qualified to teach." The Greek adjective *hikanos* comes first. The NIV translates this word as "qualified." The term essentially conveys the idea that someone or something can be viewed as sufficient or able for the task at hand. Strong defines the term as follows: "ἱκανός [*hikanos* /hik·an·os/] adj. . . .1 sufficient. 1A many enough, enough. 1B sufficient in ability, . . .[4]

The second Greek term in the phrase describes the "task at hand" or what Paul expects "reliable" people to do with what Timothy "entrusted" to them. Paul expects them to teach others to do the same. The Greek term is *didasko*. The word denotes the action of one person teaching something to another. Strong defines the term as follows: "διδάσκω [*didasko* /did·as·ko/] v. . . . 1 to teach. 1A to hold discourse with others in order to instruct them, deliver didactic discourses. 1B to be a teacher. 1C to discharge the office of a teacher, conduct one's self as a teacher."[5]

Paul commands Timothy to entrust the essential truths of the faith to reliable individuals who will carry on the process with others. This description of the disciple-making process contains four generations of disciples. Paul and the other apostles represent the first generation. Timothy represents a second generation of disciples. Timothy and his peers bridged the gap between those disciples whose lives overlapped Jesus' and all future disciples who will believe in Him by the witness of others. Reliable men stand as the third generation, and the others they teach are the fourth generation.

Paul's strategy for executing Jesus' mission of making disciples relied on a process of multiplication. Paul instructed Timothy (singular) to invest his life in men (plural). Paul expected these men (plural) to invest in others (plural). This describes a multiplicative process that has the potential to expand the faith exponentially.

The Strategy of Multiplication Explained

To illustrate how a multiplicative strategy of making disciples works, one can compare the process to an additive strategy. For example, I could choose to teach the Word of God to one hundred people per year for ten years. At the end of this ten-year period, I could claim to have made one thousand disciples. Teaching one hundred people at a time would require a classroom setting of a large group and would afford very little life-on-life interchange between me and the students. The focus would center on the transfer of information with little or no time to model behavior or follow up on what the students did with what they learned. This is an additive strategy because I simple add up my efforts at the end of each year to determine the results.

An alternative approach would require a teacher to concentrate on only a few individuals for one year. For the sake of example, let's say three. The goal of this approach becomes to teach the three disciples to replicate the process themselves by becoming individual disciple makers. At the end of year one, my expectation of these three individuals would be for them to each find three other individuals to train, while I started over with three new reliable men. If all goes according to strategy, at the end of year two, three generations, or sixteen capable disciple makers, have completed the process: me, the original three I trained in year one, the nine they trained in year two, and the three I trained in year two. This illustrates a multiplicative strategy because my efforts become multiplied through the lives of others.

Now one might say: Wait a minute. If you used an additive strategy, you would have produced 200 disciples at the end of year two, while under a multiplicative strategy, you trained only 15 new disciples. In the short run, this appears true, but the genius of a multiplicative strategy lies in the later years where the numbers expand exponentially. In this example, the break-even point is reached at the end of year five; under the additive strategy, I would have made 500 disciples, and under a multiplicative strategy, there would be 537 new disciples. Consider, however, what happens at the end of year ten: During this period I could have trained 1,000 disciples additively. Under the multiplicative strategy, I would have trained 30 disciple makers myself, but when you multiply my efforts by the efforts of 30 reliable men, we would have collectively made over 132,000 new disciples. To take this strategy one step further, if we let the strategy of multiplication run for twenty years at the rate of 3 new disciple makers a year, the entire world population of 6 billion plus could be reached for Christ. Take out a calculator and do the math if you don't believe me.

At this point, you may be thinking something like: So what! I understand Paul's command to Timothy. I accept my role for making disciples. I can even comprehend the potential of a multiplicative strategy, but how does the teaching of 2 Timothy 2:2 intersect my role as a leader? The answer: God desires you to apply the strategy of multiplying followers of Jesus Christ among those you lead.

Consider every relationship you have as a leader. Take into account every superior, subordinate, and peer that surrounds your position as a leader. Think of all the customers, suppliers, and service providers, such as bankers, lawyers, and consultants, with whom you have contact. These individuals make up your mission field for making disciples. Within this pool of relationships reside reliable individuals who God desires you to entrust spiritual truth, so they in turn can teach others. I would suggest that at this very moment there are more opportunities to make disciples among your network of relationships than you have the capacity to disciple. Being a follower of Jesus Christ who leads provides you many relationships that hold a potential for disciple making.

Every leader who desires to make disciples needs a Paul. Do you have a more spiritually mature believer entrusting spiritual truth and discipline to you? Do you have a Paul equipping you to make disciples? If you are willing to make disciples but have never been equipped, then the first step is to find a Paul. Remember, there were fifteen years of relationship and equipping that proceeded Paul's speaking of 2 Timothy 2:2. I doubt Paul would have expect this from Timothy the first time they met. Find a Paul!

Once equipped, the next step is to identify reliable men in which to invest. A multiplicative strategy for making disciples works best when implemented in a proactive and intentional manner, not a passive and reactive one. Jesus commanded His followers to initiate action that resulted in disciple making. Paul commanded Timothy to entrust in reliable men who would teach others. Jesus and Paul both spoke in the imperative, expecting their audiences to go and take action.

Modern-day followers of Jesus Christ who lead others must initiate actions that lead to disciple-making relationships and opportunities. We serve Christ with the marching orders of Jesus and Paul still in force. God expects us to proactively initiate action. Making disciples requires organization and intentional actions. A leader should always stand ready to identify the reliable men or women they strive to disciple with an eye toward them replicating the process. Can you identify such an individual in which you are intentionally investing? Find a group of reliable individuals and start the process of entrusting the truths of the faith. Keep an eye on the day that you challenge them to begin to entrust in others.

The mission focuses on making disciples. The strategy involves investing in others who in turn will do likewise. Reliable men and women represent the target. Your unique network of relationships represents a mission field that God has already prepared in advance for you. Every leader-to-follower relationship entrusted by God represents potential for making disciples.

Disciple making begins with and cannot be divorced from the life-on-life relationship whereby a spiritually mature disciple personally entrusts to others spiritual truth and disciplines. Every position of leadership involves life-on-life relationships that hold the potential to exchange spiritual truth. The opportunity to form a "Paul" to "Timothy" relationship exists all around you.

This lesson is the second of three designed to teach the Entrusted Leader core value number two: *A MISSION for leading characterized by a faithful commitment to multiplying followers of Jesus Christ that supersedes all other endeavors.* The previous lesson established that God expects every follower of Jesus Christ to personally engage in the mission of making disciples. This lesson considered the strategy of multiplying disciples by entrusting the truths of the faith to reliable men and women who can become qualified to teach others. The next lesson will go one step further and discuss how to build a specific disciple-making plan of action for each leadership platform entrusted by God.

Discussion Questions based on "The Strategy of Multiplication"
1. Based on 2 Timothy 2:2, describe why the strategy of multiplication so effectively serves the mission of making disciples.
2. Write a brief description of what it means to be a reliable person. Would other people describe you as reliable, faithful, and trustworthy? Why or why not?

3. Discuss the influence a "Paul" has had in your spiritual walk. If you have never been in a relationship with a "Paul," write out a plan to find one.
4. Describe the "Timothy" you are currently discipling. If you are not currently entrusting in the life of a "reliable man" (a Timothy), write out a plan to find one.

Jesus Christ pronounced the mission: ". . . go and make disciples. . . ."
The Apostle Paul defined the strategy: ". . . entrust to reliable men. . . ."

Disciple making begins with and cannot be divorced from a life-on-life relationship!

Every opportunity to lead involves leader-to-follower relationships that hold the potential for a disciple-making exchange of spiritual truth.

PERSONAL APPLICATION EXERCISE

Draw the network of relationships from one opportunity you have to lead others (work, home, neighborhood, as a volunteer). Do you see a potential "Timothy" to disciple?

The Platform of Leadership
Romans 13:1

Jesus Christ stated the mission: ". . . go and make disciples . . . ," and in turn the Apostle Paul outlined a strategy of multiplication: ". . . entrust to reliable men. . . ." Every position of leadership provides a platform for a leader to faithfully engage in the mission of multiplying disciples of Jesus Christ. God entrusts leadership platforms to leaders according to His eternal purposes.

"The Platform of Leadership" completes the three-lesson set designed to teach an Entrusted Leader core value number two: *A MIS-*

SION for leading characterized by a faithful commitment to multiplying followers of Jesus Christ that supersedes all other endeavors. Jesus established the mission: Make disciples! Each follower of Jesus Christ stands called to participate in this mission. The Apostle Paul gave Timothy the strategy of multiplication for making disciples. This strategy of developing life-on-life relationships with reliable men and women who can teach others still works today. God intends and desires for this mission and strategy to rise above all other endeavors and become the preeminent priority in all your leadership opportunities. God has entrusted you with various platforms of leadership that provide opportunities for you to initiate the actions necessary to make this mission and strategy a reality where you lead others.

The ENTRUSTED Leader defines a "platform of leadership" as follows: the position a leader stands upon whereby others publicly recognize a leader's authority to lead. The leader's position and authority make up the two key concepts of this definition. A leader's platform encompasses one's span of authority, sphere of influence, and realm of responsibility associated with his or her position of leadership. Keep in mind that God entrusted the influence and authority associated with your leadership platforms for His purposes, not yours.

This may sound like an obvious question, but I want you to ask yourself: How does a person acquire a leadership platform? Your answer to this question will dramatically impact how you lead others. Three possible answers exist to this question. A leader typically ascribes the origin of his or her leadership platform to self, another person, or God.

Heroic stories of success have popularized the myth of "the self-made leader" in western culture. Many leaders arrogantly ascribe all the credit for getting to the top to self. Years of hard work and sacrifice deceive many leaders into believing that they accomplished success without help from others. When asked about the origin of one's platform or authority to lead, deep down in their hearts these leaders believe in self! This view of leadership platform origin inevitably produces a self-centered leader. This egocentric leader believes he or she answers to no one but self and will lead others according to his or her own personal agenda and to satisfy one's selfish desires. This leader rarely or never considers the opportunity to impact others for Christ associated with one's platform of leadership.

Undying loyalty as one ascends the ladder solidifies the commitment of "the company man" in many organizations. These leaders willingly admit that other people contributed to their rise to leadership. They attribute the granting and keeping of their leadership platform to those in power above them. Years of loyal service and pleasing others leave many leaders feeling indebted to another for their opportunity to lead. This view of leadership platform origin inevitably produces a people-pleasing leader. The leader who strives to please thinks that he or she must answer to the whims of those above him or her in order to grab the next rung and/or protect the leadership turf already secured. The expectations that an individual perceives others to hold guide this leader's priorities and actions, even if such expectations conflict with one's personal convictions. This leader may recognize the opportunity to impact others for Christ associated with one's platform of leadership, but they rarely or never act for fear of displeasing others.

An eternal perspective guides the Entrusted Leader's view of the origin of one's leadership platform. This third option rests upon a firm belief in God Almighty, the sovereign King and Ruler of heaven and earth. Wise and humble leaders recognize the work of a higher being Who placed them on a platform of leadership. This leader believes in a sovereign and loving God. An Entrusted Leader knows that God providentially granted him or her the authority to lead others. This leader will lead according to God's standards and not self-centered desires or the expectations of others. Entrusted Leaders recognize the opportunity to impact others for Christ associated with one's platform of leadership and order their priorities accordingly.

According to the Apostle Paul, every leader owes his or her ascent to a platform of leadership to God. "Everyone must submit himself to the governing authorities, for there is no authority except that which God has established. The authorities that exist have been established by God" (Rom. 13:1). The Lord God Almighty, sovereign King and Ruler of heaven and earth, is the origin of all leadership authority.

God has established all human authority to lead others. No authority exists in the world that does not find its origin in the sovereign king and ruler of heaven and earth. An individual who occupies a platform of leadership resides there according to God's grace and purpose. Consequently the Apostle Paul commands everyone to submit to all governing authority. Disobedience to human authority constitutes rebellion against God since He established it in the first place: "Consequently, he who rebels against the authority is rebelling against what God has instituted, and those who do so will bring judgment on themselves" (Rom. 13:2).

The historical backdrop of this passage suggests that Paul had civil government leaders in mind when he wrote Romans 13:1. The first-century Roman government oppressed both Christians and Jews. Judaism advocated submission, but some were beginning to call for a rebellion. These sentiments were infiltrating the early church as well. Romans 12:1–2 introduces a lengthy lesson on what it means as a Christian to live a "transformed life" while still on earth. Paul speaks out against civil disobedience primarily because he equates such behavior as rebellion against God. Paul's logic stems from the fact that God established every position of authority and entrusted to a leader the responsibility for others. This hierarchy of leadership exists according to God's purpose and eternal will. Therefore, Christ followers must submit to all authority.

The term "governing authorities" in Romans 13:1 refers to the person who possesses a position of leadership authority. Later in the verse, Paul refers to the "authority" established by God. Paul distinguishes between these two entities that come together to form a single base of leadership activity. Paul argues that everyone must submit to those leaders in charge because God established their span of authority and placed them in the position of leadership. Furthermore, God has acted according to His eternal plan and purpose that continually unfold throughout all of human history. Consider the following examples.

Cyrus, the king of Persia, ruled the known world five hundred plus years before the birth of Christ. In the first chapter of the book of Ezra, Cyrus, a secular king, acknowledges that the Lord God Almighty had given him the kingdoms of the world over which to rule. Cyrus went on to publicly proclaim that he believed God had appointed him the task of rebuilding the temple in Jerusalem. In this example, one sees the convergence of a secular leader, a God-ordained platform of leadership, and God's purposes being worked out in human history.

God made Joseph the ruler of all Egypt in order to save a remnant of Israel (Gen. 45:4–8). Again we find an individual leader and a platform of leadership coming together to be used according to God's purposes. In Exodus 3, the reader finds a similar story of God selecting Moses to lead Israel out of the bondage in Egypt.

Lastly, consider the case of Esther. God moved this young Jewish girl from obscurity to the royal authority of queen at just the right moment in history to help avert a plot to destroy the Jewish people. Consider the words of Mordecai: "When Esther's words were reported to Mordecai, he sent back this answer: 'Do not think that because you are in the king's house you alone of all the Jews will escape. For if you remain silent at this time, relief and deliverance for the Jews will arise from another place, but you and your father's family will perish. And who knows but that you have come to royal position for such a time as this?'" (Esther 4:12–14).

The Apostle Paul assures us in Romans 13:1 that God has established every platform of leadership and the authority associated with these positions. Furthermore God places individuals on these platforms to lead others according to his purposes. A leader, the authority to lead, and God's purpose all converge to form a single leadership platform. Just as Mordecai posed the question to Esther, a Christ follower must consider: Has God placed me on a platform of leadership that affords me the authority to lead for a specific eternal purpose at a particular point in history?

Paul certainly had the leaders of Rome in mind when he wrote Romans 13:1; however, the principle of a leader occupying a God-entrusted platform of leadership can apply to every arena of life. God alone has established a hierarchy of leadership authority in all human organizations, such as family, business, government, military, church, and ministry. One can conclude that the idea of one person possessing the authority to lead others rests on a sound biblical foundation. Any organization operating without a leader acts inconsistently with God's Word.

God raises leaders in accordance with His will and purpose. Consequently, every leader must acknowledge that he or she owes his or her ascension to a platform of leadership to God. A leader should strive to determine why God has placed him or her upon a particular platform of leadership and what the Lord desires one to accomplish with his or her entrusted authority. This reality of the origin of leadership authority extends to every position of leadership one holds at home, in the marketplace, and society at large. To use a platform of leadership for selfish gain or to please others opens a leader to the possibility of leading in a fashion that runs counter to God's purposes.

How do you think God views a leader that uses his or her God-entrusted platform of leadership to promote one's selfish agenda instead of God's eternal purposes? Every leader must realize that using one's platform of leadership for personal gain is a misuse of God's investment. Consider the examples of Pharaoh (Exod. 9:16) and Belshazzar (Dan. 5) who both refused to acknowledge God's purpose connected to the platforms of leadership granted to them by God.

Every platform of leadership contains an element of opportunity and responsibility. The opportunity involves using one's authority and position of leadership to impact others for the cause of Christ. The responsibility involves a recognition that God has entrusted each platform of leadership according to His purposes, and just as we learned in the Parable of the Talents a leader will someday have to answer for what he or she did with what God entrusted.

Many people hold multiple leadership platforms simultaneously. Many men, for example, live as a husband/father, a marketplace executive, and a church elder/deacon; sit on the school board; and serve as the volunteer coach of his son's or daughter's soccer team, all at the same time. Each of these platforms of leadership carries an inherent amount of leadership authority that a leader has the right to exercise. Once again, distinction exists between a person, the authority of the position, and God's will for granting them.

Paul viewed his self-worth and identity as inseparable from his relationship to Jesus Christ. Consider his teaching to the followers of Jesus Christ in Galatia: "I have been crucified with Christ and I no longer live, but Christ lives in me. The life I live in the body, I live by faith in the Son of God, who loved me and gave himself for me" (Gal. 2:20). Paul viewed his life as eternally one with Christ. Paul did not equate the worth of his life with some temporal platform of leadership. He recognized that Jesus Christ loved him and died for him. Paul's identity was anchored to the immovable foundation of a personal relationship with his Lord and Savior. Nothing outside of Christ's presence in his life defined for Paul who he was. Paul derived his meaning and security of life from the Son of God who loved him and died for him. Consequently Paul trusted in Jesus Christ for peace of mind and meaning in life, not in his platforms of leadership or pleasant circumstances.

Paul was a tentmaker by profession (see Acts 18:1–4). No doubt Paul approached his work with the highest degree of professionalism. He identified himself, however, first and foremost as a servant of Jesus Christ. "Paul, a servant of Christ Jesus, called to be an apostle and set apart for the gospel of God. . . ." (Rom. 1:1). Paul did not let his profession of tent making define his identity or self-worth.

Paul recognized that God had set him apart for the gospel. This mission framed Paul's view of life and provided the foundation for his self-worth. Making disciples superseded all other endeavors, including tent making. Paul's discipling of Priscilla and Aquila in the tent making arena provides a good example of how a leader can use a platform of leadership according to God's will. Consider the future ministry efforts of Priscilla and Aquila found in Acts 18:18–26, 1 Corinthians 16:19, Romans 16:3, and 2 Timothy 4:19 as evidence of how Paul's strategy of multiplying disciples worked in an everyday setting.

As a leader charged with the responsibility of leading others, certainly one must faithfully satisfy his or her professional obligations to the organization for which he or she works. A Christ follower must respect the policies and authority God has placed one under in all walks of life, as we have seen in Romans 13:1. Just as I believe Paul did, followers of Christ must approach their professions with the highest regard for excellence. Within the Entrusted Leader concept resides an assumption that a follower of Jesus Christ will always strive to be the best at one's chosen profession. Again, however, just as Paul did in his tent making, the Entrusted Leader must realize a higher calling on his or her life and that one's profession does not define a Christ follower's existence.

Within the Entrusted Leader concept resides an assumption that a follower of Jesus Christ will always strive to be the best at one's chosen profession.

I want readers to get this point loud and clear: As a follower of Jesus Christ, your self-worth and identity have no correlation to whatever platforms of leadership on which you stand! Period! Your self-worth and identity cannot be separated from your relationship with Jesus Christ! Period! As a modern-day follower of Jesus Christ who leads others, no platform of leadership defines who you are. Your significance only comes from the Son of God who loves you and died for you, not whatever position of leadership you happen to hold at a given moment. Remember, God established the leadership authority you have and has entrusted this responsibility to you for His purpose. God grants and rescinds authority according to His plan and timetable.

A temporal platform of leadership progresses through time with a succession of peaks and valleys. Sometimes, the circumstances surrounding one's leadership platform seem to function well. At other times, circumstances seem troublesome. If a leader ties his or her identity and self-worth to the oscillating pattern of a temporal leadership platform, then the leader will experience a roller-coaster ride of emotions based on one's perception of circumstances. When conditions appear good, the leader will feel happy and secure. When conditions appear out of control, the leader will fall victim to stress, anxiety, and worry. Consider also the leader whose identify is so entwined with his or her platform of leadership that the very thought of possibly losing one's authority brings on stress and anxiety. Sadly, if this person does actually have a leadership platform removed from his or her life, he or she typically experiences a blow to one's identity and self-worth also.

God did not intend for the followers of Jesus Christ to live insecure lives, even in the face of unsettled circumstances. Paul learned the secret of being content in all circumstances because his identity was founded in Jesus Christ, not a leadership platform (see Phil. 4:10–14). We should follow Paul's example. Such an attitude provides the Christ follower stability in the midst of temporal ups and downs as a leader. The Christian's security and peace of mind are rooted in his or her relationship with Jesus Christ, not his or her platform as a leader.

If you truly believe that God has established all authority, that He has entrusted whatever leadership platform you have, and that He is sovereign and loving, then you too can experience the peace of mind and security Paul found by becoming content in all circumstances—good and bad. Realize that God is responsible for you being a leader— not luck, good fortune, other people, or your efforts alone. God looks for leaders who are willing to do all He asks and to acknowledge Him as the one who entrusted to a person the authority and position to lead others.

How you view the origin of leadership authority will impact how and why you lead others. A leader's platform provides an opportunity to impact others for the cause of Christ or to make disciples. Every relationship contained in your platform of leadership holds the potential for a disciple-making interchange.

Every platform of leadership you hold has the potential for making disciples. Christ followers already have relationships with potentially reliable men and women to whom one can entrust spiritual truth and disciplines. You can develop a simple plan to implement the strategy of multiplying disciples, right where you lead. This plan will work in any platform of leadership. Below is a simple five-step process that outlines a framework for developing a plan for making disciples:

Step one is to create a list of platforms you currently hold.

Step two is to pick one of these platforms and identify every person by name with whom you have a relationship. Then repeat this with all other leadership platforms.

The third step involves defining the nature of each of these relationships with the goal of identifying potential "reliable men" among whom God might be preparing for you to make disciples.

The fourth step involves establishing a detailed set of priorities and actions that will move the disciple-making process along. For example, if you identify someone who is not a Christian, you might set a priority of sharing your testimony and the gospel with this individual within the next six months. Maybe you know a new believer who has never grown spiritually. You might suggest meeting periodically to study God's Word. The point becomes to develop priorities and a plan for each relationship and implement the action steps necessary to accomplish your goal.

The last step is perhaps the most important but most overlooked. Step five is to pray for every person by name within the span of your leadership platform. Pray! Pray! Pray! Pray specifically for each platform and individual on your list. Keep a prayer notebook and/or journal.

This lesson completes our teaching on Entrusted Leader core value number two: *A MISSION for leading characterized by a faithful commitment to multiplying followers of Jesus Christ that supersedes all other endeavors.* Jesus established the mission: Make disciples! The Apostle Paul gave Timothy the strategy of multiplication for making disciples. God intends and desires for this mission and strategy to rise above all other endeavors and become the preeminent priority in all your leadership platforms.

God has entrusted you with various platforms of leadership that provide a position upon which you can stand and whereby others publicly recognize your authority to lead. Each position of leadership you hold provides a platform entrusted to you by God that contains multiple opportunities to impact others for the mission of Christ. God desires you to develop a disciple-making action plan for each platform of leadership you possess. By doing so, a leader will move toward making the Entrusted Leader core value number two a reality: *A MISSION for leading characterized by a faithful commitment to multiplying followers of Jesus Christ that supersedes all other endeavors.*

Discussion Questions based on "The Platform of Leadership"

1. Describe one or two platforms of leadership God has entrusted to you. What network of relationships is associated with each of these platforms?

2. Do you see any opportunities to encourage the spiritual growth of others associated with your platforms of leadership? How are you responding to these opportunities?

3. According to Romans 13:1, God establishes all leadership authority. What are some implications of this for all leaders, both Christian and secular?

4. What determines your self-worth and personal identity: oneness with Christ (Gal. 2:20) or one of your leadership platforms? Briefly describe the basis of your self-worth and identity. (Be specific.)

*God entrusts leadership platforms to leaders
according to His eternal purposes!*

*Every position of leadership provides a platform for a leader to
faithfully engage in the mission of multiplying disciples of Jesus Christ.*

*A vast network of relationships typically
encircles every platform of leadership.*

PERSONAL APPLICATION EXERCISE

Draw one of your leadership platforms and the network of relationships associated with it. Do you see opportunity to encourage others?

7

Approach
CORE VALUE: An APPROACH to leadership characterized by denial of self and serving others.

Two Approaches to Leadership
Mark 10:42–45

Jesus Christ "approached" leadership as a servant. He rejected the world's authoritative, power-based approach. Christ followers who lead are called to deny self, resist the temptations of power and authority, and approach leadership as a servant to all.

Jesus taught His followers to deny self and serve others as a basic approach to leadership. This way of leading requires a heart oriented on God and others instead of self.

Many styles of management exist, but there are only two approaches to leadership: Jesus' approach and the world's approach. Jesus Christ approached leadership as a servant. He rejected the world's authoritative approach. Jesus instructed His followers to lead by serving others as opposed to exercising authority over them.

Jesus instructed His followers to lead by serving others as opposed to exercising authority over them.

A "style" describes various techniques used by managers to direct others. A style helps a manager organize and administer a group's behavior to complete a particular task. A manager can legitimately alternate between various styles of management, depending on the task at hand and the experience level of those he or she oversees. Styles focus on managing people and their work activities. Hendricks and Deison point to the following styles and the situation each fits best:

1. Directing style—best for inexperienced followers.
2. Coaching style—best for discouraged or disillusioned followers.
3. Supporting style—best for experienced followers.
4. Delegating style—best for peak performers, high impact followers.[1]

The best business schools teach these techniques and others like them. Countless authors have written books describing various styles for managing people. In my opinion, however, management and leadership are different disciplines, each with a proper application. If managing people focuses on organizing and administering their activity in regard to a task, then leading people focuses on encouraging, motivating, empowering, and guiding their activity in regard to pursuing a vision and mission.

An "approach" conveys an attitude of a leader's heart in regard to leading others and describes how one views a leader in relation to those who follow. Only two approaches exist: A leader views one's role as either a servant or an authority figure. A leader sees himself or herself as either a superior, controlling others who must serve his or her self-centered agenda, or a servant, serving others and the collective good of an organization. A leader either serves those he or she leads or views followers as pawns at one's disposal. A leader who serves recognizes that real followers choose to follow voluntarily out of trust and respect. An authoritative leader forces others to follow by coercion or by exercising power and authority. The difference in these two approaches is night and day.

The approach of leading by serving is diametrically opposed to leading by exercising authority. Unlike styles of management, it would not be appropriate for a leader to switch between approaches of leadership. Typically a leader's heart is oriented toward one approach. Jesus unreservedly rejected and denounced the world's approach to leading as an authority figure. Jesus led as a servant and instructed His followers to do likewise. As modern-day followers of Jesus Christ, believers have no choice but to adopt Jesus' approach to leadership, which entails serving those we lead. Mark 10:42–45 makes the difference between Jesus' approach to leadership and that of the world crystal clear.

> [42] *Jesus called them together and said, "You know that those who are regarded as rulers of the Gentiles lord it over them, and their high officials exercise authority over them.* [43] *Not so with you. Instead, whoever wants to become great among you must be your servant,* [44] *and whoever wants to be first must be slave of all.* [45] *For even the Son of Man did not come to be served, but to serve, and to give his life as a ransom for many." (Mark 10:42–45)*

Jesus called his disciples together and gave them a lesson in leadership. This lesson is recorded in Mark 10:35–45. In my opinion, this is the single most important passage in the New Testament on the topic of leadership. This passage has two main sections bridged by a significant transitional phrase. Two significant events preceded and prompted Jesus' teaching on leadership.

In Mark 9:33–34, believers learn that an argument had erupted among the twelve apostles. Jesus confronted them on the nature of their argument. He asked them point-blank about what they had been arguing. All twelve apostles remained silent. No one gave the Lord an answer. As one can see, the apostles had argued over who among them was the greatest. The apostles debated who was the most important, the most powerful, and the most influential. Jesus gave them a preview of the lesson to come when He responded to their silence by saying: "If anyone wants to be first, he must be the very last, and the servant of all" (Mark 9:35).

A second and more immediate incident prompted a firmer response from the Lord. In Mark 10:32, Christ followers learn that Jesus was leading His disciples on a journey to Jerusalem. The apostles had come to realize that Jesus was the promised Messiah. The crowd was ready to place Him on the throne of David as king. All of Israel was looking for a warrior savior who would throw off the shackles of Roman dominance. Israel longed for the restoration of glory and power of God's kingdom on earth. Jesus' followers had seen His miraculous powers and popularity with the masses. Surely the time had come for Jesus to march into the City of David, the capital of Israel, Jerusalem, and seize the reins of power predicted by the prophets of old.

Zebedee had two sons named James and John. Jesus called these brothers, whom He named "Boanerges," to be two of His twelve apostles. This nickname meant "sons of thunder" and perhaps provides a student of God's Word some insight into their personalities. Hungry to exercise the power of their association with Jesus, they once asked the Lord, "Lord, do you want us to call fire down from heaven to destroy them?" after the people of a Samaritan village refused Jesus a proper welcome (Luke 9:54).

James and John desired power. Perhaps these two brothers ignited the discussion of who among the apostles should be called the greatest. After all, James and John were among the earliest followers of Jesus, which meant they had "seniority." They comprised two-thirds of Jesus' inner circle along with Peter. Given Peter's apparent fall from favor for rebuking Jesus (see Mark 8:33; when the Lord refers to you as "Satan," you might be out of favor), James and John perhaps had come to believe that they were the greatest among the apostles.

James and John's inflated view of their importance led to the second incident that prompted Jesus' lesson on leadership. In Mark 10:37, Christ followers find these "sons of thunder" making the following request of the Lord Jesus: "Let one of us sit at your right and the other at your left in your glory." Jesus had just finished warning the apostles that His arrival in Jerusalem would be met with betrayal, suffering, and death, followed by His resurrection. This description of Jesus' impending reception did not fit with James and John's view of a warrior savior, ready to claim the power of His earthly throne. These brothers hung dearly to their belief that Jesus' visit to Jerusalem would include being crowned king. James and John fully intended to grab two positions of power before the coronation.

Once this power play by the sons of Zebedee became known, the other ten apostles reacted very negatively. Mark tells us that the remaining apostles became indignant. The other ten apostles became very upset by James and John's request for positions of power. Jesus recognized that He had to put a stop to this infighting among his disciples. Jesus knew that between the apostles' argument about who was the greatest and James and John's request for power, these twelve had a faulty concept of leadership. The time had come for Jesus to make the essence of His approach to leadership crystal clear to the twelve apostles, and to His followers for all time.

Jesus began His lesson on leadership by describing the world's approach to leadership. Jesus said in Mark 10:42: "You know that those who are regarded as rulers of the Gentiles lord it over them, and their high officials exercise authority over them." The world's approach to leadership is characterized by the following: authority, power, controlling people, giving commands, force, manipulation, coercion, and enticement. In a nutshell, the world's approach to leadership is based on "authority." The ultimate goal of this approach is to control people according to the leader's selfish desires.

Two key phrases spoken by Jesus best describe the world's authoritative approach. He first said that Gentile leaders "lord it over them." The root Greek word is *katakurieuo*. Strong defines this term as follows: "1 to bring under one's power, to subject one's self, to subdue, master. 2 to hold in subjection, to be master of, exercise lordship over."[2] This word conveys the idea of overpowering someone to subdue and control them. *Theological Dictionary of the New Testament* says this of *katakurieuo*: ". . . the word means the exercise of, dominion against someone, i.e., to one's own advantage."[3] From this, a person can draw a picture of a leader who uses his position, power, and authority to control others for his or her selfish agenda and gains.

Jesus reinforces this image when He says: "and their high officials exercise authority over them." The root Greek term for "exercise authority" is *katexousiazo*. Strong defines the term as follows: "1 to exercise authority, wield power."[4] *Theological Dictionary of the New Testament* adds this to our understanding of *katexousiazo*: "it is likely that the word implies the tendency towards compulsion or oppression which is immanent in all earthly power, and not merely in political."[5] The world's approach contemplates a leader wielding power to force followers to submit and obey commands by compulsion.

A leader using this approach relies on one's possession of authority to force followers to obey orders and follow commands. Followers become nothing more than expendable parts to be used to accomplish the leader's self-centered agenda and goals. Leaders who use this approach exercise their authority to control followers for their own purpose and self-interest. The interest and needs of a follower are of no importance or concern to an authoritative leader.

An authoritative approach to leading exhibits a selfish approach. A leader whose heart is oriented on self will typically resort to using authority because this approach puts his or her interest first. An authoritative leader uses people for personal gain with no regard for the well-being of a follower.

Please keep in mind that there is nothing wrong with a leader possessing legitimate authority. Recall our lesson on Romans 13:1 where readers learned that God Himself has established all authority. No authority exists apart from God. He raises people up to lead according to His will. There is nothing wrong with a leader exercising his God-given authority in a certain situation. In fact, not to do so would be a dereliction of duty and responsibility. The line is crossed when the leader uses his or her authority for selfish purposes instead of God's will and the benefit of one's entire organization.

"Not so with you. Instead. . . ."

With these words in Mark 10:43, Jesus declared that He rejected the world's authoritative approach to leadership. Jesus also instructed His followers to reject this approach to leading others. Compelling others to follow by the use of force, power, enticement, or manipulation (or anything of the sort) was not an option for a follower of Christ. Authoritative leadership was not an option then and still is not an option today. The authoritative approach to leading may work in the world's system, but it has no place in God's administration. An Entrusted Leader must resist the seduction of leading with the world's approach.

Jesus quickly offered His followers an alternative approach: ". . . whoever wants to become great among you must be your servant, and whoever wants to be first must be slave of all" (Mark 10:43–44). James and John mistakenly thought greatness came from possessing a position of power and influence. These brothers assumed that sitting at Jesus' right and left hands would make them second to none, except the Lord Jesus. Jesus completely turned the tables when He described His approach to leadership. To be the kind of leader God desires to use, one must reorient his or her view of leading from self to God and others.

Jesus approached leadership as a servant. James and John desired greatness among His followers and mistakenly believed that sitting next to Jesus in His glory would make them great. Jesus clearly stated that greatness comes from serving others, not exercising authority over them. Empowering others characterizes Jesus' approach to leadership. By serving others, a leader can enable followers to contribute to the overall welfare of the organization and themselves. A leader using this approach truly views oneself as a member of a group, not the most important person in a group.

Jesus' servant approach to leading is not a reactive or passive one. Leaders who serve do not wait passively for events to unfold to see how one should react. Leading as a servant does not mean the leader foregoes taking initiative or risks. God has established every leader's authority to lead others, and not to do so constitutes an abdication of one's responsibility. Jesus did not teach His followers to be passive, reactionary leaders.

Jesus used two key terms to articulate His approach to leadership. He said one must become a servant and a slave. The root Greek term for "servant" is *diakonos*. Strong defines it as follows: "1 one who executes the commands of another, esp. of a master, a servant, attendant, minister. 1A the servant of a king."[6] Paul uses this same term to describe leaders within the church that we call deacons. A "*diakonos*" leader is one who follows the commands of Jesus and places one's selfish interest secondary to the good of the organization as a whole. Note the contrast between worldly leaders who give commands that serve their own interests first and godly leaders who execute the commands of another that serve the interests of the organization as a whole. Sadly in our culture today, people do not expect leaders to serve, nor do people expect servants to lead.

Jesus took His description of a leader a step further when He said His followers were to be slaves. The root Greek word is *doulos*. Strong defines this term as follows: "1 a slave, bondman, man of servile condition. 1A a slave. 1B metaph., one who gives himself up to another's will those whose service is used by Christ in extending and advancing His cause among men. 1C devoted to another to the disregard of one's own interests. 2 a servant, attendant."[7] To approach leadership as Jesus did requires one to willingly disregard his or her interests for the sake of others. This takes a strong faith in God and the conviction that God will watch out for the leader's interests as the leader oversees the interests of others. Jesus approached leadership as a servant and so should his followers.

You may be asking yourself: How can a person be a servant/slave and a leader at the same time? What connection exists between serving and leading? In his book *Jesus on Leadership*, Wilkes addresses this connection: "Mission (and the vision of that mission) was the connection between service and leadership."[8] The key to understanding the relationship between serving and leading lies within an organization's vision and mission. Wilkes goes on to add: "A servant leader—*serves the mission* and *leads by serving* those on the mission with him."[9] Authoritative leaders force others to serve the leader's self-centered agenda. Jesus' approach calls for leaders to serve others as all members of an organization pursue their mission and vision together. Whatever organization one leads in, it is the leader's responsibility as a follower of Christ to enable and empower those he or she leads. Empowerment comes by the leader serving his or her followers, who in turn are enabled to contribute to the maximum of their ability to help accomplish the organization's mission. This may require putting one's self-interests behind the mission of the organization and those he or she leads.

Jesus' approach to leadership can have a positive impact on any organization. Most followers work more effectively when led by a servant rather than a dictator. People prefer a leader who puts the mission of the organization ahead of his or her own self-interests. Leaders empower workers to maximize their efforts when the leader serves his or her followers instead of bossing them around. This may surprise some, but, Jesus' approach to leadership is not primarily intended to make you a better worldly leader. Jesus' approach may not maximize worldly success. Jesus not only rejected the world's authoritative approach to leadership, but He also rejected worldly missions, such as the pursuit of fame, fortune, and power. Jesus never promised that leading as a servant would result in material gains. Jesus' approach to leadership is intended for the pursuit of His mission on earth.

Jesus came to earth to serve others, not to be served. Jesus obediently laid His interests aside and gave His life according to the will of the Father. "For even the Son of Man did not come to be served, but to serve, and to give his life as a ransom for many" (Mark 10:45). Jesus completed His mission when He died on the cross. Jesus' crucifixion was an act of humility, sacrifice, and service to others. Jesus is not asking His followers to do anything He did not do.

As followers of Jesus Christ, our mission is to make disciples. Applying Jesus' approach requires a prior commitment to serve Jesus' mission of making disciples. Think back to our prior lessons on Entrusted Leader core values one and two: *A HEART willing to do all God asks* and *A MISSION for leading characterized by a faithful commitment to multiplying followers of Jesus Christ that supersedes all other endeavors.* Jesus commanded His followers to make disciples. We must decide if we are willing to do so. If we are, then the approach we must take to leading people involves the role of a servant.

Jesus rejected the world's authoritative approach to leadership. He instructed His followers to do likewise. Leading with authority is about telling people what to do and expecting them to obey. Authoritative leadership puts a leader's self-interest ahead of those of his or her followers and the organization as a whole. This approach uses power and authority that forces people to comply and obey even against their will.

Jesus approached leadership as a servant. This approach requires humility and sacrifice. Serving those one leads means putting their needs and the mission of the organization ahead of those of the leader. This approach empowers and enables people to contribute to the mission of the organization. A leader using this approach believes that those he or she leads will follow voluntarily because they recognize that the organization's mission is worth pursuing.

Discussion Questions based on "Two Approaches to Leadership"

1. Write a description of the difference between Jesus' approach and the world's approach to leadership.
2. What is the difference between a style of management and an approach to leadership?

3. Jesus said to His followers: "Not so with you. Instead . . ." (Mark 10:43). What does this teach leaders who claim to follow Jesus' instruction about which approach to leadership they should use?

4. Leading as a servant (*diakonos* or *doulos*) does not suggest a leader who is weak, passive, or only reactive. Based on the Greek concept of a servant and slave, explain how this can be so.

Jesus Christ "approached" leadership as a servant.
He rejected the world's authoritative approach.

Jesus taught His followers to deny self and serve others!

PERSONAL APPLICATION EXERCISE

Illustrate a leader-to-follower relationship you are currently in. Above this illustration, list some actions you can initiate that will serve and encourage your follower(s).

Serving Others
Philippians 2:1–8, James 1:27, Micah 6:8, John 13:1–17

Serving others as a leader requires true humility. A humble heart oriented on the needs of others proves to be a prerequisite for leading as a servant.

A higher calling than self summons a leader. This calling beckons a leader to set aside personal agendas, selfish ambitions, and vain conceit, thereby clearing the way to initiate acts of service aimed at meeting the real needs of those who follow.

The call to serve followers extends to the less fortunate. Every organization includes people who live a vulnerable and defenseless existence. Leaders who serve recognize the "widows, orphans, and foreigners" among his or her flock of followers and strives to protect them at all costs.

Jesus approached leadership as a servant. Jesus rejected the world's authoritative approach of leadership and commanded His followers to do likewise. Serving others starts within a person's heart. It requires humility, the setting aside of one's personal ambition, and placing the needs of others ahead of one's self-centered agendas. Everyone has the choice in life to be other-centered or self-centered. Choosing to serve others requires a person to orient his or her heart on God and others instead of self.

Basic nature leads humans to protect self-interests first. The natural orientation of a person's heart points toward self. Self-seeking people order their lives to satisfy the needs and desires of their heart even at the expense of others. When a person comes to know Jesus Christ as his or her personal savior, he or she becomes free from the bondage of a prideful and self-oriented life. Union with Christ makes a selfless life possible; however, one must make this choice daily. The temptation to continue a self-centered life remains after conversion. The Apostle Paul encouraged the saints in Philippi to live a life focused on serving others based on their union with Christ:

> *¹ If you have any encouragement from being united with Christ, if any comfort from his love, if any fellowship with the Spirit, if any tenderness and compassion, ² then make my joy complete by being like-minded, having the same love, being one in spirit and purpose. ³ Do nothing out of selfish ambition or vain conceit, but in humility consider others better than yourselves. ⁴ Each of you should look not only to your own interests, but also to the interests of others. (Phil. 2:1–4)*

The Apostle Paul also encouraged the Philippians to adopt the same attitude displayed by Christ Jesus. Consider Paul's description of Jesus' attitude:

> *⁵ Your attitude should be the same as that of Christ Jesus:*
> *⁶ Who, being in very nature God,*
>   *did not consider equality with God something to be grasped,*
> *⁷ but made himself nothing,*

taking the very nature of a servant,
being made in human likeness.
⁸ And being found in appearance as a man,
he humbled himself
and became obedient to death—
even death on a cross! (Phil. 2:5–8)

Paul reminded the saints at Philippi that they had experienced Christ's love when they came to know Jesus Christ as their savior. Their union with Christ provides the basis for Paul's teachings that a Christian should imitate Jesus' as a servant. A Christian's fellowship with the Holy Spirit empowers and makes such a life possible.

Followers of Jesus Christ should imitate His attitude in all respects. Understanding Jesus' attitude requires study of God's Word. The focus of this study involves Jesus' choice to adopt the very nature of a servant. Jesus exists fully divine and fully human. While the manner may be a mystery to us, the reality remains fixed that Jesus willingly let go of His divine nature and humbled Himself to take on the nature of man. Jesus carried His commitment to serve others to the point of dying on a cross. Paul challenges all followers of Jesus Christ to adopt this attitude of a servant. This attitude will require us to let go of self and humbly sacrifice our selfish desires for the sake of others.

Paul used the Greek term *doulos* for "servant" in Philippians 2:7. Jesus used the same term for "slave" in Mark 10:44 (see previous lesson: "Two Approaches to Leadership"). In the opening verse of his letter to the saints in Philippi, Paul identified himself and Timothy as *douloi Christou*, or servants of Christ. If followers of Christ are expected to live as a "*doulos*," one must understand what it means to live as a servant. A *doulos* essentially describes a person who has relinquished self-interests and serves the will and interests of another. Christians should serve Jesus Christ and others with this attitude.

We can ask ourselves what this might look like for a leader. Paul gives us some insight in Philippians 2:1–4. We should do nothing out of selfish ambition. Vain conceit should never motivate our priorities and actions. A leader must humble oneself. Leaders must view others with all humility. The leader who views others humbly will see himself or herself as no better than one's followers. As we lead others, we must look out for their interests. We cannot fall into the temptation of only considering how our own interests are protected and served by our decisions and actions. The leader who adopts selfless attitudes in relation to others, especially those he or she leads, will be on the way to imitating Christ's attitude of a servant.

Pride and selfish ambition stop a leader from becoming a servant to others. Paul encourages humility. A humble attitude provides a window through which a leader can properly view oneself in relation to others. Too lofty a view distorts the reality that in God's eyes a leader is no more important than those he or she leads. I believe God allows hardship in life to break our pride and create a humble attitude in our heart. Humility reduces our self-dependence and increases our dependence on God. Arrogance on the part of a leader works as a de-motivator to one's followers. Humility, on the other hand, inspires and empowers others to follow. Humility is a starting point for becoming a servant.

Another step to becoming a servant of others is letting go of our own personal ambitions and agendas. A leader must stop viewing every decision and action by how it impacts oneself. The pursuit of selfish ambition as priority one by a leader quickly spoils the will of those who follow. Selfish ambition also serves to de-motivate others. People do not want to follow a leader who uses other people for his or her self-centered gains. To serve others, a leader must put the collective needs of one's followers ahead of self.

Leading as a servant requires humility of heart and a sincere desire to look after the needs of others, especially the needs of weak and helpless followers. Consider for a moment the words of the prophet Micah:

> [8] He has showed you, O man, what is good.
> And what does the LORD require of you?
> To act justly and to love mercy
> and to walk humbly with your God. (Mic. 6:8)

Micah connects walking humbly before God with extending mercy and acting justly in relation to others. Leaders who serve restrain from perpetrating injustice on followers and in fact do all they can to ensure justice for even the most vulnerable of followers. Humble leaders treat others with dignity, integrity, grace, and mercy. They patiently repair and reconcile relationships, even when wronged, thereby restoring the functionality of the leader-to-follower relationship. God calls leaders to act justly, love mercy, and walk humbly.

James said that the evidence of a true follower of Jesus Christ can be seen in a person's actions toward vulnerable members of society and one's commitment to avoid the trappings of the world. "Religion that God our Father accepts as pure and faultless is this: to look after orphans and widows in their distress and to keep oneself from being polluted by the world" (James 1:27).

Widows and orphans often live a vulnerable and defenseless existence. Women who lack a husband and children who lack a father to protect them often fall prey to others. Self-centered and ambitious people use such defenseless individuals for their personal gain. Every organization has widows and orphans. These followers may not literally lack a husband or father figure to protect them, but they are just as defenseless as widows and orphans. Every organization has individuals who struggle with a variety of personal and professional challenges that leave them weak and defenseless. Part of leading as a servant involves recognizing followers who resemble "widows and orphans" and protecting them and looking out for their needs.

James also exhorted his readers to avoid the trappings of the world. Unfortunately in their zeal to garner worldly success, many leaders use the widows and orphans of an organization as a rung on the ladder of their leadership ascension. Sadly, even leaders who claim to follow Jesus Christ are guilty of using others as stepping stones on the path toward "success." To make matters worse, today's materialistic Christian community reinforces this self-promoting behavior by suggesting that worldly success metrics equate to God's blessings. "Christian" leaders have mistakenly adopted an attitude that if they are achieving worldly success, then they must be obeying God and experiencing His blessing. The average Christian layperson conveniently ignores the true metric of God's pleasure and blessing as defined by passages such as James 1:27.

Revisit Philippians 2:1–7 for a moment. One's union with Christ makes possible the adoption of Jesus' attitude and actions as a servant.

Jesus' love for us opens the door to love others. Selfish ambition and vain conceit can be replaced with humility and a concern for others only when we relinquish control of our lives to the Holy Spirit. Transformation into a leader who approaches leadership as a servant begins with an intimate relationship with Jesus Christ and cannot be separated from this bond. Jesus modeled what leading as a servant looks like to His twelve apostles. John 13:1–17 records Jesus' greatest example of how a leader serves others.

> [1] *It was just before the Passover Feast. Jesus knew that the time had come for him to leave this world and go to the Father. Having loved his own who were in the world, he now showed them the full extent of his love.*
>
> [2] *The evening meal was being served. . . . [4] so he got up from the meal, took off his outer clothing, and wrapped a towel around his waist. [5] After that, he poured water into a basin and began to wash his disciples' feet, drying them with the towel that was wrapped around him. . . .*
>
> [12] *When he had finished washing their feet, he put on his clothes and returned to his place. "Do you understand what I have done for you?" he asked them. [13] "You call me 'Teacher' and 'Lord,' and rightly so, for that is what I am. [14] Now that I, your Lord and Teacher, have washed your feet, you also should wash one another's feet. [15] I have set you an example that you should do as I have done for you. [16] I tell you the truth, no servant is greater than his master, nor is a messenger greater than the one who sent him. [17] Now that you know these things, you will be blessed if you do them." (John 13:1–17)*

In this passage, we learn much about Jesus as a leader who served others and His relationship with His followers. In this passage, Jesus models His approach to leadership as a servant. Paul suggested that a Christian's inspiration to love and serve comes from one's union with Christ. Jesus' confidence to love and serve His disciples emanated from

His relationship with the Father. The story of Jesus washing the disciples' feet reveals His love, humility, confidence, courage, selflessness, and commitment to carry God's mission for His life to the point of death on a cross.

Jesus knew that the time had come for Him to suffer, die on the cross, be resurrected, and ascend into heaven. Before He left earth, Jesus intended to show the apostles the full extent of His love for them. Jesus knew that God had granted Him all authority, that He had come from God, and that He was going to return to God. Jesus' confidence to humbly and selflessly serve His apostles was rooted in His relationship with the Father. This faith in God the Father provided Jesus the confidence to love and serve others at His own expense.

Jesus showed the apostles the extent and depth of His love for them by washing their feet. This was a thankless task performed in Jesus' day by slaves or household servants. Jesus would not have been expected to wash His apostles' feet, nor would the apostles have been expected to wash each others' feet. The apostles had dirty feet, and consequently, they had a real need. Jesus took the initiative to serve them in a manner totally unexpected from the one people called Master and Lord. Jesus encouraged His apostles to follow His example and to serve each other. If they would do so, Jesus promised they would be blessed.

Peter initially refused to allow Jesus to wash his feet. Peter did not understand his own need to be served by his Lord and Master and did not fully understand the concept of leaders who serve their followers. Jesus initiated this act of service as an example for the apostles. He wanted them to understand what it meant for a leader to initiate an act of service to humbly meet a real need of someone else.

As a follower of Christ who perhaps leads at home, in the marketplace, or the community at large, one might ask, What does serving the real needs of others look like where I lead? Please keep in mind that one must view leadership as a servant within the context of a mission. Jesus had essentially two missions when He came to earth the first time. One was to die on the cross and pay the penalty of sin, thereby making it possible for us to become reconciled to God and have union with Christ. Jesus completed this mission. The other mission was to prepare the apostles to lead the effort of making disciples. Jesus served the apostles within the context of preparing them to lead. Serving others does not mean a requirement to meet every want and need followers think they have. One leads as a servant by initiating actions that enable and empower others to participate in a mission to the maximum of their ability.

One should not view serving others as simply doing random acts of service that no one else wants to do. Serving followers does not mean one performs subservient tasks that are not expected of a leader. Leading as a servant does not mean one humbly takes out the trash, sweeps the floors, and makes the coffee.

Serving others requires meeting their real needs. As was the case with Peter and his need to have Jesus wash his feet, often followers will not recognize their own real needs. Jesus understood the implications of His mission to His disciples. Consequently, He understood their needs in the context of God's plan better than they did. As a leader, one may be in the position of understanding the mission and how it impacts his or her followers better than they do. To serve those one leads, a leader must develop a clear understanding of his or her followers' needs in the context of whatever mission the organization is pursuing together.

Developing an understanding of followers' needs requires getting to know others on a personal level. One must form an understanding of the follower's strengths and weaknesses. Part of meeting a follower's needs involves bringing his or her strengths to bear on an organization's mission effort. In areas where a follower is weak, a leader must either develop a plan of action to help the follower transform a weakness into a strength or accept his or her limitations and compensate for the shortcoming with another strength.

Another aspect of serving your followers involves getting to know their heart. Emotions such as fear, anger, insecurity, stress, anxiety, and many others can dramatically reduce a follower's contribution to the mission. A leader must know what motivates and inspires each of his or her followers and what levels of risk and responsibility one can handle. Serving real needs requires a leader to know a follower personally.

Jesus led others as a servant and expects His followers to do likewise. Paul encouraged believers to imitate Christ's attitude as a servant. A Christian's union with Christ and faith in the sovereignty of God form the foundation for serving others. An unwavering commitment to the service of Jesus' mission to make disciples provides the motivation to serve others.

A leader who serves others must be humble. A leader who believes he or she is better than his or her followers will rule them but not serve them. There is no place for vain conceit in Jesus' approach to leadership as a servant.

Serving others means a leader must set aside selfish ambition, as personal agendas get in the way of serving others. The mission a leader and one's followers pursue together must become everyone's top priority. Followers who perceive a leader using them to accomplish only what is best for the leader will not follow voluntarily.

To serve others, a leader must love his or her followers as Christ loved His disciples. A leader must get to know his or her followers intimately and must understand the real needs of a follower, sometimes better than that follower does. This often requires a leader to get involved with the dysfunctional part of a person's life. The leader has to initiate acts of service that meet the needs of his or her followers.

Leading as a servant often requires a leader to love followers who are hard to love. Jesus, for example, socialized with tax collectors and sinners. Every leader has hard-to-love followers. The leader who strives to serve others learns to love the weak follower as well as the star performer. Leaders must also look out for the needs of the most vulnerable members of the organization he or she leads. Leaders should never take advantage of the "widows and orphans" one leads. One way a leader can serve these people is to make sure no one else takes advantage of them either.

Serving others proves mightier than exercising authority over them. Serving those you lead within the context of a mission empowers and enables your followers in great ways. Entrusted Leader core value three is: *An APPROACH to leadership characterized by denial of self and serving others.* Serving others as a leader starts by humbly setting aside one's personal agendas and by initiating acts of service that meet the real needs of those who follow. Get to know the real needs of those you lead and initiate the appropriate acts of service to meet them.

Discussion Questions based on "Serving Others"

1. Explain why humility is a prerequisite for a person to lead as a servant.

2. How does selfish ambition and vain conceit inhibit the formation of healthy, functional leader-to-follower relationships?

3. Why do you think James encouraged Christians to look after the needs of orphans and widows? What characterizes a widow and an orphan, besides the obvious absence of a husband or father figure? (James 1:27)

4. Describe ways you can extend mercy, ensure justice, and display humility to those you lead (Mic. 6:8).

5. Jesus set an example for His followers when he washed the apostles' feet. What are some ways you can apply this lesson to where you lead others? (John 13:1–17).

Serving others as a leader requires true humility.

A calling higher than self beckons a leader to set aside personal agendas, selfish ambitions, and vain conceit, thereby clearing the way to initiate acts of service aimed at meeting the real needs of those who follow.

Leaders who serve recognize the defenseless and less fortunate among their flock of followers and strive to protect them at all costs.

PERSONAL APPLICATION EXERCISE

Describe any personal agendas and selfish ambitions that you may need to set aside that potentially hinder you leading as a servant. Ask God to give you insight and wisdom in this regard.

Denying Self
Mark 8:34–38

Jesus invites any leader to follow Him on the grand journey of publicly serving God's will. To keep up, a leader must be willing to set down all self-serving baggage and voluntarily pick up an instrument of self-sacrifice.

By nature, every human suffers from the curse of self-centeredness. We are inclined to protect our own self-interest first and foremost. Self-preservation and self-promotion motivate how we interact with others. Choosing to deny self and forego the pursuit of personal desires remains foreign to our minds. No one wants to willingly let go of self-serving baggage and voluntarily pick up an instrument of self-sacrifice. The price of the ticket for following Jesus starts with denying self and goes up from there.

Mankind's fall from grace left the hearts of men bent toward self and away from God. Unregenerate man is enslaved to a life focused on the gratification of selfish desires. Any thoughts of denying self are confined to short-term selfless acts that actually benefit one's self-interest in the long run. The lost have no choice but to follow the impulses of their self-centered hearts. Christians do have an alternative—one created with spiritual birth and empowered by the Holy Spirit.

Only a personal relationship with Jesus Christ frees a person from the eternal judgment of a self-centered life. Trusting that Jesus paid the penalty your selfish acts deserve when He died on the cross results in eternal freedom and forgiveness. Justification by faith does not, however, free us from the temptation, inclination, and results of living a self-centered life while still on earth. The tension between the possibility of denying self and the desire to live for self constitutes a battle that rages within the hearts of every born-again Christian. Denying self becomes something a follower of Christ must choose to do daily.

God looks for leaders willing to do all He asks. God said of David: "After removing Saul, he made David their king. He testified concerning him: 'I have found David son of Jesse a man after my own heart; he will do everything I want him to do'" (Acts 13:22). To be a leader willing to do all God asks by definition requires a choice to deny self and pick up the pursuit of whatever God asks of us.

Jesus was willing to do all God asked of Him: "My Father, if it is possible, may this cup be taken from me. Yet not as I will, but as you will" (Matt. 26:39). In His humanity, Jesus had the capacity to choose His will over the Father's will. As hard as it is to imagine, Jesus could have chosen in the Garden of Gethsemane not to go to the cross. Fortunately for mankind, Jesus chose to deny self and put the Father's will first. Jesus lived out His commitment to God's mission for His life to the point of death, the ultimate act of self-denial.

Jesus approached leadership as a servant. Jesus rejected the world's authoritative approach to leadership and instructed his followers to do likewise (Mark 10:42–45). This truth was covered in an earlier lesson ("Two Approaches to Leadership"). Jesus took the form of a servant (Phil. 2:1–8). Jesus knew His followers' real needs and humbled Himself to meet them. Jesus washed the feet of His apostles and instructed them to do the same for others (John 13:1–7).

Self-denial characterizes Jesus' entire life. Jesus' choice to put the needs of others and the will of the Father ahead of His self-interests resulted in sacrifice, suffering, and the humiliation of dragging a cross through the public streets of Jerusalem. To be counted as a follower of Jesus Christ, one must be willing to deny self, pick up a cross, and follow Him. The centerpiece of this lesson is Mark 8:34 where Jesus said: ". . . If anyone would come after me, he must deny himself and take up his cross and follow me." To fully appreciate the force of this statement, one must first understand the context within which Jesus spoke these words.

Background/Introduction to the Book of Mark

John Mark most likely authored this gospel. He had close contact with Barnabas and Paul (Acts 12, 13, 15). John Mark is most likely the same Mark who ministered with Peter in Rome in the early AD 60s (1 Pet. 5:13). Peter's life seems to have influenced the writing of the Gospel of Mark.

Mark probably wrote his account of Jesus' life in the late AD 60s. The historical backdrop was Nero's persecution of Christians and Peter's death as a martyr in AD 64. Mark wrote to Roman Gentile Christians who were facing the prospects of persecution and death for their faith in Jesus.

The events of Jesus' life as recorded by Mark were not arranged in a strict chronological order. The author did not intend to record a detailed historical account. Mark's writing style is similar to a person telling stories about a friend to make a series of points. In this case, Mark's purpose for telling these stories was to paint an accurate picture of Jesus' identity.

Mark chose this style for his gospel because it served his purpose for writing to his audience of Roman Gentile believers. These followers of Jesus Christ faced the prospects of persecution and martyrdom for the public display of their faith and were beginning to raise some fundamental questions about their faith. Their questions were: Who is this Jesus? Is following Jesus worthy of death? These questions remain relevant today.

The first eight chapters of Mark are dominated by two themes. The first picture of Jesus painted by Mark addresses Jesus' true identity and authority. Mark sought to answer the question: Who is Jesus? How a person answers this first question ultimately determines one's answer to the second: Is faith in Jesus worthy of suffering persecution, ridicule, and death?

The second theme addressed by Mark deals with the hardness of men's hearts. A heart dulled by selfishness would never fully understand who Jesus was. A heart fixed on preserving self-interest would never choose to deny self, pick up a cross, and follow Jesus to the end. Mark shows us how Jesus Himself used His teaching of God's Word and a series of miraculous acts to establish His true identity and reveal the hardness of His disciples' hearts.

The Gospel of Mark opens with Jesus extending to Simon and Andrew an invitation to follow Him: "As Jesus walked beside the Sea of Galilee, he saw Simon and his brother Andrew casting a net into the lake, for they were fishermen. 'Come, follow me,' Jesus said, 'and I will make you fishers of men.' At once they left their nets and followed him" (Mark 1:16–18). Jesus followed this invitation with a promise.

Simon (Peter) and Andrew were fishermen by profession. Jesus invited these brothers to follow Him, to watch and observe His life. Jesus told Peter and Andrew that if they accepted His invitation, their lives would be transformed into something new. They would become "fishers of men." Note that Jesus did not promise that Peter and Andrew would become better fishers of fish if they followed Him. Jesus did not promise worldly success and prosperity if they followed Him. In the context of today's world, leaders must keep in mind that following Christ and leading others as Jesus desires does not bring any guarantee of becoming better "fishers of fish," or better worldly leaders.

The intent of Jesus' invitation to follow Him was to develop His disciples into future leaders for His kingdom. The focus of the disciples' training would center on their hearts. These potential leaders did not need skills development; these men needed to grasp His true identity and then develop hearts willing to deny self and endure the price of following Jesus publicly.

The Gospel of Mark functions as a leadership development manual that records how Jesus trained His disciples. The biggest barrier to developing into the type of leaders Jesus desired them to be was not a lack of skills or knowledge. The challenge that lay before the disciples was to overcome their "hardened hearts." This need for heart development still plagues leaders today.

A hardened heart is one that has become calloused. A person with a hard heart lacks the ability to understand and apply spiritual truth to one's life. A hard heart clouds one's thinking, heightens the emotions of the flesh, and misdirects the orientation of one's will onto self.

A quick study of the synoptic gospels, especially the Gospel of Mark, reveals that Jesus did not focus his efforts on developing the functional leadership skills of His apostles. He did not spend three years communicating the latest principles of management to them. Instead, Jesus centered His training efforts on two key realities that would transform the apostles into the type of leaders to which He planned to entrust the future of Christianity. Leaders who follow Jesus start to become "fishers of men" only when they fully grasp Jesus' true identity and acknowledge a need for freedom from the bondage of a hardened/self-centered heart.

Mark 8:27–30 underscores the importance of the reality of Jesus' true identity.

> *²⁷ Jesus and his disciples went on to the villages around Caesarea Philippi. On the way he asked them, "Who do people say I am?"*
>
> *²⁸ They replied, "Some say John the Baptist; others say Elijah; and still others, one of the prophets."*
>
> *²⁹ "But what about you?" he asked. "Who do you say I am?" Peter answered, "You are the Christ."*
>
> *³⁰ Jesus warned them not to tell anyone about him. (Mark 8:27–30)*

In this passage, Mark brings the question of Jesus' identity and authority to a climax. Jesus asked His disciples how other people answered the question of His identity. In the first eight chapters, Mark painted a landscape that included many answers to this question (see 1:11, 24; 2:7–11; 3:11, 21, 22, 30; 4:41; 5:7; 6:3, 14–16, 49).

Mark opens his gospel with a pronouncement from the Father: ". . . You are my Son. . . ." (Mark 1:11). Mark goes on to quote other comments in regard to Jesus' identity and authority (some accurate and some not) that include: the Holy One of God; a blasphemer who claims to forgive sins; the Son of God; a crazy person; a man possessed by Beelzebub; a man with an evil spirit; a person in command of the wind and waves; Son of the Most High God; a carpenter—son of Mary, brother of James, Joseph, Judas, Simon, and some sisters; John the Baptist raised from the dead; Elijah; and a prophet of old. Mark recorded the opinions of a broad cross section of first-century eyewitnesses who ranged from demons to King Herod.

"Who do you say I am?" This is the question Jesus now posed to His disciples. Jesus made the question of His true identity and authority personal to His followers. The question of Jesus' identity moved from a theoretical debate among the masses to each individual disciple. Jesus knew that how His disciples answered this question in their own hearts would determine the level of their commitment to follow Him and the type of leader each would ultimately become. This remains true today. How you answer this question deep in your soul will determine how you will follow Jesus publicly and how you will lead others.

Peter answered for the group. His statement, "You are the Christ," was intellectually correct. Unfortunately, Peter and the other disciples failed to process the personal implications of this declaration. They correctly perceived Jesus' true identity and authority. These original disciples, however, misunderstood who "the Christ" really was and the nature of His messianic mission.

According to Old Testament prophecies, there was only one *Christos*. This was a singular claim. The word in Greek designates one as the Messiah, the Lamb of God that would take away the sins of the world, the ruler of God's kingdom on earth. Later in the Gospel of Mark, the high priest asked Jesus point-blank if He was the Christ to which Jesus responded: "I am" (Mark 14:61–62). Jesus' answer was nothing short of a claim of divinity, a claim that Jesus would later be mocked for as He hung on the cross (Mark 15:32). There was only one *Christos* in the Father's plan, and Jesus was the one.

Peter's pronouncement was both good news and bad news. The good news was that the disciples had finally come to recognize Jesus' true identity. The bad news was that they did not understand the "messianic mission" that inspired every act Jesus performed, including His willingness to deny self and die on the cross. Unfortunately at this point the disciples failed to comprehend the implications of following Jesus to Jerusalem. They thought Jesus was traveling to claim an earthly throne when, in reality, He was headed to the cross.

The disciples most likely had Old Testament passages such as Isaiah 9, Jeremiah 23:5–8, Ezekiel 37:22–28, Psalm 2, and Isaiah 11 in mind, all of which describe "the Christ" as a victorious "warrior king" destined for a throne. This limited view of the Messiah motivated James and John to ask for positions of power. What the disciples did not understand was that these pictures of the Christ relate to His second coming. Jesus will, in fact, literally return to earth and reign as King, but this was not the messianic mission during the disciples' lives.

The disciples could not imagine Jesus, "the Christ," as a "suffering Savior." Old Testament passages such as Isaiah 53 and Psalm 22 did not fit with the disciples' paradigm of a messiah that would come and rule over Israel and free them from the shackles of Rome. This misconception of "the Christ" would become painfully obvious to the disciples in very short order. Of note, by the time Peter wrote his first epistle, he had come to understand that the Christ would first come and suffer and that glory would follow (1 Pet. 1:10–11).

Mark 8:31–33 contains a clear picture of the suffering that lay ahead for "the Christ." Unfortunately, hearts fixed on self have a hard time accepting the reality of Jesus' true identity.

> *31 He then began to teach them that the Son of Man must suffer many things and be rejected by the elders, chief priests and teachers of the law, and that he must be killed and after three days rise again. 32 He spoke plainly about this, and Peter took him aside and began to rebuke him.*
>
> *33 But when Jesus turned and looked at his disciples, he rebuked Peter. "Get behind me, Satan!" he said. "You do not have in mind the things of God, but the things of men." (Mark 8:31–33)*

Now that His disciples had correctly identified Him as "the Christ," Jesus immediately began to correct their misunderstanding of "the Christ" and His mission. Jesus began to teach His disciples that His future included suffering, rejection by the leaders of Israel, death, and resurrection (see Old Testament references to the Messiah's suffering, death, and resurrection in Isaiah 52:14 and Psalm 16:10).

Mark tells us that Jesus began to speak "plainly" about what lay ahead. In rereading Mark 1:1–8:30, one will find that this is the first mention of the Son of Man's suffering and death. Jesus no longer spoke in parables. He wanted His followers to clearly understand the mission He was obediently pursuing and the price He was going to pay. Jesus wanted the disciples to understand that they were following Him to the grave, not an earthly throne. Modern-day believers must recognize that they too are following Christ to a grave, not a throne.

This new teaching presented more information than Peter could process. Like James and John, Peter had to have believed that all he had personally given up to follow Jesus to this point was going to be rewarded on earth as Jesus ascended to the throne of Israel. This picture of suffering, rejection, and death had no place in his concept of a warrior king. This new teaching so perplexed Peter that he pulled Jesus aside and "rebuked" Him. Peter attempted to correct what he perceived as Jesus' faulty self-perception as "the Christ." The Greek word for "rebuke" is an authoritative word. Strong defines the term as follows: "[*epitimao* /ep·ee·tee·mah·o/] . . . to tax with fault, rate, chide, rebuke, reprove, censure severely. . . . to admonish or charge sharply."[10] Peter pulled no punches at this moment. His dreams, and those of all the disciples, of power, glory, authority, and honor associated with being publicly identified with "the King" was being shattered right before his eyes.

Jesus quickly responded to Peter's strong words with a rebuke of His own. Jesus spoke to Peter but looked at all of His disciples. Jesus' message was intended for all of them. Jesus characterized Peter's mind-set as aligned with Satan. Satan tempted Jesus in the desert (Luke 4:1–13), essentially offering Jesus an alternative to God's will. Satan suggested that by following his will, Jesus could have glory without the cross, He could have power without pain and suffering, and He could have fame without being rejected. All of this appealed to the concept of "the Christ" being a warrior King, not a suffering Savior. The last thing Satan wanted was Jesus on the cross.

Peter was suggesting the same course of action—an earthly throne without suffering. Jesus knew, as Peter would later acknowledge, the real glory of a throne lay on the other side of suffering on a cross. Jesus went on to admonish Peter and the disciples that their minds were set on the things of men, not the things of God. The disciples were fixed on pursuing their self-centered agendas to gain positions of power, influence, affluence, authority, control, and fame. Jesus wanted them to understand that following Him meant a reorientation of their minds and hearts. The things of God had to become their number one priority, no matter the personal costs. The next passage of Scripture would make this point crystal clear to the disciples and to the masses who were gathered around Him.

> ³⁴ *Then he called the crowd to him along with his disciples and said: "If anyone would come after me, he must deny himself and take up his cross and follow me. ³⁵ For whoever wants to save his life will lose it, but whoever loses his life for me and for the gospel will save it. ³⁶ What good is it for a man to gain the whole world, yet forfeit his soul? ³⁷ Or what can a man give in exchange for his soul? ³⁸ If anyone is ashamed of me and my words in this adulterous and sinful generation, the Son of Man will be ashamed of him when he comes in his Father's glory with the holy angels."* (Mark 8:34–38)

In this passage, Jesus clarifies that the choice to turn away from the things of men and embrace the things of God has a price. Clearly to set aside our selfish missions in life and pursue God's mission for our life will cost us things that are dear to us. As did Jesus, one must resist the subtle alternatives offered by Satan that seem to be shortcuts or alternatives to God's will.

Jesus called His disciples and the crowd to hear what He was about to say. The significance to the inclusion of the masses is that the invitation to follow Jesus is open to anyone who was willing to pay the price. The door of discipleship, to be a learner of Jesus, is open to all; all who dare to follow Jesus' defined path. The message of the cross relates to everyone who will listen, not just a select few of committed believers.

Remember that Jesus is still speaking plainly and not in parables. Jesus introduces His definition of the requirement of following Him with a conditional phrase. Jesus says: "If anyone would come after me . . ." Clearly the use of the term "if" indicates a choice that precedes the qualification to follow. The New International Version then uses the phrase: "anyone would come after me." The Greek term for "would" is *thelo*. This is the verb form of the noun *thelema*. *Thelema* is the same term used in Acts 13:22 when God spoke of David as being a man after His heart because David was willing to do all His will (*thelema*). Perhaps a clearer translation of this conditional phrase might be "If someone chooses to orient the will of their heart on coming after me . . ."

There is another key term in this conditional phrase Christ followers must understand. Back in Mark 1:17, Jesus extended Peter and Andrew an invitation to "follow me," or "*deute opiso mou*," to "come after me." To *deute opiso* was an invitation to observe, listen, and learn. This invitation simply meant an individual could follow along with Jesus in order to find out who He was and what He was about.

The invitation to follow Jesus in Mark 8, however, possesses a different nature than the one found in Mark 1. Jesus was now raising the commitment level of being associated with him. The time for casual observation was now over, and there was a price associated with following Jesus. In this conditional phrase, Jesus said: "If anyone would come after me. . . . ." Jesus uses different terms with this invitation than His previous one. Jesus no longer extends the invitation to "*deute opiso*," or casually follow along and observe. Now the invitation includes the words *erchomai* and *opiso*. This combination of Greek terms that we translate "come after" is more the sense of being publicly identified with Jesus Christ. What Jesus says is that if you set the will of your heart to be publicly identified as His follower, then this is what it looks like. What we will see next is that following Jesus is not a path to earthly thrones, fame, fortune, and positions of authority. Following Jesus, publicly standing as His follower, has a price associated with it and Jesus is about to speak plainly about the price.

Jesus lists three actions a person must take if one wants to be publicly identified with Him. The first act requires a person to deny self. The Greek word used by Jesus is *aparneomai*. Strong defines the term as follows: ". . . to deny. . . . to affirm that one has no acquaintance or connection with someone. . . . to forget one's self, lose sight of one's self and one's own interests."[11] In Mark 8:34, this term reveals an imperative, or a command. Following Jesus requires one to completely disassociate his or her life with one's own self-interests, needs, and agenda. One must ask himself or herself: Am I willing to pay this price to be counted as a follower of Jesus?

Setting aside something to follow Jesus requires picking up something else in return. Picking up something is the second condition Jesus mentions. We let go of self and we "take up" something else. True discipleship involves letting go or putting down self-will and then picking up God's will in its place.

The Roman authorities of Jesus' day required a condemned criminal to publicly carry a cross to the spot of one's execution. This spectacle provided an act of public humiliation. With this in mind, Jesus lays out the third condition of following Him, which is picking up a cross. God's will for Jesus included a literal cross on which He was to die. This act was necessary to fulfill God's purpose in His life of offering His life as a ransom for many. God's mission for Jesus included a literal cross. God's mission for Jesus' followers involves telling others about Jesus' death on the cross.

So what does self-denial mean to those of us who are modern-day followers of Jesus Christ and leaders of others? Let me begin by stating what I think it does not mean. Denying self in the context of following Jesus should not be thought of as a short-term casual act of personal sacrifice or inconvenience. Denying self is not as simple as choosing temporary abstinence or doing without something we love.

What Jesus is demanding of those who follow Him, those who choose to be publicly identified as a follower, is a total 180 degrees turning away from the pursuit of all personal agendas, never to return to them. One must make a total and public commitment to engage everything we are and possess for the cause of Christ and to let the chips fall where they may. This commitment extends to everywhere we live and lead.

This is not to say you should quit your job, sell your possessions, give all your money away, and live in seclusion, isolated from the world. In some respects, this would be too easy. We have already suggested the possibility that you reside exactly where God wants you to lead others. Most likely, you already lead in the mission field in which God desires you to lead. What God may be waiting for is for you to stop pursuing your own interests and make the interests of others and His mission of making disciples the focus of where and why you lead others. This would be a choice to "deny self" and "pick up a cross" and follow Jesus.

One must make a total and public commitment to engage everything we are and possess for the cause of Christ and to let the chips fall where they may.

Jesus desires leaders to use every opportunity to lead others to pursue His mission for His followers, which is to make disciples. This mission must take priority over all other endeavors. The possibility exists that this choice may cost you something dear. This decision to publicly follow Jesus where you lead may result in persecution. All I can say is that I believe Jesus spoke plainly about the price of following Him.

One may also ask: Who is Jesus and how could He ask this of me? Let's go back to the purpose of the Gospel of Mark. If Jesus is asking a follower to deny self and suffer persecution, then the question becomes the same today as it was in the first century when Christians regularly faced becoming a martyr: Who is Jesus and is He worth dying for? If we truly believe Jesus is "the Christ," then the answer is a resounding YES!

Denying self requires an unwavering trust in the sovereignty and love of God. The sovereignty of God gives us the peace of mind that God is ultimately in control of all the circumstances of our lives. We rejoice in the good and bad alike because we view them all as part of God's will. Likewise if we truly believe God loves us, then take comfort that all circumstances ultimately work for our good, even though some situations appear bad.

Jesus clarified in Mark 8 that His true identity included an empty tomb, not an earthly throne. Jesus clearly explained to the apostles that the invitation to follow Him involved going to the depths of a grave, not the lofty heights of world leadership that they so selfishly craved. Jesus brought His lessons of leadership together in Mark 8:34 when He set forth the nonnegotiable terms of becoming a leader in His kingdom: "Then he called the crowd to him along with his disciples and said: 'If anyone would come after me, he must deny himself and take up his cross and follow me.'" Jesus looks for leaders who are willing to completely disassociate the attitudes and actions of one's heart from self and follow Him down the path of persecution and public humiliation on a cross. The need for and process of heart reorientation from self to God's will define how Jesus developed leaders. Any leadership development that deviates from this focus appears incomplete at best or produces leaders that ignore their heart need and rely on management techniques and leadership skills.

Jesus' message to His followers in Mark 8 did not win Him popularity points. Jesus painted a clear and truthful picture of God's will in regard to the Christ being rejected and the Savior's death on a cross.

Jesus communicated to all concerned that following Him required relinquishing one's personal goals and pursuing God's objectives. Jesus did not play to the masses and speak what the populace wanted to hear. The masses want a leadership development process that promises an end result of success, popularity, and material gain.

One of the problems in leadership development today stems from a desire to sell to the masses. The not-so-subtle message communicated in many programs suggests that if a leader follows Jesus, then he or she will receive God's blessing and become a more effective leader from a worldly point of view. These same programs conveniently omit Jesus' teachings that to emulate him as a leader, one must wash feet, rub elbows with the downtrodden, accept rejection by rulers, endure ridicule, expect to be persecuted, and carry a cross. Potential leaders do not flock to development programs that promise an end result of persecution and personal sacrifice. Herein lies the problem. Most Christian leadership development programs omit unpopular realities of Jesus' message to leaders because these truths tend to drive away prospects.

Denying self requires one to set aside all personal desires and ambitions and follow Jesus' example of pursuing God's will regardless of the personal price involved. To become the leader God desires you to be requires you to set aside the pursuit of personal gain and make serving others and God's mission of making disciples the top priority wherever you lead.

Discussion Questions based on "Denying Self"

1. Who do you say Jesus Christ is? Using evidence provided in the Gospel of Mark, support your view of Jesus. Are you willing to face persecution, ridicule, and even death based on your view of Jesus' true identity?
2. In what ways might a hardened heart inhibit a person from becoming a biblically sound leader useful to God? Briefly describe the hardness/softness of your heart.
3. What does it mean to "deny self" as a condition of following Jesus?
4. Discuss how setting aside your personal agendas might impact how you lead others.

Following Jesus requires a leader to set down all self-serving baggage and voluntarily pick up an instrument of self-sacrifice.

No one wants to willingly let go of self-serving baggage and voluntarily pick up an instrument of self-sacrifice.

The price of the ticket for following Jesus starts with denying self and goes up from there.

PERSONAL APPLICATION EXERCISE

Briefly describe one self-centered agenda you currently hold with a tight grip. Illustrate how this inhibits your leader-to-follower relationships. If you were to "deny self" and let go of this agenda, how might your leader-to-follower relationships improve?

Stability
CORE VALUE: The STABILITY for leading created by applying a balance of skills, character, and compassion.

A Leader's Need for Skills
Psalm 78:72 and 2 Timothy 1:6

A leader needs skills.

A person's skill set must relate directly to one's sphere of leadership responsibility. A businessman needs business skills; a doctor, medical training; a lawyer, knowledge of the legal system; a teacher, training as an educator; and even a mother and a father need parenting skills to effectively fulfill their roles as leaders.

Leading others without the appropriate ability, expertise, and experience is reckless and foolish. Never let it be suggested that one can simply "love Jesus" and be excused from leading others with skilled hands. The Entrusted Leader model strives to develop one's core values as a complement to a leader's skills, not a substitute for them.

God expects a leader to diligently pursue the expertise necessary to master one's chosen profession/leadership responsibility. Skills come from a combination of God-given ability and experiences that build a reservoir of knowledge, confidence, and proficiency. Wise leaders recognize their God-given ability and initiate experiences that help transform this ability into a God-honoring skill.

An Entrusted Leader is a person of vision who faithfully serves the investment God has "entrusted" in one's life by using skills, character, and compassion to encourage others toward a common goal while upholding an Entrusted Leader's core values. This definition of a leader appeared earlier in chapter 3. The Parable of the Talents in Matthew 25:14–30 inspires the notion of a leader faithfully serving God's entrusted investment in one's life. The concept of a leader creating stability for leading by applying a balance of skills, character, and compassion finds inspiration in the description of David found in Psalm 78:72: "And David shepherded them with integrity of heart; with skillful hands he led them."

David led others skillfully with character and compassion. Leading others requires a combination of appropriately developed skills and core values that produce biblically sound leadership behaviors. Leadership stability and balance increase when a skilled leader applies the benefits of character and compassion that come only from a spiritually transformed heart.

An Entrusted Leader needs skill, character, and compassion in equal measure. A deficiency in any one of the three creates instability. A leader may get away with relying on one or two of these traits in the short term, but in the long term, cracks will appear that compromise one's stability and balance while leading others. The stresses and pressures of leading can only be withstood by developing skills, character, and compassion in equal measures.

An Entrusted Leader needs skill, character, and compassion in equal measure. A deficiency in any one of the three creates instability.

The ENTRUSTED Leader focuses on the development of a leader's heart and core values. The presence of biblical character and compassion provide evidence that such development has transpired during one's life. *The ENTRUSTED Leader* makes no attempt to develop functional leadership skills or knowledge. This leadership program assumes that the participants either have or will develop the leadership skills and knowledge necessary to be a leader in their chosen profession. This chapter will, however, discuss a leader's need for skills in the context of biblically sound leadership practices and behaviors. In addition, and perhaps most importantly, this chapter discusses skills in conjunction with a leader's need for character and compassion to create leadership stability and balance.

The primary emphasis of this book resides on the development of a leader's heart and core values. The reader should not, however, construe this to mean that only character and compassion are required to be an effective leader in God's administration. Appropriate leadership skills and knowledge must also be developed apart from the Entrusted Leader program. The core values and biblical practices/behaviors of leadership contained in this book serve to complement a leader's professional skills, not supplant them. An Entrusted Leader must possess appropriate functional skills to lead as God desires and intends.

The psalmist Asaph said of David in Psalm 78:72: ". . . with skillful hands he led them." David skillfully led Israel. An Entrusted Leader should lead others skillfully as well. Two questions immediately arise: What do we mean by the term "skill"? From where do "skills" come?

Merriam-Webster's Collegiate Dictionary defines the term "skillful" as: "possessed of or displaying skill."[1] This same dictionary defines a "skill" as:

> *2a the ability to use one's knowledge effectively and readily in*
> *execution or performance*
> *b dexterity or coordination especially in the execution of learned*
> *physical tasks*
> *3 a learned power of doing something competently: a developed*
> *aptitude or ability (language skills)*[2]

The concept of being skillful encompasses a person's intellectual capacity to use learned knowledge and a person's natural or acquired physical dexterity to perform some activity. Skills involve both intellectual and physical ability. Excellence in either area can set a person apart from others. A person does not necessarily have to possess both to be "skillful" in an area of expertise.

The Hebrew term used by Asaph in Psalm 78:72 describes David's leadership as *těbûnâ*. This word functions as a derivative of the Hebrew term *bîn*. The *Theological Wordbook of the Old Testament* defines *bîn* as follows: "understand, consider, perceive, prudent, regard. . . . Its main English usage means 'understanding' or 'insight.' . . . *bîn* includes the concept of distinguishment that leads to understanding. bîn is a power of judgment and perceptive insight and is demonstrated in the use of knowledge.[3] The *Dictionary of Biblical Languages* says of *tĕbûnâ*: "1. capacity for discerning a right course of action 2. capable to perform a craft."[4]

A person can distinguish oneself by acquiring a superior skill. Refined physical dexterity can result in a person being able to pass a football, hit a baseball, putt a golf ball, or shoot a basketball better than the next guy. A skilled artist can paint a picture, a skilled musician can play an instrument, and a skilled craftsman can forge metals in a manner more appealing to the eye and ear than others. Consider the wisdom found in Proverbs 22:29:

> [29] *Do you see a man skilled in his work?*
>   *He will serve before kings;*
>   *he will not serve before obscure men. (Prov. 22:29)*

The same applies to intellectual dexterity as well. People who can gather and assimilate data and knowledge often gain an advantage in professions such as business, law, medicine, and education. These examples, and many others like them, have the potential to distinguish an individual from others on the basis of superior skills. These types of physical and intellectual skills, however, do not necessarily make one a "skillful" leader.

The *Dictionary of Biblical Language*'s definition quoted earlier includes the idea that a person with a "skill" has the capacity to discern the right course of action. David distinguished himself as a skilled musician. He could propel a stone using a sling with deadly accuracy. He excelled in tending his family's sheep. When it came to leading Israel with "skilled hands," however, I have to believe that the aptitude that set David apart from other potential leaders was the "skill" of knowing the right course of action. Knowing and choosing to follow the right course of action become critical when one leads as God intends and desires. This skill requires one to view leading from God's point of view.

To skillfully lead others, a person must resist the temptation of focusing on "self" and view circumstances with the goal of choosing a course of action that serves the real needs of one's followers within the context of advancing God's mission.

One of the most common mistakes made by organizations involves promoting to a position of leadership a "skilled" individual based on superior performance alone. A person who possesses exceptional ability in a certain field may not be able to teach, guide, encourage, and inspire others to perform accordingly. The best salesperson does not always make the best sales manager. Do not assume that individual star performance naturally translates into the skill of leading others to do the same.

A leader has to be able to see the entire playing field. A leader has to be able to see how a myriad of seemingly unrelated variables actually interconnect. Leaders must see clearly the reality of a situation, not just how they want circumstances to be. Once the whole landscape is properly discerned, a skilled leader can embark on a proper course of action for all members of an organization. Skilled leaders have the ability to see the right course of action for a given situation and the ability to mobilize their followers to walk the path with them.

One might ask at this point: From where do "skills" come?

The development of a person's skill set comes from a unique combination of two factors. How these two factors conjoin in one's life determines what a person is good at and sets them apart from every other human being. In 2 Timothy 1:6, the Apostle Paul encourages his young protégé, Timothy, to develop his skills when he says: "For this reason I remind you to fan into flame the gift of God. . . ." What do you think Paul meant when he referred to "the gift of God" in Timothy's life? What do you think Paul meant when he encouraged Timothy to "fan into flame" his gift?

The presence of a skill in one's life results from a combination of ability and experience. A skill forms by the conjoining of God-given ability and experience. Each person has the opportunity to "fan into flames" (experience) the latent potential residing in "the gift of God" (ability) unique to one's life. Ability alone may distinguish a person from others, but not until experience polishes ability does a truly superior skill form.

Ability comes from God. Each person ever created by God has a unique set of talents. Some refer to this as "giftedness." Paul reminded Timothy that the talents in his life constituted a gift from God. God created each person exactly according to His plan and purpose for one's life. Each individual has the perfect set of ability to accomplish all God intended for his or her life. People often get into trouble when they use their ability to pursue a purpose God did not intend, or they pursue a purpose that they do not have the ability to accomplish. Evidence of a God-given ability can be seen in activities that come naturally to a person, what someone loves to accomplish, and the tasks a person can perform with minimal stress and anxiety. Ability takes into consideration a person's physical, mental, and emotional talents and limits. Leaders who excel typically have honestly assessed their own ability, applied their strengths, and stayed away from situations that expose their weaknesses.

Experience embodies the human activity that helps transform a God-given ability into a skill. Human initiatives such as the repetition of practicing a physical movement, the discipline of studying information that expands one's knowledge and understanding, and the observation of others using a skill are all examples of how a person uses experience to help transform ability into a skill. Often the gaining of such experiences comprises activities a person must initiate and persevere in to acquire. At other times, unexpected circumstances arise that one must respond to that provide an experience that can be drawn upon for the rest of someone's life. The more often one utilizes an ability and gains experience, the faster the combination becomes a skill.

A skillful leader knows how to choose the right course of action. Frequently this insight comes from past experiences. The formation of an experience base typically includes successes and failures. Wise leaders learn from their mistakes and do not repeat them when such circumstances arise again. Wise leaders learn what works and what does not work in given situations. This is how experience contributes to transforming ability into skill.

The Bible states clearly that ability comes from God. These gifts from God are diverse, in individual and unique combinations, and freely given by grace.

⁷ I wish that all men were as I am. But each man has his own gift from God; one has this gift, another has that. (1 Cor. 7:7)

*⁶ We have different gifts, according to the grace given us. If a man's gift is prophesying, let him use it in proportion to his faith. ⁷If it is serving, let him serve; if it is teaching, let him teach; ⁸ if it is encouraging, let him encourage; if it is contributing to the needs of others, let him give generously; if it is leadership, let him govern diligently; if it is showing mercy, let him do it cheerfully."
(Rom. 12:6–8)*

*⁴ There are different kinds of gifts, but the same Spirit.
(1 Cor. 12:4)*

In all three of these passages, the Greek term for "gift" is *charisma.* Strong defines this term as "a favor with which one receives without any merit of his own."⁵ The story of Bezalel and Oholiab illustrates the reality that God gives people ability by grace. God distributes ability to people according to His purpose; people do not acquire ability from God through merit.

¹ Then the LORD said to Moses, ² "See, I have chosen Bezalel son of Uri, the son of Hur, of the tribe of Judah, ³ and I have filled him with the Spirit of God, with skill, ability and knowledge in all kinds of crafts— ⁴ to make artistic designs for work in gold, silver and bronze, ⁵ to cut and set stones, to work in wood, and to engage in all kinds of craftsmanship. ⁶ Moreover, I have appointed Oholiab son of Ahisamach, of the tribe of Dan, to help him. Also I have given skill to all the craftsmen to make everything I have commanded you: ⁷ the Tent of Meeting, the ark of the Testimony with the atonement cover on it, and all the other furnishings of the tent— ⁸ the table and its articles, the pure gold lampstand and all its accessories, the altar of incense, ⁹ the altar of burnt offering and all its utensils, the basin with its stand— ¹⁰ and also the woven garments, both the sacred garments for Aaron the priest and the garments for his sons when they serve as priests, ¹¹ and the anointing oil and fragrant incense for the Holy Place. They are to make them just as I commanded you." (Exod. 31:1–11)

³⁰ Then Moses said to the Israelites, "See, the LORD has chosen Bezalel son of Uri, the son of Hur, of the tribe of Judah, ³¹ and he has filled him with the Spirit of God, with skill, ability and knowledge in all kinds of crafts— ³² to make artistic designs for work in gold, silver and bronze, ³³ to cut and set stones, to work in wood and to engage in all kinds of artistic craftsmanship. ³⁴And he has given both him and Oholiab son of Ahisamach, of the tribe of Dan, the ability to teach others. ³⁵ He has filled them with skill to do all kinds of work as craftsmen, designers, embroiderers in blue, purple and scarlet yarn and fine linen, and weavers—all of them master craftsmen and designers. ¹ So Bezalel, Oholiab and every skilled person to whom the LORD has given skill and ability to know how to carry out all the work of constructing the sanctuary are to do the work just as the LORD has commanded." (Exod. 35:30–36:1)

God commanded Moses to lead Israel in the task of building a tabernacle, so the Lord God Almighty could dwell among them: "Then have them make a sanctuary for me, and I will dwell among them. Make this tabernacle and all its furnishings exactly like the pattern I will show you" (Exod. 25:8–9). In Exodus 25–30, the reader will find a detailed description of the tabernacle and its furnishings that Moses and the people of Israel were to construct.

By grace, God chose Bezalel and Oholiab and filled them with skill, ability, and knowledge in all kinds of crafts. God filled all the craftsmen of Israel with skills in order to build the tabernacle and its furnishings. Ability comes from God. The Lord intends for people to use their ability according to God's purposes. How do you think God might have reacted to a craftsman of Israel who refused to work on the tabernacle because he or she was too busy pursuing selfish gain?

Peter taught that a follower of Christ should use his or her gifts to serve others and to administer God's grace so that God is praised and glorified: "Each one should use whatever gift he has received to serve others, faithfully administering God's grace in its various forms. If anyone speaks, he should do it as one speaking the very words of God. If anyone serves, he should do it with the strength God provides, so that in all things God may be praised through Jesus Christ . . . " (1 Pet. 4:10–11). God gives a leader ability in order to enable the leader to serve God's purposes and other people. The leader who uses his or her gifts to ingratiate self first and foremost does so contrary to God's Word and His will.

God-given ability becomes a God-honoring skill through experience. The latent potential of a person's ability transforms into useful expertise through diligence and disciplines such as study, practice, application, asking questions, watching others, and use, just to name a few. Neglecting to use one's gift inhibits the development of a skill. The Apostle Paul understood that a skill comes from a combination of ability (a gift) and experience. Consider his advice to Timothy: "Do not neglect your gift, which was given you through a prophetic message when the body of elders laid their hands on you. Be diligent in these matters; give yourself wholly to them, so that everyone may see your progress" (1 Tim. 4:14–15).

Paul recognized the God-given ability in Timothy's life, knowing that the full potential of Timothy's gift would come forth only with experience. Paul encouraged Timothy to avoid the temptation to neglect his gift and instructed Timothy to be diligent and to give himself wholly to the things God had given him the ability to do. Paul knew that with experience, Timothy's ability would progress in such a way that others would notice. Using and practicing the disciplines associated with one's God-given ability result in a skill reaching its full potential in one's life.

Consider what Solomon said about the need to hone one's ability into a skill through the hard work and dedication of preparation in Ecclesiastes 10:10: "If the ax is dull and its edge unsharpened, more strength is needed but skill will bring success." The mundane task of sharpening an ax produces a sharper edge and more efficient work. In the same way, the discipline of gaining experience helps transform an ability into a useful skill.

The story of David and Goliath provides a good illustration of how past experience helps refine a God-given ability and produce a skill. Keep in mind that past experiences pave the way for future confidence. Also, practicing a discipline ahead of time leads to familiarity and proficiency. God-given ability and past experience intersected, resulting in David's triumph over Goliath.

> *36 Your servant has killed both the lion and the bear; this uncircumcised Philistine will be like one of them, because he has defied the armies of the living God. . . . 38 Then Saul dressed David in his own tunic. He put a coat of armor on him and a bronze helmet on his head. 39 David fastened on his sword over the tunic and tried walking around, because he was not used to them.*
>
> *"I cannot go in these," he said to Saul, "because I am not used to them." So he took them off. 40 Then he took his staff in his hand, chose five smooth stones from the stream, put them in the pouch of his shepherd's bag and, with his sling in his hand, approached the Philistine. . . .*
>
> *48 As the Philistine moved closer to attack him, David ran quickly toward the battle line to meet him. 49 Reaching into his bag and taking out a stone, he slung it and struck the Philistine on the forehead. The stone sank into his forehead, and he fell facedown on the ground. (1 Sam. 17:36–49)*

God gave David the hand-eye coordination and strength to use a sling and a stone. David had the natural ability that allowed him to become proficient with a sling. While the text does not say so per se, given his profession as a shepherd, one can presume that David had plenty of time and opportunity to practice using a sling to propel a stone with deadly speed and accuracy. Such practice and experience helped turn his ability into a skill that he had confidence in.

Conversely, David was not familiar with the armor and sword of a trained military man. David did not have confidence using such instruments because he had no experience with them. Consequently, David rejected the use of Saul's armor and sword when offered them.

God has given you a unique set of abilities that he expects you to develop and use to their fullest potential. God intends to use you as a leader and to bring these abilities to bear accordingly.

Skillful leaders know what they are good at doing and where their God-given abilities lie. Skillful leaders humbly recognize areas in which they lack talent. You need to honestly appraise your strengths and weaknesses if you want to be the "skillful" leader God desires and created you to be. Many ways exist to increase your understanding of your God-given abilities, such as prayer, honest personal introspection, recognizing past experiences—good and bad, talking to friends and colleagues who know you well, and professional "skills" inventories or surveys that profile your abilities. Taking such initiatives to honestly assess your God-given ability will help you become the leader God desires.

Once you have an accurate assessment of your set of abilities, you will be in a position to gain the experience required to transform your abilities into skills. You can gain experience in a variety of ways, such as practicing a certain discipline, reading and studying the writings of others, observing and learning from others with similar skills, and finding a mentor who will guide and teach you. Fan into flame the gift God has given you. Take initiatives that promote experience.

Skills, character, and compassion work in concert to create stability and balance for an Entrusted Leader. The presence of a skill in a person's life comes from a combination of God-given ability and experiences that generate confidence and proficiency. Recognize your God-given ability and initiate experiences that help transform this ability into a God-honoring skill.

David led Israel skillfully, choosing the right course of action that served God's purpose for His people. Knowing the right course of action requires selflessness. Circumstances must be viewed according to God's purposes, not one's selfish ambition and desires. A leader must consider the impact on those who follow when selecting a course of action. This is what skillful leaders do.

Discussion Questions based on "A Leader's Need for Skills"

1. Describe or list some gifts of God (natural ability) you recognize in your life.
2. What actions can you initiate to further the development of your ability into a skill?
3. Explain why knowing the right course of action might be an important skill for a person as he or she leads other people.
4. Discuss why possessing a God-given ability that has not been developed by experience reduces a person's effectiveness and skill as a leader.

A leader needs skills that relate to one's sphere of responsibility.

*Attempting to lead others without appropriate
skills is reckless and foolish.*

*Skills come from a combination of God-given ability and experiences
that build a reservoir of knowledge, confidence, and proficiency.*

PERSONAL APPLICATION EXERCISE

Illustrate how your skills as a leader might serve and encourage one leader-to-follower relationship you currently have.

A Leader's Need for Character
Psalm 78:72 and Psalm 51:10

A leader needs character.

A leader's character directly influences every choice he or she makes. The threads of a leader's character ultimately weave a pattern of priorities, attitudes, and actions one initiates in every leader-to-follower relationship. No relationship escapes the influence (good or bad) of a leader's level of integrity and orientation of one's moral compass.

The presence of character in a leader contains a mixture of moral behavior and courageous acts. A leader must first display genuine integrity to gain a follower's trust and respect. Others willingly follow the leader who confidently and courageously communicates the right course of action an organization should take. An Entrusted Leader is a person of vision who faithfully serves the investment God has "entrusted" in one's life by using skills, character, and compassion to encourage others toward a common goal, while upholding an Entrusted Leader's core values.

Remember that the concept of a leader creating stability for leading by applying a balance of skills, character, and compassion finds inspiration from the description of David found in Psalm 78:72: "And David shepherded them with integrity of heart; with skillful hands he led them."

Modern-day culture does not fully appreciate the value of a leader possessing a balance of skills, character, and compassion. In fact, many have completely separated a leader's ethical behavior from his or her role as a leader. The prevailing societal attitude suggests that it does not matter what a leader does in one's personal life as long as the job gets done. This attitude is a byproduct of a dualistic worldview; the idea that the world can be cleanly divided between the material and the spiritual. The Bible rejects and refutes this philosophy. God's Word rejects any notion that the impact of a person's character can be compartmentalized and limited to one area of life without impacting another. Dualism stands inconsistent with the reality of life. One cannot lead skillfully in the marketplace and ignore one's need for character and compassion.

In today's leadership environment, people have elevated skills to a place of prominence that eclipses both character and compassion. Results matter more than method. The means by which a leader achieves results justifies the end. The prevailing attitude exists that if a skilled leader must compromise his or her personal convictions, then so be it. Society has a convenient way of turning a blind eye to the cold-hearted treatment of followers as long as the leader gets results.

Skills dominate the current landscape when the focus turns to developing, choosing, and promoting leaders. Most institutions of higher learning have sophisticated curricular offerings designed to teach leadership and management skills. Unfortunately, these same institutions have no clue how to develop a leader's heart and core values, from which character and compassion spring. Almost all secular and many religious institutions of higher learning reject the Bible as an educational resource. Lasting character and compassion only emerge when a leader's heart has been transformed by the absolute truth of the Word of God. The secular philosophy of relativism, which most schools now readily accept and teach, leaves them with no permanent foundation upon which to teach a leader an enduring code of ethics or a logical reason to treat others with compassion. This limiting set of circumstances has produced a generation of leaders who place a premium on skills and discount the value of character and compassion.

Envision a leader standing on a platform being supported by three columns. The platform represents the leadership position the leader holds. One column represents the leader's skills while the other two columns represent character and compassion. Ideally, a leader will possess these three qualities in equal measure. Such a situation results in a level, stable, and balanced platform of leadership upon which a leader can stand. See Figure 8.1.

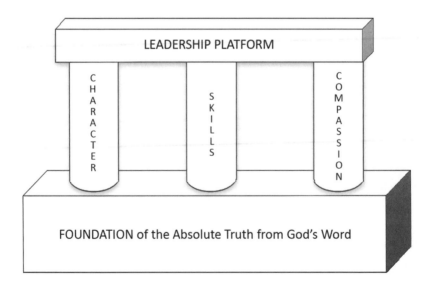

Figure 8.1 Foundation and Support for an Entrusted Leader

Figure 8.1 represents the balance and stability created when a leader's platform rests on character, skill, and compassion equally. A skill forms when God-given ability combines with experience. Institutes of higher education teach leadership and management skills. Character and compassion spring from a heart transformed by the Word of God. When a leader chooses the world's priority of developing skill and ignores the development of compassion and character, his or her platform of leadership will look more like Figure 8.2.

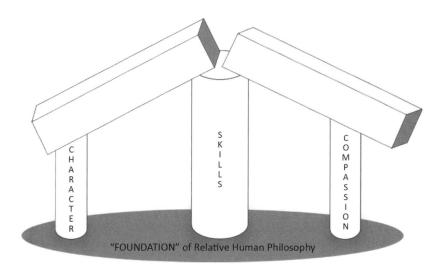

Figure 8.2: An unstable and out-of-balance platform of leadership

Development of character and compassion lag behind skill development in the leader who trusts in the shifting sands of relative human philosophy. Such a leader runs the risk that one day the pressures associated with leading will compromise his or her decision-making and result in the fracture of one's platform. Many choices demanded of a leader rest outside the realm of leadership and management skills. Such decisions require a leader with strong and stable convictions that come from character and compassion. The collapse of a leader's platform may appear less catastrophic than Figure 8.2 portrays. Sometimes the negative impact of character and compassion deficiencies is more subtle, such as a slow erosion of credibility and believability; a lack of trust, confidence, and loyalty; or a reduction of productivity because follow-ers resist giving their full effort. Leadership that relies only on skills eventually becomes unstable and unbalanced.

Some would say that character and compassion go hand in hand and cannot be separated. One might suppose that character and com-passion develop in equal measure as a leader's heart transforms. This proposition sounds logical. Observation and experience, however, sug-gest otherwise. Character and compassion do not develop in equal mea-sure. I have encountered individuals who have hearts of gold and drip with compassion for others but live an ethically immoral lifestyle. By the same token, I have encountered people who are morally impeccable and beyond reproach ethically but relate in a cold, unloving, and un-sympathetic manner to everyone around them. I believe a leader must consider both one's character and compassion as he or she develops. This lesson will focus on character. The next lesson will consider a lead-er's need for compassion.

David led others skillfully with character and compassion. Lead-ing others requires a combination of appropriately developed skills and core values that produce biblically sound leadership behaviors. Lead-ership stability and balance increase when a skilled leader applies the benefits of character and compassion that only come from a spiritually transformed heart.

The psalmist Asaph said in Psalm 78:72: "And David shepherded them with integrity of heart. . . ." David led Israel with integrity of heart. Integrity speaks to the core of David's character. The Hebrew term translated as "integrity" is *tom*. Swanson defines this term as follows: "blamelessness, integrity, innocence, i.e., a state or condition of moral goodness in a life."[6] I like the idea of a leader having "moral goodness." In this regard, I use the term "character" when speaking of the "moral goodness or integrity" of an Entrusted Leader. Reflect on this for a mo-ment and answer the following questions: How do you define "charac-ter"? What does it mean that a leader possesses "character"?

Merriam-Webster's Collegiate Dictionary says of the term "charac-ter": ". . . the complex of mental and ethical traits marking and often individualizing a person, . . . moral excellence and firmness. . . ."[7] Keep in mind the idea of a leader having "moral excellence and firmness" and read David's words recorded in Psalm 51:10: "Create in me a pure heart, O God, and renew a steadfast spirit within me."

In Psalm 51:10, David speaks of two aspects of a person's character as he asks God to strengthen his character in two ways. The request from David involved creating a pure heart within him. The second petition contemplated renewing a steadfast spirit. From this passage, the reader learns that a person's character has not only a moral or ethical aspect but also a courageous aspect. When most people think of a leader's character, he or she typically focuses on one's moral or ethical behavior. A leader's character, however, also encompasses one's courage to lead others.

Psalm 51 records David's lament after being confronted by the prophet Nathan for having committed adultery with Bathsheba. David recognized that his sin left him morally unclean before God and caused him to be unstable and insecure in his own mind and spirit. Think about your own life for a minute: Doesn't unconfessed sin leave us feeling unclean and insecure? Isn't this a natural result of sin separating us from the Lord God Almighty?

Character: "A Pure Heart"

The Hebrew word for heart, *leb*, refers to a person's inner makeup: intellect, emotion, and will. David understood that authentic moral character, what he called a "pure heart," involved more than simple outward conformity to a code of ethics. David knew his inner nature needed to become "purified" and that the evidence of such would be a change in his moral attitudes and behaviors.

The Hebrew word for "pure" is *tahor*. Strong defines this term as: "pure, clean. 1A clean (ceremonially—of animals). 1B pure (physically). 1C pure, clean (morally, ethically)."[8] A person only becomes "ceremonially clean" through a personal relationship with Jesus Christ. Conformity to rules will not create the "pure heart" David desired. Once a person receives Jesus as Lord and Savior, however, his or her character will change from the inside out and display moral attitudes and behaviors consistent with following Christ. Developing moral character involves avoiding sinful behaviors and adopting wholesome behaviors. In Colossians 3:1–17, the Apostle Paul paints an ideal picture of what the moral character of a follower of Christ should look like.

> [1] Since, then, you have been raised with Christ, set your hearts on things above, where Christ is seated at the right hand of God. [2] Set your minds on things above, not on earthly things. [3] For you died, and your life is now hidden with Christ in God. [4] When Christ, who is your life, appears, then you also will appear with him in glory.

> [5] Put to death, therefore, whatever belongs to your earthly nature: sexual immorality, impurity, lust, evil desires and greed, which is idolatry. [6] Because of these, the wrath of God is coming. [7] You used to walk in these ways, in the life you once lived. [8] But now you must rid yourselves of all such things as these: anger, rage, malice, slander, and filthy language from your lips. [9] Do not lie to each other, since you have taken off your old self with its practices [10] and have put on the new self, which is being renewed in knowledge in the image of its Creator. [11] Here there is no Greek or Jew, circumcised or uncircumcised, barbarian, Scythian, slave or free, but Christ is all, and is in all.

> [12] Therefore, as God's chosen people, holy and dearly loved, clothe yourselves with compassion, kindness, humility, gentleness and patience. [13] Bear with each other and forgive whatever grievances you may have against one another. Forgive as the Lord forgave you. [14] And over all these virtues put on love, which binds them all together in perfect unity.

> [15] Let the peace of Christ rule in your hearts, since as members of one body you were called to peace. And be thankful. [16] Let the word of Christ dwell in you richly as you teach and admonish one another with all wisdom, and as you sing psalms, hymns and spiritual songs with gratitude in your hearts to God. [17] And whatever you do, whether in word or deed, do it all in the name of the Lord Jesus, giving thanks to God the Father through him. (Col. 3:1–17)

A Christian's character rests on one's union with Jesus Christ. As followers of Christ, we need to focus our hearts and minds on heavenly things, not earthly things. A person's moral attitude and behavior will reflect whatever he or she feeds into his or her brain. The Apostle Paul said in Colossians 2 that when a person receives Jesus Christ as Lord, he or she is set free from following human rules and legalism. This does not, however, give one license to live a morally corrupt life. In Colossians 3, Paul describes what holy living looks like.

Paul instructed followers of Jesus Christ to "put to death" whatever belongs to our earthly nature. What follows is a list of the immoral attitudes and behaviors from which Christians are to turn away: sexual immorality, impurity, lust, evil desires, greed, anger, rage, malice, slander, filthy language, and lying. I do not take this as an all-inclusive list of immoral behaviors but as representative of the attitudes and behaviors a Christian must banish from one's life. Such behaviors would most certainly damage the leader-to-follower relationship.

Paul clearly describes the type of moral character that a follower of Jesus Christ should have. Paul says that believers should "clothe yourselves" with them. People see the physical clothes a believer wears. Similarly others should see these attitudes and behaviors in a Christ follower's life as well. These characteristics are: compassion, kindness, humility, gentleness, patience, forgiveness, love, unity, peace, thankfulness, wisdom, and gratitude. As with Paul's list of immoral attitudes and behaviors, I do not consider this an all-inclusive list of moral attitudes and behaviors. Paul's lists clearly contrast the outward appearance of the person who follows one's sinful nature and the outward appearance of a follower of Christ. The leader who displays the moral character Paul expects from a follower of Christ will have a positive impact on his or her relationship with those he or she leads.

A leader's moral behavior truly reflects the inward condition of his or her heart or character. Most secular institutions and organizations call this ethics.

A leader's moral behavior truly reflects the inward condition of his or her heart or character. Most secular institutions and organizations call this ethics. The world's basis for ethical behavior rests on the shifting sands of relativism, and worldly leaders function void of any absolute inward moral compass. Consequently, such a leader's moral behavior becomes limited only by what others deem as legal, company policy, socially acceptable, or, in some cases, simply whatever a leader thinks he or she can get away with.

A follower of Jesus Christ must resist the temptation of one's character being defined by relative, situational ethics. The leader who claims to follow Jesus Christ must allow his or her character to be shaped and defined by God's Word, and God's Word alone! The Bible stands firmly as the absolute standard of behavior that supersedes societal norms, company policies, and self-desire. A leader must be guided by an absolute, biblically based moral compass of right and wrong that points to what's right even when no one else is watching. Consider what David said in this regard in Psalm 119:9: "How can a young man keep his way pure? By living according to your word."

Character: "A Steadfast Spirit"

In addition to a pure heart, David asked God to "renew a steadfast spirit" in him. "Steadfast" comes from the Hebrew word *kuwn*. Strong defines this term as follows: "1 to be firm, be stable, be established. 1A (Niphal). 1A1 to be set up, be established, be fixed."[9] A leader must be of a firm and stable character. A leader cannot be insecure or of two minds. Such security of conviction and courage comes only from a steadfast spirit established and rooted in God.

A leader's sense of security and courage also reflects the inward condition of a leader's heart or character. Every leader who moves through life separated from God by sin and relies solely on self will eventually encounter a giant that overwhelms his or her self-confidence. Facing such a giant alone can leave a leader feeling insecure, indecisive, and afraid. Trusting that God ultimately controls all circumstances and is bigger than all earthly giants provides a leader with a sense of security and courage rooted in someone bigger than self. A leader must have the courage to take full responsibility for the lives of those that follow. Leaders get credit for results—good or bad! A leader must initiate appropriate action depending on the circumstances and not wait to simply react. Leaders give clear directions to others and do not wait for someone else to give directions. Leaders do not waver or second-guess decisions. Leaders make the hard decisions and choices no one else wants to make. Leaders do not compromise their convictions on controversial issues, even when their views run counter to popular opinion. Leaders take calculated risks. Bold leadership actions take courage and are not for the weak of heart.

Courage of character stems from God's presence, not raw bravery rooted in self. Real confidence does not come from arrogance, pride, or an inflated view of self. The basis of such courageous character is a firm belief in the sovereignty and providence of God. A good example of such courage appears in the story of David and Goliath.

> [45] David said to the Philistine, "You come against me with sword and spear and javelin, but I come against you in the name of the LORD Almighty, the God of the armies of Israel, whom you have defied. [46] This day the LORD will hand you over to me, and I'll strike you down and cut off your head. Today I will give the carcasses of the Philistine army to the birds of the air and the beasts of the earth, and the whole world will know that there is a God in Israel. [47] All those gathered here will know that it is not by sword or spear that the LORD saves; for the battle is the LORD's, and he will give all of you into our hands." (1 Sam. 17:45–47)

David's courage to fight Goliath, and essentially lead Israel in battle, came from his trust in the sovereignty of God, not his own skill or strength. David proclaimed that Goliath placed his trust in human-fashioned armaments. Goliath relied on his fighting skills (self). David stood up to this giant based on his faith in the Lord Almighty. Goliath defied the God of the armies of Israel, while David gave God all the credit for the victory over this giant. David understood that God intended and desired to work through him as a leader so that the "whole world" would know that God exists in Israel.

God desires and intends to use you in the same manner He used David. God wants to make His presence known through you to those you lead. Trusting in God, not self, and standing courageously before whatever giants you face constitutes one way to make God known to others. David's faith and trust in God's sovereignty resided in David's heart long before he faced Goliath. If you trust in whatever human armament makes you successful today, someday you will face a giant bigger than your skills. The result will be a quick melting away of your courage. Trust in God, and no such giant will ever steal your courage.

Fear paralyzes a leader. Being scared causes a leader to become indecisive, unsure, and insecure. Followers can sense this in a leader instantly. Nobody wants to trust his or her fate to a leader who lacks courage. Joshua assumed the leadership of Israel upon Moses' death. Joshua's first challenge as a leader involved leading Israel on a campaign to enter the promised land. This meant displacing the current residents whom forty years prior Israel had seen as unbeatable giants. God said to Joshua: "Have I not commanded you? Be strong and courageous. Do not be terrified; do not be discouraged, for the LORD your God will be with you wherever you go" (Josh. 1:9). Joshua's courage resided with God, not self.

If your courage as a leader is anchored to "self"-confidence, you will eventually reach the limits of your skills to face giants. If your courage extends beyond "self"-confidence into the reaches of a limitless and all-powerful God, you will never face a giant too big. This does not guarantee you will always emerge victoriously, but it does provide unsurpassed peace that God controls all circumstances no matter the situation.

I want to challenge you to get alone with God and ask Him to clearly reveal to you the makeup of your character. *Be careful, for this may be painful at first!* As David prayed, ask God to create in you a pure heart and a steadfast spirit (Ps. 51:10). Ask God to reveal to you any moral attitudes and behaviors you harbor in your heart that are inconsistent with God's biblical standards. Ask God to show you where your trust resides in the human armament of your own skills, rather than trusting in God's sovereign control over the circumstances of your life.

A leader needs character to complement his or her skills. The presence of character in a leader is a mixture of moral behavior and courageous acts. An Entrusted Leader's credibility links directly to one's moral character. An Entrusted Leader's decisiveness links directly to one's courage. God's Word remains the only absolute standard for a leader's moral attitudes and behavior. God's sovereignty serves as the only reliable basis for a leader's courage and confidence.

Discussion Questions based on "A Leader's Need for Character"

1. Using Psalm 51 as an inspiration, write a petition asking God to purify your heart.
2. Using Psalm 51 as an inspiration, write a petition asking God to create a steadfast spirit within you.
3. Using Colossians 3 as an inspiration, describe the potential impact on a leader-to-follower relationship if a leader "put to death" sinful behavior and, in turn, "clothed" oneself with wholesome attitudes and behaviors.
4. Describe the damaging effects fear can have on a leader's relationship with others.

Character directly impacts every choice a leader makes!

*The orientation of a leader's moral compass
influences every relationship.*

Character is a mixture of moral behavior and courageous acts.

PERSONAL APPLICATION EXERCISE

Describe an ideal vision of a leader's moral character and courageous character. What can you do to encourage the development of your character in light of this ideal vision of a leader's character?

A Leader's Need for Compassion
Psalm 78:72 and Matthew 22:36–40

A leader needs compassion.

Authentic compassion starts with a leader's love for God and then flows unconditionally to others. God desires a leader to be a vessel through which He pours His love to others. Compassion helps generate loyalty, harmony, and stability for a leader among his or her followers.

Selfless leaders normally have great empathy for others, while self-centered leaders care only for themselves. A leader who lacks compassion makes decisions based on how choices impact self with little or no regard for the impact on followers. Uncaring leaders garner little or no respect, loyalty, trust, or credibility from followers.

A leader needs compassion to help create balance and stability for leading others.

An Entrusted Leader is a person of vision who faithfully serves the investment God has "entrusted" in one's life by using skills, character, and compassion to encourage others toward a common goal, while upholding an Entrusted Leader's core values.

The concept of a leader creating stability for leading by applying a balance of skills, character, and compassion finds inspiration from the description of David found in Psalm 78:72: "And David shepherded them with integrity of heart; with skillful hands he led them."

David "shepherded" those he led. The Lord instructed David to lead Israel as a shepherd: "You will shepherd my people Israel, and you will become their ruler" (2 Sam. 5:2). Shepherding a flock involves feeding, nurturing, and protecting the sheep. Leading others involves understanding the needs of, caring for, and protecting those that follow. Leading as a shepherd produces trust, respect, and loyalty within the leader-to-follower relationship.

The Hebrew term for "shepherded" found in Psalm 78:72 comes from the root word *raah*. Strong defines this term as follows: "1 to pasture, tend, graze, feed . . . 1A1A to shepherd. 1A1B of ruler, teacher (fig).

1A1C of people as flock (fig) . . . 2 to associate with, be a friend of. 2A to associate with. 2B to be companions."[10] The basic concept behind this word relates to the relationship a shepherd has with a flock of sheep. A good shepherd has compassion for the helplessness of his sheep and cares for them. In the Old Testament, *raah* describes how God intends a leader to view one's relationship with those who follow. The idea of a leader of people being a shepherd communicates God's desire for a leader to have compassion for his or her followers and to care for them. *Raah* is used in Psalm 78:72 to describe David's compassion for those he led.

The motif of a shepherd is used throughout the Bible to describe the type of leader God desires to use: "Then I will give you shepherds after my own heart, who will lead you with knowledge and understanding" (Jer. 3:15). God wants shepherd-leaders to care for and lead His people. God desires to use selfless leaders who will compassionately care for the needs of others. In contrast, God warns of judgment on leaders who uncaringly use followers for selfish gain.

> [7] *'Therefore, you shepherds, hear the word of the LORD:* [8] *As surely as I live, declares the Sovereign LORD, because my flock lacks a shepherd and so has been plundered and has become food for all the wild animals, and because my shepherds did not search for my flock but cared for themselves rather than for my flock,* [9] *therefore, O shepherds, hear the word of the LORD:* [10] *This is what the Sovereign LORD says: I am against the shepherds and will hold them accountable for my flock. I will remove them from tending the flock so that the shepherds can no longer feed themselves. I will rescue my flock from their mouths, and it will no longer be food for them." (Ezek. 34:7–10)*

At the core of a shepherd-leader resides a compassionate heart. Compassion for others fuels the actions of a leader who cares for and protects his or her followers. Only a selfless leader with a heart oriented toward others will lead compassionately.

Perhaps more than any other trait, people want to follow a leader who they believe truly cares for them. Followers long to trust that a leader has their best interests at heart. People want to follow a leader who displays compassion for others. The leader who truly empathizes with his followers wins their support. The individual who can relate to and sympathize with the struggles of others gains respect and loyalty. A leader cannot fake authentic compassion; this trait only flows from a selfless heart truly committed to serving others.

Sadly, present society remains short on compassion. We have become a selfish and self-centered people. Individuals ruthlessly protect their individual rights at the expense of others. A dog-eat-dog world exists where people fight to take care of "number one." A sense of entitlement motivates many to take whatever they can grab from others. A sense of feeling abandoned by their leaders makes people gravitate to self-protection. The rat races most people run leave them so wound up that they lash out in anger at anyone who is in their way or who impedes their progress. Incredibly, such selfish and cold-hearted behavior seems as likely these days among people who claim to follow Jesus as those who do not. Even Christians seem to extend very little compassion to others outside the context of a ministry situation where compassion is expected. Let's consider a definition of "compassion."

Merriam-Webster's Collegiate Dictionary says of the term "compassion": "sympathetic consciousness of others' distress together with a desire to alleviate it."[11] This definition contains two vital aspects necessary to understand what compassion means. The first concerns an awareness of others. A good leader selflessly works on understanding the circumstances of his or her followers. In contrast, a selfish leader never takes his or her eyes off self long enough to gain a clear picture of why his or her followers struggle. The second concerns a desire to impact the circumstances of one's followers in a positive fashion. Leaders have to be able to relate to their followers and must desire to help them. Understanding the needs of others and desiring to relieve sufferings combine to generate compassion.

Selfless love resides at the heart of compassion for others. Extending compassion requires one to act on love for another with no expectation of personal gain. Unconditional love is basically unnatural for humans. True compassion for others extends from a heart that overflows with the love of God. Allowing God to love others through you becomes the key to having compassion for them.

Christian scholars often refer to Matthew 22:37–39 as "the Great Commandment." Jesus spoke these words in response to the question: "Teacher, which is the greatest commandment in the Law?" (Matt. 22:36)

> *37 Jesus replied: "'Love the Lord your God with all your heart and with all your soul and with all your mind.' 38 This is the first and greatest commandment. 39 And the second is like it: 'Love your neighbor as yourself.'" (Matt. 22:37–39)*

Jesus answered by quoting two seemingly unrelated Old Testament passages. The first passage quoted by Jesus comes from Deuteronomy 6:5: "Love the LORD your God with all your heart and with all your soul and with all your strength." The second quote comes from Leviticus 19:18: "Do not seek revenge or bear a grudge against one of your people, but love your neighbor as yourself. I am the LORD."

The Deuteronomy passage quoted by Jesus became well known by the people of Israel in His day. Students of the Old Testament commonly call this passage of Scripture "The Shema." The emphasis of this Old Testament Scripture involves a person's devotion to God with the totality of one's being and commitment. Loving God with all one's heart, soul, and mind depicts a relationship with God of the most intimate nature. Jesus begins His answer with a statement that marked a person's love for God as the most important relationship in every human's life. This love should permeate every bit of a person's being. The health and vitality of every human relationship depends on the health and vitality of our relationship with God.

One might consider the Leviticus passage quoted by Jesus as more obscure than the Deuteronomy passage. This verse resides in the middle of a long list of laws Moses gave to Israel that describe what holy living looks like. The Deuteronomy and Leviticus passages were not commonly linked together as Jesus did in Matthew 22. In doing so, Jesus essentially summed up the Ten Commandments and the subsequent laws of Israel. Love for God and love for others lies at the foundation of all Old Testament Scriptures according to Jesus. Consider Walvoord's and Zuck's comments on Matthew 22:34–40:

> *When the Pharisees heard that Jesus had answered the Sadducees,*
> *they quickly sent a representative, a well-versed expert in the*
> *Law, to Jesus with a question . . . Which is the greatest command-*
> *ment in the Law? This question was being debated among the*
> *religious leaders at the time and various commandments were*
> *being championed as the greatest. Jesus' quick reply summarized*
> *the entire Decalogue. He replied that the greatest commandment*
> *is to love the Lord . . . God with all one's heart . . . soul, and . . .*
> *mind (cf. Deut. 6:5). He added that the second commandment is*
> *to love one's neighbor as oneself (cf. Lev. 19:18). The first sum-*
> *marizes the first table of the Law, and the second summarizes the*
> *second table. Jesus said, All the Law and the Prophets hang on*
> *these two commandments, that is, all the Old Testament develops*
> *and amplifies these two points: love for God and love for others,*
> *who are made in God's image.*[12]

From Jesus' connection of these two Old Testament passages, one concludes that a total and intimate love relationship with God becomes the starting point for all healthy human interaction. When a person loves God with all his or her heart, soul, and mind, he or she begins to see others as God sees them. As love for God grows in a person, love naturally overflows to others. The truth remains that God begins to love others through the person that loves God. A person's capacity to love others directly relates to one's love for God. Loving God with all our heart, soul, and mind does two things that impact our love for others: Love of God shifts the focus of one's life from self to God and others, and loving God generates a reservoir of God's love that naturally flows to others.

Love for God grows in a person's heart the better one gets to know Him. Activities such as Bible study, prayer, worship, and fellowship with other Christians expand one's understanding of God's love and His ways. The more time a person spends alone with God, the better one knows Him and the deeper love grows. The leader who truly loves God with all his or her heart, soul, and mind will extend love and compassion to those who follow. Consider the examples of David and Jesus who both sought time alone with God the Father.

David
³ *In the morning, O LORD, you hear my voice;*
   in the morning I lay my requests before you
   and wait in expectation. (Ps. 5:3)

Jesus
³⁵ *Very early in the morning, while it was still dark, Jesus got up,*
   left the house and went off to a solitary place, where he prayed.
   (Mark 1:35)

Humans by nature love self. People typically order their lives to satisfy any number of real or perceived personal needs and approach relationships with others selfishly. Most people's first thought involves what they can get from a relationship with other people that might satisfy some need or desire. Jesus described the human heart as follows: "For from within, out of men's hearts, come evil thoughts, sexual immorality, theft, murder, adultery, greed, malice, deceit, lewdness, envy, slander, arrogance and folly" (Mark 7:21–22). For the most part, this list describes unloving acts of human interaction that one initiates at the expense of another.

God created mankind in His image. Consequently, we do have the capacity to love others and extend compassion to them. Sin, however, inhibits man's ability to love others selflessly. A personal relationship with Jesus Christ liberates a person from the bondage of sin that inhibits love and compassion. Loving God with all our heart, soul, and mind opens the gate for God to love others through us selflessly and compassionately.

Most people have little trouble loving "self." We order the priorities and actions of our lives to serve selfish interests. We may not always love what we do, but typically deep down inside, we love ourselves. By nature, people tend to love themselves first with all other priorities falling in line after self. Loving others involves choosing to put the needs of others ahead of our natural inclination to place self first.

Loving others as yourself involves more than mere emotions. This type of love requires a reordering of priorities. Loving others requires initiating actions on the behalf of others in order to meet their needs.

Who qualifies to be your "neighbor"? Who does Jesus expect us to love as ourselves? The Greek term for "neighbor" used by Jesus was *plesion*. Consider how Strong describes who our neighbors are: ". . . according to Christ, any other man irrespective of race or religion with whom we live or whom we chance to meet."[13] Anyone we happen to meet or associate with during the normal course of a day qualifies as our neighbor. Certainly for the leader, every single follower qualifies as a "neighbor" that Jesus commands us to love.

We have already discussed that the depth of a person's love for God increases in proportion to the time invested in getting to know God and His ways better. The same is true for human-to-human relationships. The more time a leader invests in getting to know another person, the greater the understanding he or she has for them. The better a leader understands others, the greater his or her capacity for love and compassion becomes.

Jesus' teaching on the Great Commandment has very practical application to the leader-follower relationship. An Entrusted Leader needs compassion to balance one's skills and character. True compassion for one's followers starts with and cannot be separated from a loving relationship with God. The more a leader fosters intimacy with God, the more he or she is able to display the love of God to one's followers. Prayer, worship, and Bible study deepen a leader's relationship and intimacy with God, which in turn increases one's compassion for others. Learn how to love God with every bit of your being.

Compassion requires an understanding of the needs of others. Every follower qualifies as a leader's neighbor. Compassionate leaders take time and initiate the action necessary to develop a clear understanding of the needs of his or her followers. Compassion does not end with understanding but requires action. The compassionate leader not only understands the needs of one's followers, he or she seeks to serve them by satisfying these needs. Learn how to love your neighbors like you love yourself.

The presence of compassion in a leader starts with a love for God that flows unconditionally to others. How a leader treats his or her followers dramatically impacts the leader-to-follower relationship. God desires a leader to nurture, care for, and protect followers just as a shepherd does for his or her flock. A compassionate leader's actions indicate understanding, empathy, and kindness toward followers. Compassionate leaders typically find that their followers return their love with loyalty, respect, and trust.

Discussion Questions based on "A Leader's Need for Compassion"

1. What is compassion and where does true compassion originate from?
2. Describe some of the potential benefits a leader might receive when he or she extends compassion to others.
3. What does it mean to love God with all your heart, soul, and mind?
4. What does it mean to love others as yourself?

A leader needs compassion.
Authentic compassion starts with a leader's love for God
and then flows unconditionally to others.

Selfless leaders normally have great empathy for others,
while self-centered leaders care only for themselves.

Compassion helps to create balance and stability for leading others.

PERSONAL APPLICATION EXERCISE

In your reader's journal, describe some actions you can initiate that will deepen your love for God and in turn strengthen your compassion for those who follow you.

9

Lifestyle

CORE VALUE: A LIFESTYLE that is beyond reproach and publicly demonstrates faith, hope, and love.

Living beyond Reproach
1 Timothy 3:1–7

Followers watch leaders very closely. The public's opinion and image form based on the words spoken, emotions expressed, attitudes demonstrated, and actions taken by a leader.

The leader who lives beyond reproach leaves no opportunity for followers to suspect a lack of self-discipline or self-control. Living beyond reproach helps create a positive public image and opinion of a leader.

A leader's lifestyle stands on public display. The higher one ascends on the leadership ladder, the greater the public visibility. How others view one's personal life directly impacts his or her credibility and respect as a leader. God does not require perfection; however, He does insist that a leader maintain a lifestyle free from the appearance of attitudes and actions inconsistent with His Word. Suspicions of illicit behavior should never swirl around the life of a leader who claims to follow Jesus.

The Entrusted Leader concept requires a healthy relationship between the leader and the follower. Respect and credibility characterize healthy relationships. Leading as a servant depends on others who follow voluntarily. A leader's lifestyle either enhances his or her respect and credibility with followers or erodes them.

Some suggest a leader's personal life does not impact his or her ability to lead others. I emphatically reject this notion. A leader's personal lifestyle directly impacts one's ability to lead others. Poor choices can damage a person's admiration for a leader's exceptional professional skill and diminish one's respect and credibility.

God expects a leader to display publicly a lifestyle that leaves no opportunity for followers to suspect a lack of self-discipline or self-control. Followers do not respect or trust a leader whom they suspect cannot manage his or her personal affairs. Suspicion that a leader's personal life is in disarray creates insecurity among followers. Why should followers believe that a leader can oversee the complexity surrounding others if the leader cannot control his or her own life?

God expects a leader to display publicly a lifestyle that leaves no opportunity for followers to suspect a lack of self-discipline or self-control.

God's standard for a personal lifestyle exceeds that of the world. We live in a culture that sets the moral bar based on what the majority deems socially acceptable. Over the past fifty plus years, the world has lowered the moral bar. God's biblical standard, however, has not changed. God holds a leader to a higher standard because God understands the impact a leader's personal life has on the lives of others.

According to the Apostle Paul, one who chooses the role of a leader desires a noble task. The desire to serve as a leader becomes a good and honorable intention. To remain noble, however, a leader must live above reproach. A leader must not only live a life free of wrongdoing, but also a leader must avoid any behavior that might raise a question or suspicion of wrongdoing. Paul illustrates what this means in 1 Timothy 3:1–7. Paul starts with a challenge to live "above reproach." What follows this exhortation is a long list of attitudes and actions that characterize how "living above reproach" might apply to one's life. His description of being "above reproach" equates to what I call a "socially blameless lifestyle."

> [1] *Here is a trustworthy saying: If anyone sets his heart on being an overseer, he desires a noble task.* [2] *Now the overseer must be above reproach, the husband of but one wife, temperate, self-*

controlled, respectable, hospitable, able to teach, ³ not given to drunkenness, not violent but gentle, not quarrelsome, not a lover of money. ⁴ He must manage his own family well and see that his children obey him with proper respect. ⁵ (If anyone does not know how to manage his own family, how can he take care of God's church?) ⁶ He must not be a recent convert, or he may become conceited and fall under the same judgment as the devil. ⁷ He must also have a good reputation with outsiders, so that he will not fall into disgrace and into the devil's trap. (1 Tim. 3:1–7)

Paul said: ". . . the overseer must be above reproach. . . ." The context of Paul's instruction concerns church leaders. The application of a lifestyle above reproach, however, extends to every arena in which a follower of Christ leads, including the home, marketplace, and society in general. To fully appreciate why a leader must live above reproach, one must understand the role of an overseer.

The Greek term used by Paul in 1 Timothy 3:2 that the New International Version of the Bible translates as "overseer" is *episkopos*. Strong defines this word as follows: ". . . a man charged with the duty of seeing that things to be done by others are done rightly. . . ."[1] The basic idea is that a leader watches over, cares for, protects, and ensures the integrity, accuracy, and purity of an activity. A leader charged with this public responsibility must also live this prescribed way privately or forfeit his or her credibility with others.

A leader must live beyond reproach. This characteristic is not optional for a leader. In order to be the type of leader God desires, one must live a socially blameless lifestyle. Given the noble nature of the task of leading, God requires an honorable lifestyle. Paul suggests for a follower of Christ that leading and living above reproach go hand in hand and remain inseparable. Paul rejected the idea that a person might appear excellent as a leader and less than excellent morally. Leaders bear the responsibility for setting the moral bar for those he or she leads. Followers will respond in kind to a leader's lifestyle based on the attitudes and actions observed, not just the words spoken.

Living "above reproach" means to adopt a personal lifestyle that provides no opportunity for blame or criticism. Such a person guards against behavior that others might question, misunderstand, or misconstrue. Living a socially blameless life involves avoiding life choices that discredit or disgrace a person.

One must realize that in some situations, simply abstaining from a behavior may not suffice to appear above reproach. For example, the Bible states clearly that drunkenness remains a sin. The abuse of alcohol will discredit and disgrace a leader. Simply abstaining from drunkenness may not be enough for a leader, however. A Christ follower may find that in some circumstances total abstinence from the consumption of alcohol provides the only alternative to avoid the appearance of drunkenness. The purpose of Paul's charge to appear above reproach involves protecting the respect and credibility of leaders who follow Christ.

Merriam-Webster's Collegiate Dictionary defines the noun "reproach" as: "1: an expression of rebuke or disapproval . . . 3: a cause or occasion of blame, discredit, or disgrace" and the verb: "1: to express disappointment in or displeasure with (a person) for conduct that is blameworthy or in need of amendment."[2] Reproach characterizes the person who has chosen conduct deemed disgraceful and blameworthy. Such behavior brings discredit and needs amending. Conduct that provokes reproach destroys a person's credibility and respect with others.

Paul instructs leaders to live above reproach. Leaders must behave carefully so as to avoid the appearance of conduct deemed by others to be unacceptable. To do this, one must display behavior that cannot be misconstrued by others. For example, simply visiting a bar may lead to the appearance of drunkenness. Leaders must avoid any appearance that damages one's credibility with followers, even if the conduct stands totally innocent in nature.

Living above compromising situations and choices means to be so far removed that no association can be made. For a leader, this means avoiding any and all situations or relationships that could possibly give the appearance of wrongdoing. For example, a leader should never allow himself or herself to be alone for an extended period of time with a member of the opposite sex. Even if the relationship is 100 percent innocent, the appearance alone raises questions and diminishes credibility. Living above reproach requires one to exceed innocence and to avoid situations that might be misconstrued.

What follows Paul's charge to leaders to be above reproach is a long list of attitudes and actions that directly impact a leader's credibility and respectability with others. The moral excellence of a leader's private life directly impacts the health of the leader-to-follower relationship. Questionable attitudes and behaviors damage the respectability of a leader. After encouraging leaders to adopt a lifestyle that is above reproach, Paul lists specific areas of a person's life in which a leader must publicly display noble and honorable behavior. A deficiency in any one of these areas opens a leader to reproach.

The first area Paul discusses concerns the marriage relationship. Paul says a leader must be "the husband of but one wife." By God's design, the man functions as the leader of this union. This passage provides a principle of leadership that applies to male and female leaders alike. The marital relationship generates the most intimate and sacred of all human relationships. A couple enters this union with covenantal promises intended to endure a lifetime. Male and female leaders can apply the following principle based on this passage: A leader who does not respect his or her commitment to the marriage relationship cannot be counted on to respect the leader-to-follower relationship. Followers who observe a leader who will casually ignore or disregard his or her intimate marriage relationship have no choice but to wonder if this leader will also disregard a less intimate professional relationship. Such unfaithfulness inspires suspicion and insecurity on the part of followers and damages a leader's credibility and respect.

Paul next turns to the moral quality of temperance. *Merriam-Webster's Collegiate Dictionary* defines the term "temperate" as follows: "marked by moderation . . . keeping or held within limits: not extreme or excessive . . . moderate in indulgence of appetite or desire, moderate in the use of intoxicating liquors . . . marked by an absence or avoidance of extravagance, violence, or extreme partisanship."[3] Moderation signifies a lifestyle under control. Excessive behavior of any kind suggests a lack of discipline and restraint. A temperate leader builds credibility with followers when he or she imposes personal limits of behavior on himself or herself that appear consistent with God's standards.

Initiating control of one's self-centered desires is a mark of maturity. Unfortunately most people rely on limits set by others, such as governmental laws or organizational policies. The leader that demonstrates the maturity of self-control builds respect and admiration among his or her followers. The person who cannot control his or her personal selfish desires, however, leaves no reason for his or her followers to trust that he or she can lead.

Hospitable people extend comfort and kindness to guests and strangers alike. The person who displays hospitality to others gives generously of his or her time, energy, and worldly goods. Typically, a hospitable person focuses selflessly on serving the needs of others with no expectation of reward. Hospitable acts performed by a leader communicate an attitude of kindness and generosity to his or her followers. Followers view the leader as open and approachable. This type of behavior promotes a healthy leader-to-follower relationship.

A drunkard loses all respect in the eyes of others. Everyone knows that the faculties of a drunk are seriously impaired. A leader who allows drugs or alcohol to control his or her judgment has no right to expect others to voluntarily follow. Drunkenness destroys credibility. The appearance of drunkenness raises questions of respect in the minds of others.

A violent and quarrelsome leader strikes fear into the hearts of those who follow. Most followers will seek to avoid contact and conflict with such an individual. No real relationship can exist with his or her followers when a leader resorts to physical, verbal, or emotional abuse. Scared and downtrodden people resist following abusive leaders.

Paul starts his list of reputation builders and busters with the marriage commitment. Faithfully loving one's spouse enhances one's reputation in the eyes of others. Paul ends this list of reputation builders and busters with a condemnation of the love of money. Please note that Paul does not condemn the possession of money. Being wealthy is not a sin; loving money is. Lovers of money often behave in a greedy and covetous manner. No amount of money satisfies one who craves prosperity. The pursuit of wealth consumes his or her every action, thought, and motive. The gain of money often drives leaders to use their followers to this end. This one-sided existence forges an unhealthy leader-to-follower relationship. Followers do not respect leaders consumed with acquiring personal fortune.

Living above reproach, beyond the slightest suspicion of moral compromise, remains essential for today's leader. God's absolute biblical standards shine in stark contrast to the world's standards of moral relativism. To function as the leader God desires, you must learn and apply God's biblical standards to your lifestyle. To make these standards a regular part of your lifestyle, two practical steps will start the process.

The first step one must take concerns a choice of the will. A leader must decide which moral bar will shape one's lifestyle. The world's relative standards appeal to man's sinful heart because this lifestyle embraces the false idea that each individual gets to decide for himself or herself what is right and wrong. In the world's system, living above reproach becomes an irrelevant concept because if one's behavior raises suspicion by another, then that person is considered to be judgmental or intolerant. Sadly, much of this thinking has infiltrated the evangelical community as well.

God's biblical standards allow no room for relative moral behavior. God's moral bar remains absolute and fixed and does not fluctuate according to the tides of what society deems to be acceptable behavior. As a follower of Jesus Christ who leads others, you have a choice. You must decide which moral bar will shape your lifestyle. The decision you make on this issue will determine whether or not you live above reproach.

The second step assumes that a leader chooses to allow God's biblical standards to shape one's lifestyle. If one makes such a choice, then he or she bears the responsibility of learning and obeying God's Word. The Bible makes God's moral bar clear. Living above this bar will result in a lifestyle that can be said to be "above reproach."

God expects a leader to publicly display a lifestyle that leaves no opportunity for followers to suspect a lack of self-discipline or self-control. In 1 Timothy 3:1–7, the Apostle Paul challenges leaders to live above reproach. He exhorts leaders to adopt certain social attitudes and actions that will enhance credibility and respect with one's followers. To be the leader God desires, you too must accept the challenge to live above reproach.

Those you lead are watching. Every word spoken, action taken, attitude displayed, and emotion expressed by a leader receives public scrutiny. You can go a long way toward building credibility and respect with those you lead by publicly displaying faithfulness to your most intimate relationships, temperance, self-control, hospitality, sobriety, gentleness, peace, and a satisfaction with God's provisions.

Discussion Questions based on "Living beyond Reproach"

1. Write a brief description of the biblical concept of living beyond reproach.
2. Explain how and to what degree God's standard of living revealed in 1 Timothy 3:1–7 shapes your lifestyle.
3. Describe how a leader's lifestyle impacts one's leader-to-follower relationships.
4. How can a leader's lifestyle impact a follower's perception of the leader's personal self-control and self-discipline?

Followers watch leaders very closely.
A leader's lifestyle stands on public display.

The public's opinion and image of a leader forms
based on words spoken, emotions expressed, attitudes
demonstrated, and actions taken.

The leader who "lives beyond reproach" leaves no opportunity for
others to suspect a lack of self-discipline or self-control and builds a
positive public image, respect, and credibility with others.

PERSONAL APPLICATION EXERCISE

Write words and phrases that describe an ideal leader's lifestyle that you think satisfies the challenge to live beyond reproach. What kind of words, attitudes, emotions, and actions would you expect to see in such a leader?

Being Salt and Light
Matthew 5:13–16

God expects a leader to exert a positive moral influence on society.

Leaders who sense a higher calling will stand courageously in the face of moral decay and darkness.

Leaders influence others. Leaders exert this influence in the context of the public's eye. People watch leaders like a hawk to determine the authenticity of his or her moral influence. Even those unaffected by a leader will watch and pronounce judgment on his or her actions and decisions. Influence and visibility go hand in hand with leadership and work in tandem to provide the leader an opportunity to impact the world in which he or she leads.

God endorses the noble activity of leading others. God has ordered the affairs of men whereby one guides the activities of another. God intends for a leader to influence his or her followers directly and society at large indirectly and raises up leaders in every arena of human endeavor to display His truth and glory. God has raised you up in the marketplace to publicly influence those you lead and those who watch you lead.

God desires to use each follower of Jesus Christ as a leader and looks for leaders willing to represent His interests in all walks of life. God's design for human society contemplates the leadership of those who faithfully follow His One and Only Son, Jesus Christ. Throughout human history, God has raised up earthly leaders for all to see in order to demonstrate His truth and presence in the world. One should not think that God raises up leaders only for the Church. God looks for leaders who will faithfully serve Him in every arena of life such as the family, the marketplace, government, and education. God desires you to influence others and visibly represent His interests everywhere you lead.

God desires to use each follower of Jesus Christ as a leader and looks for leaders willing to represent His interests in all walks of life.

The leader-to-follower relationship constitutes the essence of leadership. Within the context of this relationship, God intends for a leader to privately and publicly exert influence that promotes the greater good of mankind. Leaders should illuminate God's presence in a manner that attracts others and should flavor God's truth in a manner tasteful to others. Mankind resides in a dark and decaying world. Only God's love extended through human relationships, such as a leader to a follower, can penetrate and dissipate this darkness and stave off the moral decay of this world.

God expects leaders who claim to follow Jesus to demonstrate professional excellence. Whatever profession you choose, you should strive to be the best you can be. The public display of exceptional skill and knowledge in a given field of human endeavor brings glory to God. Followers respect and ascribe credibility to the leader who they believe to be outstanding at what he or she does. Such professional excellence sets the stage for a leader to influence others. Typically influence gained by excellence does not extend beyond one's temporal professional arena.

Influence, however, does not have to end with the temporal. God calls leaders who follow His Son to a grander purpose than professional excellence. Temporal professional excellence opens the door for a leader to exert influence on others that is eternally significant. Every leader-to-follower relationship stands as an opportunity to publicly display God's love and grace in a dark world. The leader-to-follower relationship can serve as a conduit to spread God's truth that counteracts the evils that so readily permeate the inhabitants of earth. Recognition that God desires and intends to use you as a leader in this regard brings real meaning to your role as a leader. God intends you to be salt and light in the marketplace, at home, and everywhere you lead others.

Jesus Christ said of His disciples: "You are the salt of the earth . . . You are the light of the world." Jesus stated that his followers are salt and light, not that they were in the process of becoming such or should somehow strive to become so. Jesus expects His followers to function in society as salt and light. Consider the following words of Jesus Christ and what it means to be salt and light to the world.

13 "You are the salt of the earth. But if the salt loses its saltiness, how can it be made salty again? It is no longer good for anything, except to be thrown out and trampled by men.

14 "You are the light of the world. A city on a hill cannot be hidden. 15 Neither do people light a lamp and put it under a bowl. Instead they put it on its stand, and it gives light to everyone in the house. 16 In the same way, let your light shine before men, that they may see your good deeds and praise your Father in heaven." (Matt. 5:13–16)

Salt not only acts as a seasoning agent that adds flavor to food, but also acts as a preservative that inhibits the decay of food. Commentators debate which of these uses Jesus might have had in mind when He instructed His followers to be the salt of the earth. When I consider the role of a leader, I think both apply metaphorically.

Salt adds flavor to food, making bland food taste better. Salt increases the appeal of food and leaves people hungry and thirsty for more. Leaders can have a similar effect on their followers. The leader-to-follower relationship represents a ripe opportunity for whetting others' appetite for the things of God. How a leader conducts himself or herself professionally can make a follower hungry and thirsty to experience God's love firsthand. Professionally skilled leaders who serve others with character and compassion act as a seasoning agent that adds a godly flavor to the world within which they lead.

Salt slows the spread of decay and preserves a food's freshness. Leaders can have a similar effect on the culture of one's organization. The leader-to-follower relationship represents an ideal environment for the spreading of God's truth and goodness to others. How a leader acts will either inhibit or encourage moral decay. Professionally skilled leaders who serve others with character and compassion act as a preserving agent that inhibits the spread of evil and corruption.

Followers of Jesus Christ need to act as salt throughout the earth. The Greek term for "earth" is *ge*. The root of this word refers to the soil, ground, or land of the planet Earth. *Ge* can also, however, refer to the people or inhabitants of the planet Earth. In Matthew 5:13, Jesus is referring to the people. Followers of Jesus are to be salt among all the inhabitants of Earth. Consider Swanson's definition of *ge*: "1. earth, the surface of the whole earth . . . 2. land, in contrast to sea . . . 5. people, inhabitants of the earth, mankind."[4]

Followers of Jesus are to act as salt among the peoples who inhabit the earth. Salt tastes best when mixed evenly into a food item and preserves only what it comes into contact with; consequently salt must be spread over the entire surface of a food to inhibit decay. Jesus desires His followers to spread out and mix with the masses of humanity in order to inhibit moral decay and promote a thirst and hunger for God's grace and truth. Leaders who follow Jesus have ample opportunity to provide both benefits of salt to those they lead.

Sadly, many leaders who claim to follow Jesus fail to preserve or flavor the environment in which they lead. Moral corruption abounds unchallenged. No behavior exists that leaves a follower hungry or thirsty to learn of one's faith in God. These leaders have lost their saltiness and make no contribution to God's eternal purpose of spreading His presence among the peoples of the earth. Salt is not a neutral agent; salt either flavors and preserves or it doesn't. God does not entrust leadership to followers of Jesus for them to be neutral. It is not good enough for a leader to mix among followers with no regard for standing against moral decay or attracting them to God's grace and mercy.

Light dissipates darkness and makes the world more clearly visible. Light illuminates so people can see more clearly and guides one's path in the night. A beacon of light far in the distance can provide direction for someone lost in the wilderness. The light of distant stars makes humans wonder what lies beyond the planet Earth.

Jesus said of Himself: "While I am in the world, I am the light of the world" (John 9:5). Jesus later explained the significance of His light: "Then Jesus cried out, 'When a man believes in me, he does not believe in me only, but in the one who sent me. When he looks at me, he sees the one who sent me. I have come into the world as a light, so that no one who believes in me should stay in darkness'" (John 12:44–46). The light of the Father shines through Jesus, revealing God's presence. This light drives away the spiritual darkness that keeps mankind blinded to God's love and truth.

Jesus instructed His followers to function as lights. Metaphorically speaking, leaders who claim to follow Jesus should function as a beacon of God's light to those they lead. Just as a lamp rests on a stand, so also leaders operate on a highly visible platform. This visibility affords a leader an opportunity to shine brightly for God. Followers close and afar can receive the benefit of spiritual enlightenment that helps them see God more clearly. As light from a star, seeing God's light shine through you as a leader draws attention to what might lie beyond the light. Others should see a Christ follower's light and be drawn to the source, which is God's presence within them.

Jesus instructed His followers to be light to the world. The Greek word for "world" is *kosmos*. The basic idea of this term relates to an orderly arrangement of something, such as an orderly government, the arrangement of the stars, or the order of the universe. The word also refers to the people who inhabitant Earth. Consider Strong's definitions of *kosmos* that explain both of these uses:

> *"1 an apt and harmonious arrangement or constitution, order, government. 2 ornament, decoration, adornment, i.e. the arrangement of the stars, 'the heavenly hosts', as the ornament of the heavens. (1 Pet. 3:3) 3 the world, the universe. 4 the circle of the earth, the earth. 5 the inhabitants of the earth, men, the human race. 6 the ungodly multitude; the whole mass of men alienated from God, and therefore hostile to the cause of Christ. 7 world affairs, the aggregate of things earthly."*[5]

I believe Jesus had the inhabitants of the world in mind as the target of His followers' light. Jesus wants the light of God to shine upon the ungodly masses who live alienated and hostile to God. The ruler of this world holds men in darkness and encourages their rebellion. As followers of Jesus, we have the opportunity to let our light dissipate this darkness and make God's presence more visible.

God's enemy wants Jesus' followers to believe that they should conceal their light. Jesus warned against this suggestion. Just as it makes no sense to place a lamp under a basket, so also it makes no sense for a follower of Jesus to hide the light of God's presence from the world. For a leader who claims to follow Jesus, the leader-to-follower relationship comes into view. As a leader, God desires you to shine spiritual light on those who follow you. When a follower of Jesus faithfully illuminates the world around him or her with God's light, our Father in heaven receives praise.

As a follower of Jesus Christ who leads, Jesus has called you to be salt and light in every relationship. So how do Christ followers do this? The first step is to recognize that you are on public display. Followers near and far are watching you. Those you lead watch how you treat others, how you make decisions, how you live your personal life. You are in the public eye and on a platform of leadership entrusted to you by God.

Secondly, you must keep in mind that you cannot be salt or light to people with whom you never have contact. God desires a leader to mix with the people of this world without losing one's saltiness or allowing the world to dim his or her light. God desires you to build authentic relationships with your followers and to look for opportunities to bring the light of God's love to their lives. Too many Christians either avoid contact with non-Christians altogether or conceal their faith in a manner that provides no salt or light.

Thirdly, when you encounter other people of the world, remember to carry God's salt and light with you. The evils of this world are thwarted when we spread the truth of God's word. Boldly living according to and proclaiming God's Word preserves society and stops moral decay. In the same way, a leader must display the light of God's love in one's own life in such a way that the illumination attracts others to God. A Christian's life does not provide salt and light; God's word and love shining through them does.

God expects a leader to display a positive moral influence for all to see. Leaders are visible and influential in regard to others. The relationship a leader has with his or her followers provides a ready-made opportunity to spread God's word and love to others. The leader who provides the salt of God's truth and word to his or her followers acts to preserve moral goodness and stop the spread of moral decay. The leader who shines the light of God's love on his or her followers draws attention to God's presence and dissipates the darkness of this world.

Jesus wants His followers who lead to courageously stand up to moral decay and darkness so all who watch them lead know and praise God the Father.

Discussion Questions based on "Being Salt and Light"

1. Describe two common uses for salt. Explain how functioning as "salt" might apply to your role as a leader.
2. What does light do? Explain how being a "light" might apply to your role as a leader.
3. Based on Matthew 5:13–16, describe the responsibility a follower of Jesus Christ carries to act as a positive moral influence on society.

God expects a leader to exert a positive moral influence on society. Leaders who sense a higher calling will act as salt in the face of moral decay and shine as a light in the face of spiritual darkness.

PERSONAL APPLICATION EXERCISE

Describe one specific action you have initiated in the past or can initiate in the future that exerts a positive moral influence on those you lead. Explain how this action serves the function of salt or light.

A Public Display of Faith, Hope, and Love
1 Corinthians 13:13

Faith, hope, and love should undergird everything a leader does! These outward expressions of a leader's inward condition encourage followers like nothing else.

Faith, belief, and trust in the providential activity of a higher being generate a sense of confidence that naturally radiates from a leader to a follower.

Hope, optimism, and positive thinking expressed by a leader help to inspire an expectation of good fortune among followers.

Love, a selfless and unconditional commitment directed toward others, creates an unbreakable bond of unity between a leader and his or her followers.

The importance of a lifestyle that is beyond reproach and that publicly demonstrates faith, hope, and love comes down to a matter of how a leader appears to others. To sustain credibility and trust, a leader must live beyond reproach. No appearance of wrongdoing should ever be associated with a leader. A leader must broadcast the clear image of God's light on the world. Others must perceive the positive moral influence associated with the saltiness of a leader's lifestyle. The followers come away with feelings of faith, hope, and love and will feel warmly toward the one they view as their leader.

A direct correlation exists between how followers perceive a person and his or her effectiveness as a leader. Even the slightest hint of an illicit attitude or action erodes a leader's credibility and trustworthiness with others, thereby reducing his or her leadership effectiveness. A leader builds confidence with followers by the public display of behavior, not hollow words through which even the most casual observer can see. Leaders stand on highly visible platforms for all to see. A leader's lifestyle forms an image in the minds of others that directly impacts his or her effectiveness.

Have you ever considered how you appear to others, to those you lead? How do you want others to perceive you? How do these same people really perceive you? Can you say with confidence that these two perceptions are one and the same? Is how you think and want others to perceive you the same as how people really perceive you? The answers to these questions directly impact your ability to lead others.

Many people expend much time, energy, and money carefully crafting an image they want others to perceive. Politicians, entertainers, and other high-profile leaders commonly employ a marketing approach to creating a public appearance. Unfortunately, often the real private lifestyle of such people does not match the façade of their public image. Once exposed as a fake, everyone quickly sees that what's inside this leader does not correlate with the outside.

A leader's appearance is the outward expression of an inward condition of his or her heart. A leader's real image can most clearly be seen by how he or she treats those who follow. Followers pick up clues and pronounce judgment on the inward condition of a leader's heart based on how they perceive their leader's treatment of others.

Jesus taught His followers the importance of a lifestyle where one's outward appearance and inward condition match. Jesus instructed His disciples to avoid the hypocrisy of the Pharisees whose lives were characterized by the outward conformity to a religiously expected lifestyle but whose hearts remained full of greed and self-indulgence. God expects a leader who claims to follow Jesus to first clean up one's inside, which will in turn clean up one's outward appearance as well.

> [25] *"Woe to you, teachers of the law and Pharisees, you hypocrites! You clean the outside of the cup and dish, but inside they are full of greed and self-indulgence.* [26] *Blind Pharisee! First clean the inside of the cup and dish, and then the outside also will be clean.*

> [27] *"Woe to you, teachers of the law and Pharisees, you hypocrites! You are like whitewashed tombs, which look beautiful on the outside but on the inside are full of dead men's bones and everything unclean.* [28] *In the same way, on the outside you appear to people as righteous but on the inside you are full of hypocrisy and wickedness."* (Matt. 23:25–28)

Jesus desires the outward expression of our lifestyle to reflect the inward condition of a heart transformed by His presence. When Jesus takes hold of a leader's heart (core values), his or her outward appearance begins to change. Jesus stated that one's outward appearance of this inward transformation would be so obvious to others that the entire world would know that a person lives as a disciple of Jesus. Do you know what outward expression Jesus claimed would distinguish His followers from all others?

Love displayed openly and genuinely for all to see distinguishes a person as a true follower of Jesus Christ. By love, the world will know Jesus' followers. This presupposes that Jesus' followers demonstrate this love as they interact in the world: "By this all men will know that you are my disciples, if you love one another" (John 13:35). Would people who follow you recognize you as a follower of Jesus based on an outward appearance of love?

The world honors strength, authority, and power, not love. Many leaders who claim to follow Jesus give lip service to love but openly display strength, authority, and power as the basis of their leading. Those who follow worldly leaders would characterize them as powerful and authoritative but not as loving. Jesus intends for the outward appearance of His followers who lead to publicly display the inward change that has taken place within their hearts—a change marked by love first but also evidenced by a strong sense of faith and hope. "And now these three remain: faith, hope and love. But the greatest of these is love" (1 Cor. 13:13).

The Apostle Paul painted a clear picture of what a heart transformed by God's love looks like in relation to others. The leader who relates to others in the manner described in 1 Corinthians 13 will greatly encourage his or her followers.

> [1] *If I speak in the tongues of men and of angels, but have not love, I am only a resounding gong or a clanging cymbal.* [2] *If I have the gift of prophecy and can fathom all mysteries and all knowledge, and if I have a faith that can move mountains, but have not love, I am nothing.* [3] *If I give all I possess to the poor and surrender my body to the flames, but have not love, I gain nothing.*
>
> [4] *Love is patient, love is kind. It does not envy, it does not boast, it is not proud.* [5] *It is not rude, it is not self-seeking, it is not easily angered, it keeps no record of wrongs.* [6] *Love does not delight in evil but rejoices with the truth.* [7] *It always protects, always trusts, always hopes, always perseveres.*
>
> [8] *Love never fails. But where there are prophecies, they will cease; where there are tongues, they will be stilled; where there is knowledge, it will pass away.* [9] *For we know in part and we prophesy in part,* [10] *but when perfection comes, the imperfect disappears.*

[11] When I was a child, I talked like a child, I thought like a child, I reasoned like a child. When I became a man, I put childish ways behind me. [12] Now we see but a poor reflection as in a mirror; then we shall see face to face. Now I know in part; then I shall know fully, even as I am fully known.

[13] And now these three remain: faith, hope and love. But the greatest of these is love. (1 Cor. 13)

Eloquent speech without love produces nothing but a lot of noise. Such a life may draw the attention of others, but this existence remains void of substance. In the same way, superior spiritual insight, a strong faith, and personal sacrifice all come to nothing without love. Outward expressions of a religious lifestyle can all be faked to draw attention to self. Love cannot be faked. True love originates in a heart transformed by a personal relationship with Jesus Christ and the presence of the Holy Spirit. God desires the outward expression of love to mirror the inward condition of your heart.

The Greek language uses multiple words to convey various forms of love. The word used by the Apostle Paul in 1 Corinthians 13 is *agape*, which describes a selfless love extended based on what's best for another. In contrast to *agape* is *eros*, which describes a love intended to satisfy one's selfish desires. The world lives by *eros*. Followers of Jesus live by *agape*. Eros is self-centered love, while *agape* is other-centered love. *Theological Dictionary of the New Testament* contrasts *eros* (Ἔρως) and *agape* (Ἀγαπᾶν) as follows:

Ἔρως is a general love of the world seeking satisfaction wherever it can. Ἀγαπᾶν is a love which makes distinctions, choosing and keeping to its object. Ἔρως is determined by a more or less indefinite impulsion towards its object. Ἀγαπᾶν is a free and decisive act determined by its subject. . . . Eros seeks in others the fulfillment of its own life's hunger. Ἀγαπᾶν must often be translated "to show love"; it is a giving, active love on the other's behalf.[6]

As a follower of Jesus Christ, the ability to selflessly extend a giving and active love (*agape*) on another's behalf originates with God. For God initiates this sacrificial approach to love and enables us to love others in the same way. God's love for mankind has stood the ultimate test of selflessness so proven by God's willingness to sacrifice His own son on mankind's behalf. "For God so loved the world that he gave his one and only Son, that whoever believes in him shall not perish but have eternal life" (John 3:16). Because God extends *agape* to us, we can extend *agape* to others.

God desires selfless love to rule the leader-to-follower relationship. When a leader chooses to lead by serving others, one must rely on others following voluntarily. People must feel secure in a leader's love (*agape*) if they are to voluntarily follow. Followers must be convinced in their minds that the leader truly cares for their well-being and has their best interests at heart. People want to know that the leader respects their value and worth. This *agape* coming from a leader to a follower must be real and not just empty words or a fake image.

In 1 Corinthians 13, the Apostle Paul describes in very practical terms what *agape* looks like in human relationships. This picture of love is commonly recited at weddings in the context of a husband and wife marriage relationship. This picture of love can also be applied to the leader-to-follower relationship. The leader who extends *agape* as described by Paul in 1 Corinthians 13 creates a real appearance to others that will compel them to follow voluntarily. As you read the list below, take note of the selfless and even sacrificial nature of love described by Paul. Imagine the positive impact a leader can have when followers realize they are being led with love like this.

- Patient
- Kind
- Not envious
- Not boastful
- Not proud
- Not rude
- Not self-seeking
- Not easily angered
- Keeps no record of wrongs

- Does not delight in evil
- Rejoices in truth
- Always protects
- Always trusts
- Always hopes
- Always perseveres
- Never fails

The Apostle Paul concludes 1 Corinthians 13 by listing three permanent outward expressions that should be publicly evident in the lifestyle of every follower of Jesus Christ. These three outward expressions that indicate a person has a mature relationship with Jesus Christ are faith, hope, and love. Followers of a leader who claims to follow Jesus Christ should recognize the presence of faith, hope, and love in the life of their leader. Would those who follow you describe you as a person of faith, hope, and love?

Jesus taught that natural man's inward condition is rotten and that the outward expression of one's heart makes him or her unclean. ". . . What comes out of a man is what makes him 'unclean.' For from within, out of men's hearts, come evil thoughts, sexual immorality, theft, murder, adultery, greed, malice, deceit, lewdness, envy, slander, arrogance and folly. All these evils come from inside and make a man 'unclean'" (Mark 7:20–23). The Apostle Paul described the outward expressions of man's sinful nature as follows: "The acts of the sinful nature become obvious: sexual immorality, impurity and debauchery; idolatry and witchcraft; hatred, discord, jealousy, fits of rage, selfish ambition, dissensions, factions and envy; drunkenness, orgies, and the like . . ." (Gal. 5:19–21). The leader whose lifestyle remains under the control of his or her sinful nature cannot help but outwardly express attitudes and actions described by Jesus and Paul. The leader who submits control to the Holy Spirit, however, will progressively mature in Christ and outwardly express attitudes and actions of faith, hope, and love.

We have already defined love. *Agape* describes a selfless love extended based on what's best for another. The Greek word for faith is *pistis*. Strong defines *pistis* as follows:

". . . conviction of the truth of anything, belief; in the NT of a conviction or belief respecting man's relationship to God and divine things, . . . the conviction that God exists and is the creator and ruler of all things, the provider and bestower of eternal salvation through Christ . . . a strong and welcome conviction or belief that Jesus is the Messiah, through whom we obtain eternal salvation in the kingdom of God."[7]

The Greek word for hope is *elpis*. Strong defines *elpis* as follows: *". . . expectation of good, hope . . . in the Christian sense . . . joyful and confident expectation of eternal salvation."*[8] Leaders who are inwardly controlled by the Spirit will outwardly demonstrate faith, hope, and love to others. The absence of the outward expressions of faith, hope, and love indicate a life that inwardly has not yielded to the control of God's Holy Spirit.

Paul stated that of the three, love is the greatest. *Agape*, selflessly acting based on what is best for another, motivates a follower of Jesus to enter the world's marketplace and to lead as a servant. *Pistis*, the conviction that God exists as the sovereign king and ruler of heaven and earth, and *elpis*, a positive attitude of expecting to see the goodness of God in one's life, motivate a follower of Jesus to stay in the world's marketplace and lead as a servant when circumstances get difficult.

We live in a world today that embraces the philosophy of relativism. This relative worldview rejects the existence of absolute truth. The person who embraces a relative view of life will eventually spiral downward to a life that reflects no faith, hope, or love, as Paul described.

Relativism rejects the possibility of faith in an absolute, divine being. If you follow relative philosophy to a logical conclusion, then one must conclude that nothing absolute or divine exists in the universe. Relativism says that there is no God and that man is alone in the universe; consequently "faith" is impossible because no object of faith exists. The logical conclusion of this philosophy inevitably exhibits self-centeredness because one believes that nothing greater than self exists.

Relativism also impacts hope. This philosophy states that no eternal, supernatural, or sovereign being exists and that chaos and random chance rule the universe, not an absolute and divine creator. Man is left with no choice but to conclude that the course and events of the universe are out of control. This view of life leaves one with no hope. The logical conclusion of this worldview leaves a person feeling despair, depression, and helplessness.

Lastly, relativism impacts love. Relative ethics state that there exists no absolute right or wrong in the universe. This philosophy says that the situation dictates the rightness or wrongness of a person's moral behavior. The logical conclusion of this philosophy leads to unbridled sensuality. According to relativism, each person lives free to satisfy the desires of his or her heart because each individual has the ability to define what is right for them. This view of life destroys the biblical concept of *agape*. A relative, self-centered, and sensual view of love will result in broken relationships and deep emotional pain.

In Galatians 5, the Apostle Paul says that followers of Jesus have been called to freedom. This freedom yields a lifestyle of serving one another as opposed to a lifestyle of indulging our sinful nature. Paul explains that an inward yielding of one's heart to the Holy Spirit provides the key to an outward expression of a lifestyle marked by faith, hope, and love. Simply striving to resist the impulses of the sinful nature does not produce faith, hope, and love. Submission to the leading of the Spirit, Who works to conform us into the image of Christ, results in the desired outward lifestyle.

As a leader who follows Jesus, you must step back and honestly assess how others view you. Consider asking your followers for some honest feedback. See if they describe you in terms consistent with faith, hope, and love. If you hear, however, words more along the line of one's sinful nature, consider this a red flag.

Yielding to the Spirit becomes for the most part a function of a person's spiritual discipline. The more consistently you practice disciplines such as Bible study, prayer, fellowship, service, and worship, the more the Holy Spirit works in your life. The evidence of this work is a stronger faith, unwavering hope, and selfless love for others.

Faith, hope, and love should undergird every action and decision initiated by a leader who claims to be a follower of Jesus. Conveying these marks of spiritual maturity toward others impacts a leader's effectiveness more positively than striving to create a façade of being in charge. God's will for an Entrusted Leader directs him or her to self-lessly love those he or she leads, not just boss them around and tell them what to do. Read and meditate on 1 Corinthians 13 and ask God to open your eyes to ways to apply all sixteen descriptors of love listed by the Apostle Paul to the relationship you have with your followers.

We live in a culture dominated by the philosophy of relativism. This relative worldview has left many, even some of your followers, drowning in brokenness and despair. The leader-to-follower relationship represents an opportunity entrusted by God to publicly demonstrate faith, hope, and love. The leader who has yielded to God's Spirit and displays the fruit of the spirit will over time encourage, enable, and empower his or her followers. A leader who allows the sinful nature to rule his or her actions and decisions will discourage, deflate, and de-motivate followers with, in the words of Paul: ". . . hatred, discord, jealousy, fits of rage, selfish ambition, dissensions, factions, and envy; drunkenness, orgies, and the like . . ." (Gal. 5:20–21). I encourage you to look for ways to extend faith, hope, and love to every leader-to-follower relationship you encounter. If you do so, your followers will notice the difference between you and a leader who follows the ways of the world and will be greatly encouraged.

Discussion Questions based on "A Public Display of Faith, Hope, and Love"

1. Paul characterized a person who speaks well but does not extend love to others as nothing more than a noisemaker (1 Cor. 13:1). Explain what you think he meant and the discouraging impact this might have on a leader's relationship with followers.

2. In 1 Corinthians 13:4–8, Paul lists sixteen descriptors of how love appears in a person's life. List all sixteen descriptors of love and ask yourself: Do the people who follow you recognize these sixteen traits of love in your lifestyle?

3. In 1 Corinthians 13, Paul concludes by listing three permanent outward expressions that should be seen in the lifestyle of a follower of Jesus Christ. What are they?

   To what degree do you think those you lead observe these three outward expressions in your lifestyle and what can you do to make them more evident to others?

4. Describe in your own words what "love" looks like to you in a leader-to-follower relationship.

Faith, hope, and love should undergird everything a leader does.
Faith generates confidence that radiates from a leader to a follower.
Hope inspires an expectation of good fortune among followers.
Love creates an unbreakable bond of unity in a
leader-to-follower relationship.

PERSONAL APPLICATION EXERCISE

Describe one act of faith, one act of hope, and one act of love that you can express to others that will encourage the hearts of those you lead.

10

Fortitude
CORE VALUE: The FORTITUDE for leading built on the love and sovereignty of God and the discipline of prayer.

Faith in the Love and Sovereignty of God
Mark 4:40–41 and 1 Samuel 17

Fear paralyzes a leader. Faith in the love and sovereignty of God empowers a leader.

Every leader will eventually encounter a situation too big to control by one's sheer willpower. Sensing a lack of control, self-reliant leaders often become trepid, timid, insecure, anxious, stressed, and agitated. Fear and insecurity are symptoms of a leader's lack of faith in God's ability to compassionately control all situations. The leader who trusts in God's love and sovereignty can face adverse circumstances free from the bondage of fear or anxiety.

Fear paralyzes a leader. Being afraid leaves a leader indecisive. A leader intimidated by adverse circumstances often fails to initiate the appropriate action required for a given situation. People often abdicate their responsibility to lead when facing the dread of impending danger. Many irrational behaviors flow from the person who leads with a mind in the grip of panic.

Insecurity opens the door for doubt and anxiety. Leaders who speculate on countless things that might happen often fall victim to emotional bondage and stress. "What if" thinking will unnerve the leader who dwells on improbable events in an unforeseen future. Circumstances that a leader perceives as beyond one's control typically cause digression into a feeling of anxious concern. The anticipation of doom and gloom often explains why a leader displays an agitated attitude. The uncertainties of what might happen drive many leaders to second-guess decisions and retrace actions already concluded.

God desires leaders who follow Jesus Christ to lead others without being bound by fear, insecurity, doubt, and anxiety. The word that best fits the internal strength that God intends you to lead from is "fortitude." *Merriam-Webster's Collegiate Dictionary* defines fortitude as follows: ". . . strength of mind that enables a person to encounter danger or bear pain or adversity with courage."[1]

One may wonder: Where does the state of mind come from that enables a leader to face adversity with courage? How does a person obtain fortitude? To some extent, each individual has a certain capacity to face difficulties inherent in his or her personality. Everyone, however, encounters circumstances that exceed this inherent capacity for courage. When this happens, emotions of fear, insecurity, doubt, and anxiety will take over in a person's heart and mind, resulting in poor decisions and irrational behavior. Fortitude for leading starts by trusting in a God whose infinite power and control exceed all temporal circumstances.

Real fortitude, the state of mind that enables a person to lead others decisively in the midst of overwhelming danger and adverse conditions, depends on a faith that truly trusts in the love and sovereignty of the Lord God Almighty. Do you believe God loves you unconditionally and always puts your best interests first? Do you believe that God is the Creator of and sovereign King and Ruler over all heaven and earth? Then we must also believe that all circumstances are under God's control and that everything that happens works for our greater good and well-being. Fortitude based on God's love and sovereignty frees a leader from fear, insecurity, doubt, and anxiety.

Real fortitude, the state of mind that enables a person to lead others decisively in the midst of overwhelming danger and adverse conditions, depends on a faith that truly trusts in the love and sovereignty of the Lord God Almighty.

Jesus went to extreme lengths to establish in the hearts and minds of His followers the full extent of His love and true identity. The twelve apostles witnessed Jesus perform many miracles. These miraculous acts clearly demonstrated Jesus' divine control over nature, diseases, death, and the demonic world. Jesus' disciples, however, allowed circumstances beyond their control to overwhelm their trust in His love and faith in His sovereignty. The result of this lack of faith by the apostles in Jesus' love and sovereignty resulted in feelings of fear and insecurity, which surprised and disappointed Jesus. Consider the circumstances surrounding the time Jesus calmed a raging storm.

> *35 That day when evening came, he said to his disciples, "Let us go over to the other side." 36 Leaving the crowd behind, they took him along, just as he was, in the boat. There were also other boats with him. 37 A furious squall came up, and the waves broke over the boat, so that it was nearly swamped. 38 Jesus was in the stern, sleeping on a cushion. The disciples woke him and said to him, "Teacher, don't you care if we drown?"*

> *39 He got up, rebuked the wind and said to the waves, "Quiet! Be still!" Then the wind died down and it was completely calm.*

> *40 He said to his disciples, "Why are you so afraid? Do you still have no faith?"*

> *41 They were terrified and asked each other, "Who is this? Even the wind and the waves obey him!" (Mark 4:35–41)*

Fortitude for leading others comes only from an unwavering faith in the love and sovereignty of God. A leader who follows Jesus must trust that God controls every circumstance and that He has the leader's best interests at heart. Jesus showed the disciples the extent of His compassion for mankind and the unlimited scope of His supernatural power. The disciples witnessed Jesus' miracles firsthand and had no reason to be paralyzed by fear and anxiety. The account of Jesus calming the storm was one of many circumstances Jesus allowed in order to teach the disciples about His love and sovereignty. These lessons should have produced a faith evidenced by fortitude.

The group of disciples in the boat on the lake included professional fishermen whose livelihood depended on fishing these waters. These anglers were skilled at both fishing and navigating a boat. No doubt the disciples possessed a familiarity with the waters they sailed the night Jesus calmed the storm. No doubt these fishermen had encountered difficult circumstances such as storms many times before. Surely they had successfully traversed these waters in the midst of rain and wind before. This tempest, however, constituted no ordinary storm. Mark described it as a "furious squall," a storm capable of sinking their boat. The intensity of this storm surpassed these fishermen's experience and ability to navigate a boat. This shortfall of professional ability to prevent their boat from swamping left the disciples fearful of drowning. This set of adverse circumstances led these followers of Jesus to question His love for them and His ability to protect their lives.

Every leader, regardless of his or her skill level, will face circumstances that exceed their experience and ability. The leader who relies on "self" will experience fear and anxiety as he or she comes to realize a situation exists beyond his or her control. I believe God allows such overwhelming circumstances to arise to demonstrate His love and sovereign control, to lessen one's reliance on self, and to deepen a person's faith and trust in the Lord. God desires leaders to trust in Him. When followers rely on God, all fear and doubt melt away and leaders can face adverse conditions with lasting fortitude.

The disciples' fear prompted two questions: "Teacher, don't you care if we drown?" and "Who is this? Even the wind and the waves obey him!" These two questions reveal a twofold lack of faith and trust in Jesus. First of all, the disciples questioned Jesus' love and concern for their well-being. Secondly, the disciples did not fully grasp that Jesus could miraculously control all circumstances, even the weather. Do you feel the presence of Jesus' love where you lead others? Do you rely on His miraculous power when facing circumstance beyond your control? If not, do you try to navigate difficult times alone and rely on self, only to wind up fearful and anxious?

Jesus had demonstrated His love and sovereignty many times for the disciples to witness first-hand. Jesus had also extended love and compassion to total strangers. In addition, Jesus had performed numerous miracles that proved no circumstance was beyond His ability to control. Jesus taught the masses with parables, but He taught His disciples in a straightforward manner.

After He calmed the storm, Jesus asked His disciples why they were afraid. Jesus commented that He was surprised that they still lacked faith. The disciples had been following Jesus long enough to witness numerous miracles. By this time, they should have clearly understood Jesus' unconditional love for sinners. Consider the following events recorded by Mark prior to the story of Jesus calming the storm:

- Jesus drives out an evil spirit (Mark 1:23–28).
- Jesus heals Simon's mother-in-law and others (Mark 1:29–34).
- Jesus heals a man with leprosy (Mark 1:40–45).
- Jesus heals a person with paralysis (Mark 2:1–12).
- Jesus states his commitment to sinners (Mark 2:17).
- Jesus heals on the Sabbath (Mark 3:4–6).
- Jesus teaches the disciples in a straightforward manner (Mark 4:33–34).

After all the disciples had seen Jesus do and after all He had taught them, they should have felt secure in His love for them and His ability to control any circumstance they faced. Perhaps you have experienced God's unconditional love in your life. Perhaps you have seen him accomplish the miraculous in past circumstances. Do you have faith and peace or do you regularly feel abandoned and afraid?

Fear, doubt, anxiety, and insecurity all constitute warning signs that a person trusts in self and not God. The intensity of fear goes up as one perceives circumstances spinning beyond his or her ability to control. God does not want Christ followers to live or lead bound by these emotions. However, God does not expect us to generate some internal bravery as an offset to fear. God wants us to truly relinquish self-reliance and trust in Him.

For example, King David encountered circumstances that had frozen other men with fear. "Then the Philistine said, 'This day I defy the ranks of Israel! Give me a man and let us fight each other.' On hearing the Philistine's words, Saul and all the Israelites were dismayed and terrified. . . . As he was talking with them, Goliath, the Philistine champion from Gath, stepped out from his lines and shouted his usual defiance, and David heard it. When the Israelites saw the man, they all ran from him in great fear. . . . David said to Saul, 'Let no one lose heart on account of this Philistine; your servant will go and fight him'" (1 Sam. 17:10–11, 23–24, 32). David did not possess bravery superior to that of the other Israelites; rather he possessed a deeper faith and trust in the Lord God Almighty, which came out as real fortitude. The depth of David's faith in God can be seen in how he approached the adverse circumstances that surrounded his encounter with Goliath.

> [45] *David said to the Philistine, "You come against me with sword and spear and javelin, but I come against you in the name of the LORD Almighty, the God of the armies of Israel, whom you have defied. [46] This day the LORD will hand you over to me, and I'll strike you down and cut off your head. Today I will give the carcasses of the Philistine army to the birds of the air and the beasts of the earth, and the whole world will know that there is a God in Israel. [47] All those gathered here will know that it is not by sword or spear that the LORD saves; for the battle is the LORD's, and he will give all of you into our hands." (1 Sam. 17:45–47)*

David's faith empowered him to face Goliath fearlessly. David truly believed God would dictate the outcome of the battle according to His will and purpose. Faith in the sovereignty and love of God made it possible for this future leader of Israel to stare adversity in the face and not flinch. Once the fight with Goliath was won, David's faith in God provided a source of encouragement for the other Israelites. No longer "dismayed and terrified," the soldiers of Israel eagerly engaged the enemy.

> [50] *So David triumphed over the Philistine with a sling and a stone; without a sword in his hand he struck down the Philistine and killed him.*

⁵¹ David ran and stood over him. He took hold of the Philistine's sword and drew it from the scabbard. After he killed him, he cut off his head with the sword.

When the Philistines saw that their hero was dead, they turned and ran. ⁵² Then the men of Israel and Judah surged forward with a shout and pursued the Philistines to the entrance of Gath and to the gates of Ekron. Their dead were strewn along the Shaaraim road to Gath and Ekron. ⁵³ When the Israelites returned from chasing the Philistines, they plundered their camp.
(1 Sam. 17:50–53)

The path to leading with fortitude is not mustering up levels of superhuman self-confidence and courage. No matter how self-assured a leader becomes, there will always arise circumstances, "furious squalls," or "Goliaths" that exceed one's skills and melt away one's courage. The only way a leader can avoid becoming paralyzed by fear and insecurity involves letting go of self-reliance and embracing an unwavering faith in God.

A wise leader recognizes his or her need to trust God. A leader must build the solid foundation of an intimate and trusting relationship with God before the storms of leading rise into an uncontrollable tempest. God solidified David's faith in the Lord's love and sovereignty long before the day he faced Goliath. As a follower of Jesus who leads others, God desires you to have faith like David. A deeper faith in God comes from spiritual discipline and devotion. The next lesson in *The ENTRUSTED Leader* focuses on prayer and how prayer leads to fortitude in leading.

Fear paralyzes a leader. Insecurity leaves a leader feeling doubtful and anxious. Such negative emotions result in a lack of initiative, poor decisions, and irrational behavior on the part of a leader. God does not expect a leader to muster the self-will, courage, and strength to supersede feelings of fear and doubt. God does, however, expect a leader to let go of self-reliance. God desires a leader to trust and follow Him.

God intends leaders to lead with fortitude: ". . . strength of mind that enables a person to encounter danger or bear pain or adversity with courage."[2] Lasting fortitude for leading comes only from faith in the love and sovereignty of God. The leader who trusts in God's love and sovereignty will be able to face adverse circumstances without fear or anxiety.

Discussion Questions based on "Faith in the Love and Sovereignty of God"

1. The disciples' fear of their boat being swamped by a furious storm prompted them to ask two questions, one before Jesus calmed the storm and one after: "Teacher, don't you care if we drown?" (Mark 4:38).

2. "Who is this? Even the wind and the waves obey him!" (Mark 4:41). These two questions reveal a fundamental lack of faith and trust in Jesus in two regards. Comment on the two aspects of faith in Jesus that the disciples lacked at this point.

3. Think of a situation (i.e., "furious squall") you have faced in your profession that threatened to swamp your boat. Describe how you felt in the midst of this storm.

4. Do you struggle with any level of fear, doubt, anxiety, or insecurity in regard to where you lead others? Comment on how a lack of faith in the love and sovereignty of God might impact your courage and peace of mind as a leader.

5. The Israelites faced a warrior too big for their conventional fighting skills and armament. Their perception of an adverse situation left them frozen with fear. Explain how David had the fortitude to face Goliath alone.

Fear paralyzes a leader.

Faith in the love and sovereignty of God empowers a leader.

Fear and insecurity are symptoms of a leader's lack of faith in God's ability to compassionately control all situations.

The leader who trusts in God's love and sovereignty can face adverse circumstances free from the bondage of fear or anxiety.

Personal Application Exercise

Describe a circumstance currently causing you to feel fear, insecurity, doubt, or anxiety as a leader. Write out a prayer in your own words that focuses on God's love for you and His sovereign control of this circumstance.

Prayers that Lead to Peace and Courage
Philippians 4:4–7

Prayer remedies anxiety and creates peace and courage. The fortitude that springs from prayer guards a leader's mind and heart from dysfunctional thoughts and feelings.

God's Word encourages a leader to pray about all circumstances. The power of prayer extends beyond obvious religious issues into every facet of life a leader might encounter. Pray about everything, especially what relates to where you lead others!

Anxiety chokes the life out of a leader. Anxious thoughts leave a leader feeling emotionally, physically, intellectually, and spiritually exhausted. The leader who unduly worries about immediate circumstances often wallows in self-doubt and inactivity. The very thought of a situation that might exceed one's ability to control produces an apprehension that stops a leader in his or her tracks. The leader who suffers from stress runs the risk of making poor and impulsive decisions. Anxiety slowly erodes one's ability to lead others boldly and effectively.

The ill effects of worry compromise and damage a leader's relationship with his or her followers. In contrast, mutual respect characterizes a healthy leader-to-follower relationship. The leader who treats others with gentleness gains respect from those who follow. Internal anxiety very often erupts from a leader in the form of harsh treatment of others. Emotionally dysfunctional leaders often take out their insecure feelings on innocent followers. Leaders with pent-up stress sometimes lose control and lash out with mean-spirited communication and behavior.

These misdeeds and other anxiety-related behaviors negatively impact the leader's relationship with his or her followers.

Anxiety indicates an immature faith in God. Worry exhibits a warning sign that a leader has placed his or her trust in an entity other than God. Self-reliance stems from pride and tempts a person to take control. When a leader loses a sense of control, anxiety starts to build. Reliance on God stems from humility and leads a person to trust. When faith in God becomes real, peace and joy take over a person's heart. Anxiety and worry imply that God lacks love and control (sovereignty). Peace indicates that a person feels secure in God's love and control.

Fortitude for leading comes from prayer.

Fortitude for leading comes from prayer. Prayer frees a leader from anxiety and worry. A leader who claims to be a follower of Jesus Christ must pray about every situation! Prayer creates intimacy with God and deepens a leader's understanding of God's love. Time alone with the Lord God Almighty broadens one's view of His infinite sovereign control of all circumstances. Fortitude and peace come from the power of prayer. Prayer provides an antidote for anxiety. Consider the implications of taking Philippians 4:4–7 literally and applying this promise where you lead others.

> [4] Rejoice in the Lord always. I will say it again: Rejoice! [5] Let your gentleness be evident to all. The Lord is near. [6] Do not be anxious about anything, but in everything, by prayer and petition, with thanksgiving, present your requests to God. [7] And the peace of God, which transcends all understanding, will guard your hearts and your minds in Christ Jesus. (Phil. 4:4–7)

Paul commands his readers to "Rejoice!" He repeats this statement to underscore the importance of being filled with joy and gladness regardless of one's circumstances. An intimate relationship with the Lord God Almighty provides the basis for such rejoicing, even in the face of persecution and trials. The context of rejoicing for Paul contemplated the presence of adversity, not the absence of troublesome circumstances.

Real faith in God changes the vantage point from which a person views difficulty from his or her finite capacity to cope with stress to God's infinite sovereign control and unconditional love. Paul commands followers of Jesus Christ to "rejoice in the Lord always," not just when things are going well and we feel in control of our surroundings.

As a leader, you will face adversity. Just as David faced Goliath, you will encounter "giant" situations that appear to exceed your leadership experience and/or skill. Saul and his men responded to Goliath with fear and panic. Difficult situations should not diminish a leader's joy or result in irrational decisions and actions. The presence of anxiety and worry in the heart and mind of a leader suggests too much dependence on self and too little faith in God. When adversity comes, faith in God's love and sovereignty frees a leader from the stress and worry of trusting in one's own abilities alone.

Gentleness should mark the life of every follower of Jesus Christ. Every person you encounter should get the sense that you deal with others fairly, equitably, and mildly. The Greek word used by the Apostle Paul is *epieikes*. Strong defines this term as: ". . . equitable, fair, mild, gentle."[3] The leader whom others view as fair, equitable, and mild has laid the groundwork for a healthy relationship with those who follow. The leader whom others view as unfair, inequitable, and harsh will soon lose the respect and credibility of those who follow. Gentleness comes from a heart fixed on God and others. The lack of gentleness when dealing with others indicates a heart fixed on self. *Epieikes* is much more than being tender and nurturing, however; this term carries the idea of always doing the right and fair thing in regard to others even if the right thing is not to one's own advantage. The gentle (fair, equitable, mild) and selfless leader fosters healthy relationships with those who follow.

The Apostle Paul states that a follower of Jesus Christ should not suffer from the ill effects of anxiety. A continuous barrage of anxious thoughts and feelings can literally damage a person's physical and mental well-being. Constant worry opens the door for insecurity and doubt, which cause a leader to second-guess his or her decision making. Anxiety can poison the leader-to-follower relationship in a number of ways. Anxious leaders often treat their followers harshly and unfairly. A leader burdened by stress or anxiety often gravitates to self-serving decisions and actions. These and other such harmful attitudes and actions on the part of a leader result in damage to the leader-to-follower relationship.

Paul commands his readers: "Do not be anxious about anything. . . ." The Greek word for "anxious" is *merimnao*. Strong defines the term as: ". . . to be anxious . . . to be troubled with cares . . . to seek to promote one's interests."[4] Paul wrote these words in the imperative, as a command to be followed, not a self-help suggestion for peaceful living. One may ask: How can this be? How can I control my feelings of anxiety? After all, who doesn't want freedom from the troubled feelings of one's cares?

In this passage, there are two key insights that will help a leader counteract the dysfunctional feelings associated with anxious thoughts. The first insights relate to the link between self-centered thoughts and stressful feelings. A *merimnao* (anxious) person promotes his or her self-interests ahead of all others. Feelings of stress, worry, and anxiety typically well up in a person's heart when thoughts arise that suggest one's interests are being threatened. Freedom from the bondage of worry starts when a person relinquishes control of one's interest to God and trusts Him fully regardless of the apparent circumstances.

The second key to offsetting anxiety relates to a disciplined prayer life. Paul states that followers of Jesus Christ should pray about everything. This command to pray about everything stands in stark contrast to Paul's previous command to not be anxious about anything. Prayer provides freedom from anxiety! This antidote for anxiety extends to all circumstances. No matter what a leader faces, the opportunity for prayer exists. As a follower of Jesus Christ who leads others, you should pray about everything, especially any situation that produces anxiety.

The topic of how to pray effectively goes beyond the scope of this lesson. Many good books exist that strive to improve a Christian's prayer life. The relevant point for a leader concerns the need to adopt the discipline of regularly going before God to thankfully pray and make requests of God for all circumstances that relate to every opportunity to lead and that generate anxiety. Pray about everything!

Anxiety attacks a person's mind and heart. The leader who carries a responsibility for the lives of others becomes particularly vulnerable to this threat. Paul tells followers of Jesus Christ that the natural result of a disciplined prayer life remains twofold. The prayerful leader experiences a peace from God that transcends all understanding. Note that Paul did not say that prayer necessarily changes our circumstances, thereby reducing our stress. Prayer changes our view of circumstances from our finite temporal perspective to God's miraculous and infinite perspective. Focusing on God's love and sovereign power results in peace.

Another benefit of prayer actually comes from the first result of peace. This peace that surpasses all understanding: ". . . will guard your hearts and your minds . . ." (Phil. 4:7). The Greek word for "guard" is *phroureo* (froo-reh-o). Strong defines this term as follows: "[*phroureo* /froo·reh·o/] . . . to guard, protect by a military guard, either to prevent hostile invasion, or to keep the inhabitants of a besieged city from flight."[5] Prayer serves to stand guard over a leader's emotions (heart) and thoughts (mind). Prayer reorients a leader's heart and mind off self and onto God. Prayer produces peace that protects a leader from the invasion of insecure thoughts that result in fear and anxiety.

Prayer connects a leader with the love of the God who ". . . so loved the world that he gave his one and only Son, that whoever believes in him shall not perish but have eternal life" (John 3:16). The God who loved you enough to sacrifice His own Son stands ready to extend the comfort of His love into the most difficult of circumstances. Prayer reminds a leader that God cares what happens and will not abandon one to his or her own strength to resolve difficult circumstances. Prayer keeps fresh in a follower of Christ's heart and mind that God is actively working, that God has a unique plan for a leader's life that includes stressful situations, and that nothing can separate us from the love of God. Prayer connects a leader to God's infinite love that enables one to peacefully endure hardship. Consider the words of the Apostle Paul from Romans 8:28–39:

> [28] And we know that in all things God works for the good of those who love him, who have been called according to his purpose. [29] For those God foreknew he also predestined to be conformed to the likeness of his Son, that he might be the firstborn among many brothers. [30] And those he predestined, he also called; those he called, he also justified; those he justified, he also glorified.

31 What, then, shall we say in response to this? If God is for us, who can be against us? 32 He who did not spare his own Son, but gave him up for us all—how will he not also, along with him, graciously give us all things? 33 Who will bring any charge against those whom God has chosen? It is God who justifies. 34 Who is he that condemns? Christ Jesus, who died—more than that, who was raised to life—is at the right hand of God and is also interceding for us. 35 Who shall separate us from the love of Christ? Shall trouble or hardship or persecution or famine or nakedness or danger or sword? 36 As it is written:

"For your sake we face death all day long; we are considered as sheep to be slaughtered." 37 No, in all these things we are more than conquerors through him who loved us. 38 For I am convinced that neither death nor life, neither angels nor demons, neither the present nor the future, nor any powers, 39 neither height nor depth, nor anything else in all creation, will be able to separate us from the love of God that is in Christ Jesus our Lord. (Rom. 8:28–39)

Prayer connects a leader with the infinite power of the God who created the universe and is the sovereign King and Ruler of heaven and earth. God answers to no other being, and He works His plan for mankind according to His own will. No circumstances exist outside His knowledge or control. God's power extends over every detail of every situation, and nothing happens except what He allows to happen according to His plans and purposes. God is all-powerful and sovereign. Prayer helps align one's heart and mind to the reality that no matter how stressful a situation seems, all circumstances exist within God's sovereign control and is part of His will for a person's life. Consider the Apostle Paul's words to this effect in Ephesians 1:11–12: "In him we were also chosen, having been predestined according to the plan of him who works out everything in conformity with the purpose of his will, in order that we, who were the first to hope in Christ, might be for the praise of his glory."

Fortitude for leading rests on the knowledge that God loves you and that He is actively controlling all circumstances according to His plan and for His glory. Prayer brings to mind God's love and sovereign control. Prayer reminds a believer of these realities and generates peace that chases away fear, doubt, stress, worry, and anxiety.

A disciplined prayer life yields the fruit of peace for a leader. Order, routine, and focus characterize a disciplined prayer life. Paul said to pray about everything. The discipline of prayer easily applies to a leader's life and routine. To get started, all you need to do is organize your prayers in an orderly fashion. Remember Paul said that prayer can be extended to "everything." Anything that causes you anxiety should be taken to God in prayer in as specific terms as possible. Once the leader prays, the knowledge of God's love and sovereign control over all stressful situations leads to peace, even if the circumstances never change.

Anxiety disables a leader. Stress contributes to poor decisions, misguided initiatives, and dysfunctional behavior on the part of a leader. Anxious thoughts cause self-doubt and indecisiveness. Worry creates a passive leader. Anxiety can compromise the leader-to-follower relationship, thereby reducing a leader's effectiveness.

The Apostle Paul commands followers of Christ, including leaders, to not be anxious about anything. No situation or circumstance, regardless of its level of difficulty, should cause a leader who follows Christ to experience stress and worry. Anxious thoughts and feelings come from a lack of trust and faith in the Lord God Almighty. One of the remedies for anxiety is prayer. Prayer exercises one's faith and trust in God.

The Apostle Paul also commanded followers of Christ, including leaders, to pray about everything. No situation or circumstance, regardless of its perceived eternal insignificance, should be excluded from one's prayer list. Present every request to God, especially items that cause you to experience anxious thoughts and feelings.

Prayer does not obligate God to improve difficult circumstances in our favor. Praying about everything may not change a stressful situation, but prayer will change one's perspective of the situation at hand. Prayer gets a leader's eyes off the finite limits of self and onto God's love, sovereignty, and infinite power. In the midst of anxious moments, prayer generates a peace that surpasses all understanding and guards one's heart and mind from anxious thoughts and feelings.

Authentic fortitude for leading rests on the peace of mind that God loves you and that He is in complete control of every detail of your life. Nothing happens outside God's perfect plan for your life, even painful trials and tribulations. A disciplined prayer life connects a leader to God and bolsters one's courage and confidence. Pray about everything you face as a leader in order to experience God's peace that surpasses all understanding.

Discussion Questions based on "Prayers that Lead to Peace and Courage"

1. In light of Paul's command to rejoice in the Lord's presence at all times, what impact should difficult circumstances have on a leader's joy and what does the presence of anxiety and worry suggest about a leader facing a tough situation?

2. Paul wants all people to see "gentleness" in the life of a follower of Jesus. Explain how the presence of "gentleness" in a leader might serve to encourage those who follow.

3. Paul states that a follower of Jesus Christ should not suffer from the ill effects of anxiety. Discuss how anxiety affects you as a leader and what you do to counteract it.

4. Paul states that a follower of Jesus Christ should pray about "everything." Do you think "everything" includes circumstances you face as a leader? Discuss how you integrate prayer into your role as a leader.

Prayer remedies anxiety and creates peace and courage.

The fortitude that springs from prayer guards a leader's mind and heart from dysfunctional thoughts and feelings.

Pray about everything, especially what relates to where you lead others.

PERSONAL APPLICATION EXERCISE

List "everything" that is currently generating anxious thoughts and feelings in your life as a leader. Be as specific as possible. Establish a routine to pray for these items on a regular basis. For example, take five minutes at the start of every workday to pray for these and any other stressful circumstances you will face in a day.

The Discipline of Prayer and Leading with Fortitude
Mark 1:35

Jesus made prayer a priority. The Son understood the value of starting the day by conversing with the Father! If Jesus made the discipline of prayer an integral part of His life, then shouldn't we?

King David also made prayer a priority, and he expected God to answer.

A disciplined prayer life helps a person lead with fortitude. Prayer empowers a leader with courage and confidence for the challenges of leading others.

Fortitude comes from prayer. The responsibility of leading others can leave a person feeling discouraged and alone. The adage "It's lonely at the top" often rings true for the leader who faces tough decisions and adverse circumstances alone. A disciplined prayer life helps a person lead with fortitude because prayer connects a leader to God's perspective and power. Prayer generates peace, courage, and the fortitude to lead others.

God does not intend for you to shoulder the burden of leadership solely upon the strength of your finite skills, abilities, and personality. God stands ready to help. A leader gains access to God's infinite power through consistent and disciplined prayer. Boldly coming to God's throne enables a leader to accomplish the good works that God purposed and prepared in advance for the leader to accomplish. The leader who neglects the opportunity of prayer essentially has ignored the surest resource of infinite power and wisdom available to help him or her guide others. Leaders don't have to go it alone!

Effective leaders normally possess self-discipline. People who take ownership and responsibility for their own growth typically excel as a leader. Excellent leaders order priorities that improve their efficiency in leading others. They do whatever it takes to become the best leader possible. Excellent leaders constantly work to perfect their skills and abilities. They govern and control their own attitudes and behaviors. They set and live by standards far above the social norms. They pay attention to details, and their work ethic remains second to none. They live orderly and organized lives. These self-imposed disciplines rule every area of an effective leader's life. For a leader who desires to emulate Christ, self-discipline should rule one's prayer life as well.

As a follower of Christ, disciplined prayers enhance a person's leadership efforts. God desires you to make prayer a daily priority. A routine of coming before the Lord in an orderly fashion yields much fruit. Make your requests known to God and wait expectantly for Him to answer. A disciplined prayer life helps a person lead with fortitude. Wise leaders adopt the discipline of prayer and make prayer the number one priority in every opportunity for leading.

The noteworthy leaders of the Bible called out to God in prayer. They believed in the power of prayer. The saints of old trusted that God heard and answered the prayers of His leaders. No circumstance was too small or insignificant to pray about. These leaders expected to see God's hand move in response to their prayers. They ordered their lives so as to make prayer a priority in their daily routine.

The discipline of prayer can be broken down into two simple components: the priority of prayer and the expectation of prayer. The leader who strives to follow Jesus Christ can benefit greatly by integrating these two simple components of a disciplined prayer life into his or her daily routine. Read the following passages of Scripture and consider the priority Jesus placed on getting away to pray alone.

> [35] *Very early in the morning, while it was still dark, Jesus got up, left the house and went off to a solitary place, where he prayed. (Mark 1:35)*

> [23] *After he had dismissed them, he went up on a mountainside by himself to pray. When evening came, he was there alone. . . . (Matt. 14:23)*

> [15] *Yet the news about him spread all the more, so that crowds of people came to hear him and to be healed of their sicknesses.* [16] *But Jesus often withdrew to lonely places and prayed.*
> *(Luke 5:15–16)*

The Priority of Prayer

Jesus routinely retreated from the crowds that constantly surrounded Him to pray alone. He sought solitary places where He could talk to His Heavenly Father privately. Jesus started many days in the predawn darkness talking to God. He concluded many days praying alone late into the night. Jesus made prayer and time alone a priority.

Modern technology (cell phones, e-mail, airline travel, etc.) has accelerated communication, compressed time, and eliminated the lag time leaders used to have to sit and think before acting. People now expect instantaneous decisions in line with the rapid flow of information. The pace of the marketplace races at mind-boggling speeds. The global arena never sleeps. Recognize that you lead in an environment that has surpassed most leaders' cognitive ability to keep up. To survive, you must carve out alone time in your schedule and then protect it with all diligence. Time alone with God must be a priority that every leader who follows Christ does not compromise.

The leader with good intentions to pray but no follow-through receives no benefits. Talking about prayer but failing to execute is a waste of breath. Reading "how to" books on prayer leaves a leader still powerless unless he or she implements what one learns. No amount of good intentions, talk, or knowledge about prayer can substitute for actually getting alone to talk to God. The leader who follows Christ must make prayer a priority on a daily basis.

Most leaders possess packed schedules. Leaders typically have more demands on their time than they can possibly satisfy. Busy leaders can list countless good activities that seem to demand precedence over praying. It is very easy for a leader to believe that the to-do list must be addressed first in a day instead of the prayer list. The urgency of the moment easily convinces one that prayer must come later, after present circumstances get resolved. Unfortunately, later rarely or perhaps never comes for such a leader, so prayer goes undone. Time alone with God in prayer must be the top priority of every leader who claims to follow Jesus Christ.

Leaders often rely on a high level of self-confidence and self-reliance. They typically believe in their own ability to resolve problems and accomplish tasks. A "can-do" attitude and a belief that "I can handle anything on my own!" permeates action-oriented leaders. Past experiences and successes create a false sense of being able to handle any situation. Confident leaders must remain careful, however, for the temptation exists to ignore prayer and turn to self first. Such leaders subtly adopt a feeling that no need exists to tap into God's unlimited resources. Self-reliance can lead to an attitude of not needing to make prayer a priority, or not needing to access God's supernatural power. Pride convinces leaders that they can handle adversity on their own and that they are too important and busy to stop and pray. An absence of prayer creates a subtle and deceptive trap that leaders who follow Christ wisely avoid.

Jesus made prayer a priority. Jesus routinely removed Himself from others and talked with the Father. Jesus retreated from the hustle and bustle of a busy schedule and the crowds around Him. What a mystery: Jesus, the second member of the trinity, fully God and fully man, recognized a need to make prayer a priority. Any leader who claims to follow Jesus Christ must take note of the discipline and priority of prayer that dominated Jesus' schedule. If Jesus needed to pray, how much more do leaders who claim to follow Him need to pray?

The temptation to give in to a busy schedule and not pray is great. The temptation to believe we can handle things on our own without prayer is great. The weakening of a leader's life as a result of neglecting prayer is slow and subtle but sure. The erosion of a prayer-less leader's strength continues until the day he or she wakes up to a problem too big to handle. Leaders who follow Jesus would be wise to follow Jesus' example and make prayer their top priority within the framework of a busy schedule.

Jesus often spent time alone with God and prayed (see Luke 5:16). Jesus routinely prayed. His prayer life indicated a sense of order, discipline, and forethought. Jesus did not just react to circumstances; rather He prayed in advance for God's will to be done. Jesus did not wait to pray in the face of adversity and danger. Prayer regularly dictated Jesus' schedule. Jesus did not ignore time alone with God nor did He treat prayer as an afterthought or add-on to His schedule. Leaders who follow Jesus must incorporate prayer as part of their regular daily routine.

Jesus expected prayer to make a difference. David also prayed with the expectation that he would see God's hand move in response to prayer. Read Psalm 5:1–3 and take notice of David's expectation that God would answer his prayers.

> ^{1} Give ear to my words, O LORD,
>   consider my sighing.
> ^{2} Listen to my cry for help,
>   my King and my God,
>   for to you I pray.
> ^{3} In the morning, O LORD, you hear my voice;
>   in the morning I lay my requests before you
>   and wait in expectation. (Ps. 5:1–3)

The Expectation of Prayer

King David understood the benefit of going before the Lord Almighty in prayer in the morning. God stands ready to hear prayers every hour of the day, but the discipline of an early morning conversation with God allowed David to present his requests before the affairs of the day became a distraction. Like all busy leaders, surely David faced the temptation of getting his day started based on his own strength and initiative. David resisted this temptation, for he knew that the best use of these early hours in a day was to pray about the circumstances he faced before taking action.

Many of David's prayers are recorded in the book of Psalms. Very often his prayers focus on God and contain words of praise, worship, and thanksgiving. One such example is Psalm 100:4–5: "Enter his gates with thanksgiving and his courts with praise; give thanks to him and praise his name. For the LORD is good and his love endures forever; his faithfulness continues through all generations." Starting a time of prayer with praise, worship, and thanksgiving tends to get one's focus off self and immediate circumstances and onto God and His faithfulness and provisions in past circumstances. Acknowledgment of the greatness of God reorients one's mind and heart off self and onto God.

In Psalm 5:1–3, however, David focuses on his requests. With praise, worship, and thanksgiving as the entry into God's presence, David puts his expectation that God will respond to his requests in the forefront. In this passage, one finds David's trust and faith in God's love and sovereignty on display. David petitioned God in the morning and fully believed that God would hear his cry and move His hand in response. David's prayer was not some formal religious ritual; no, David cried out to God for help in the midst of adverse circumstances and fully expected help to come.

David did not simply react emotionally to a bad situation with a desperate cry for help. David ordered his thoughts and prayers and presented them to God at the start of the day. This morning routine of prayer suggests that David possessed self-discipline and a sense that prayer had to be the top priority every day. Leaders should take note of David's discipline of prayer, for this is an easy discipline to incorporate into one's daily schedule. Leaders who desire to follow Jesus have the opportunity to apply David's example and start every day with prayer. Leaders should make a simple list of items that they face and make praying the first activity of each day.

David said: ". . . I lay my requests before you . . ." (NIV). The New American Standard Bible translates this quote a little differently: ". . . I will order my prayer to You. . . ." The Hebrew word for "lay" (NIV) or "order" (NASB) is *arak*. Strong defines this term as follows: ". . . to arrange, set or put or lay in order, set in array, prepare, order, . . . to arrange or set or lay in order, arrange, state in order, set forth (a legal case). . . ."[6] The word means to present something in an orderly and disciplined fashion. David approached his prayer life with a sense of discipline. David "laid" or "ordered" his prayers before God.

Once David presented his orderly prayer requests before God, he waited to see God move. The NIV says David would "wait in expectation." The NASB says that David would: "eagerly watch." The Hebrew term for "wait" (NIV) or "watch" (NASB) is *tsaphah*. Strong defines the term as follows: ". . . to look out or about, spy, keep watch, observe, watch . . . to watch, watch closely."[7] The root of this word carries the sense of a watchman looking out to the horizon for any evidence of approaching danger. David made his petitions to God first; then David stood as a watchman fully expecting to see signs of God's hand moving in his favor.

Leaders by nature are people of initiative and action. Most leaders feel so secure and confident in their ability that they do not hesitate to launch a course of action to meet a situation. Acting without the preface of prayer can lead one to rash and foolish actions. While taking initiative has its place, a wise leader lays his plans before God first and waits expectantly to see how God in turn will move. Leaders must wait patiently on God and not simply take matters into their own hands.

Waiting expectantly on God to answer prayer comes down to the objective of a leader's faith. Either a leader trusts in his or her own ability to handle circumstances correctly or a leader trusts more in God's ability to handle circumstances and expectantly waits. A vast difference exists between formulating your own plan and asking God to bless decisions as you move forward, and asking God to initiate action and standing as a watchman looking for God's hand and then joining in His plan. Do you really expect to see God move in response to your prayers? Or are you quick to initiate your own actions and hope God blesses them?

A disciplined prayer life characterized many great leaders of the Bible. The belief that God hears and responds to prayer bolstered the fortitude of these praying leaders. These leaders faced difficult situations and adverse circumstances with courage as a result of trusting that God's hand would move in response to their prayers. Their relationship with God developed such that they acknowledged the limits of their finite strength and cried out to the Lord God Almighty to bring His infinite power to bear on tough issues. Consider the following list of great praying leaders from the Bible:

- Abraham (Gen. 20:17)
- Isaac (Gen. 25:21)
- Jacob (Gen. 32:9–11)
- Moses (Exod. 8:30–31)
- Samuel (1 Sam. 8:6–7)

- David (2 Sam. 7:18)
- Solomon (1 Kings 8:22–23)
- Hezekiah (2 Kings 19:15)
- Nehemiah (Neh. 1:1–4)
- Daniel (Dan. 6:10)
- Jonah (Jon. 2:1)
- Jesus (Mark 1:35)
- Disciples (Acts 1:13–14)
- First-century disciples (Acts 2:41–42)
- Stephen (Acts 7:59)
- Peter (Acts 9:40)
- Cornelius (Acts 10:1–2)
- Paul (Acts 26:29

As a follower of Christ, adopting the discipline of prayer will lead to fortitude for leading. The first step involves making prayer a priority. I recommend starting every day with prayer. Avoid the temptation of diving into your to-do list first and keep sacred a few minutes alone with God before you begin. Come before the Father in an orderly fashion with your prayers well thought out. I recommend committing them to writing in a notebook so they can be easily recalled and answers can be noted. Expect God to answer. Wait patiently and expect God to move. Watch for signs and circumstances that indicate God's hand at work.

Fortitude for leading rests on the love and sovereignty of God. The discipline of prayer connects a leader to the Lord and produces peace and courage. A disciplined prayer life helps a person lead others with fortitude. Leaders who desire to follow Jesus should make prayer a priority in their schedule and wait expectantly for God to answer.

Discussion Questions based on "The Discipline of Prayer and Leading with Fortitude"

1. What does David's morning routine of prayer tell us about his self-discipline and priorities? How can you apply this same discipline and sense of priority where you lead?

2. What did David do once he made his request before God? Compare and contrast "waiting in expectation" on the Lord to answer a prayer and rushing off to initiate actions based on one's own wisdom and understanding of a situation.

3. Do you really expect to see God's hand move in response to your prayers? Are you willing to wait in expectation, or are you more inclined to pray and then initiate your own action? Explain your answer.

4. Explain the difference between asking God to bless your plan of action and moving forward compared to asking God to initiate his plan of action and waiting expectantly.

Jesus made prayer a priority.

King David also made prayer a priority and he expected God to answer.

A disciplined prayer life helps a person lead with fortitude. Prayer empowers a leader with courage and confidence for the challenges of leading others.

Fortitude comes from prayer.

Personal Application Exercise

In your reader's journal, list several items you can pray about that relate to a leader-to-follower relationship(s) you currently have. Commit to starting every day discussing them with the Lord and then wait expectantly and watchfully for God to move.

Worldview

CORE VALUE: A WORLDVIEW founded on absolute truth and the words of Jesus Christ.

A Biblical Worldview
Psalm 119:97–106 and Romans 12:2

A biblical worldview illuminates the path to discovering God's will and ways. Internalizing God's Word will transform how a person looks at leading others.

Seeing others through God's eyes will change how you approach every leader-to-follower relationship. A leader who desires to follow Christ must commit to developing a biblical worldview through a disciplined routine of studying God's Word.

Every leader possesses a "worldview." How a person views the world directly influences how he or she leads others. A worldview provides a lens through which a person peers into his or her circumstances. A worldview serves as a preset filter through which someone receives and interprets bits of information about one's surroundings. Simply stated, a "worldview" shapes what a person believes to be true about the world in which mankind exists.

A "worldview" shapes what a person believes to be true about the world in which mankind exists.

A leader's attitudes and actions ultimately spring from one's view of the world. A leader responds to his or her surroundings based on how he or she interprets truth. A faulty worldview invariably produces flawed leadership. A dysfunctional view of one's circumstances results in a dysfunctional leader. A worldview consistent with the truth and reality of human existence creates a strong foundation for effective leadership. Consequently, to lead as God intends, one must embrace a view of the world consistent with God's revelation of Himself and His creation.

A person's behavior always correlates to one's worldview. A person whose worldview has excluded the existence of God will live and act unrestrained and unaccountable to a higher being. Such a person only restricts behavior to what benefits self or what one believes he or she can get away with. A person whose worldview excludes God finds no reason to know or obey His Word. Such a person lives to gratify the selfish desires of the flesh with no regard to a higher sense of right and wrong. One's worldview ultimately dictates his or her attitudes and actions toward others. This outcome remains inescapable! A leader's worldview will shape how he or she leads others.

Sincerely believing a premise about the world in which humans live does not necessarily make the premise true. A wise leader contemplates questions such as: Is what I believe about the world true? Does my worldview match with objective reality? Do my ideas regarding my surroundings align with God's revelation of Himself in creation and His Word? For example, some might say that people are basically good but make bad choices because they lack education. This premise leads one to emphasize education under the assumption that bad choices will vanish once people have been educated. The problem with this view of mankind is that this worldview neither matches objective reality of society and creation nor aligns with God's revelation of man in the Bible. Human nature remains basically self-centered and not good. People make bad decisions and choices based on a sinful nature, not a lack of education. Man needs both justification and sanctification, not more education, to modify one's behavior. If one believes people are basically good and only need education, he or she will lead differently than the leader who sees people as sinful and fallen creatures.

Many influences compete to shape a person's view of the world in which he or she leads. Every leader gets bombarded with ideas that seem to fit with reality but in fact fail the test of truthfulness. Modern communications have flooded our minds with thoughts that seem right on the surface but prove to be false when closely examined. A leader can select from a wide range of sources by which to formulate one's worldview, such as religion, science, media/movies/television, entertainers, newspapers/books, art, music, education, friends, popular trends, family heritage, socio-ethnic origin, athletics, and the Internet. Sadly, these elements of secular culture impact the worldview of the average follower of Christ way too much.

A leader who follows Christ must honestly assess and then carefully craft a worldview that produces attitudes and actions consistent with how God desires a person to lead.

A leader who follows Christ must honestly assess and then carefully craft a worldview that produces attitudes and actions consistent with how God desires a person to lead. Only one source exists that remains consistent with objective reality of the universe and God's revelation of Himself. This source is the Bible. God's will is for followers of Christ to view the world through His Word. We call this a biblical worldview. Read Psalm 119:97–106 and consider how God's Word impacted the thinking of David.

> *97 Oh, how I love your law!*
>   *I meditate on it all day long.*

> *98 Your commands make me wiser than my enemies,*
>   *for they are ever with me.*

> *99 I have more insight than all my teachers,*
>   *for I meditate on your statutes.*

> *100 I have more understanding than the elders,*
>   *for I obey your precepts.*

> [101] I have kept my feet from every evil path
>   so that I might obey your word.
>
> [102] I have not departed from your laws,
>   for you yourself have taught me.
>
> [103] How sweet are your words to my taste,
>   sweeter than honey to my mouth!
>
> [104] I gain understanding from your precepts;
>   therefore I hate every wrong path.
>
> [105] Your word is a lamp to my feet
>   and a light for my path.
>
> [106] I have taken an oath and confirmed it,
>   that I will follow your righteous laws.
>   (Ps. 119:97–106)

God's Word saturated David's conscious thoughts. This state of mind provides evidence that David regularly fed God's Word into his mind and heart. Since David nourished his soul with Scripture, he could meditate on God's Word all day long. God's Word filtered every observation and decision and colored every judgment and evaluation David made in the course of a day. David's view of the world came through the lens of God's Word permeating his mind. David possessed a biblical worldview. The mind of a leader who follows Christ should be so saturated with God's Word that every attitude and action spring from this biblical view of the world.

The commands of the Lord provide wisdom for a leader. The Bible speaks to how a leader should lead and relate to others. David recognized that a commitment to know God's commands made him wiser than his enemies. God's statutes provided David insight that surpassed the knowledge gained from temporal human teachers. David's understanding of the reality of the world exceeded that of his elders because his knowledge and wisdom came from the revelation of the one who created the world. This same wisdom, insight, and understanding can help a Christ follower lead others with a clearer and more accurate view of the world than other leaders.

God's Word not only provides wisdom for leading but also protects a leader from immoral decisions and actions that may very well cause one to fail as a leader. David recognized that obeying God's Word kept his feet from following an evil path. General observation suggests that more leaders fail because of evil behavior than fail from a lack of leadership skills. A commitment to obey God's Word serves to shield a leader from such potential career-ending attitudes and actions.

A big difference exists between knowing God's Word and obeying God's Word. The possession of knowledge alone provides a leader little or no significant benefits. Obedience to God's Word gives a leader wisdom and keeps one off an evil path. These benefits only come from obedience. A person must apply and adhere to God's Word in order for this knowledge to bear fruit in one's life.

The Word of God tasted sweet to David. He hungered for God's Word. The consumption of Scripture satisfied the taste buds of his mind. Is the intake of Bible knowledge a pleasurable experience to you? Is the taste of God's Word in your heart and mind sweet like honey? The creation of a biblical worldview requires a disciplined intake of God's Word. A leader who follows Christ must acquire a taste for studying and knowing the Scriptures. Every leader's daily routine should include the discipline of feeding passages of the Bible into one's mind. God's Word can taste as pleasurable as eating something sweet, like honey.

God's precepts gave David understanding. Looking at life through the lens of God's truth helped David see the reality of the world accurately. This clear perception afforded David understanding. A biblical worldview helps a leader know right from wrong. Such a black and white view of issues helps a leader to recognize the deceit of a wrong path. David said that God's precepts led him to "hate" every wrong path. A leader with a biblical worldview despises any situations contrary to God's Word and takes steps to totally disassociate oneself from them. The Hebrew term for "hate" is *sane*. The *Theological Wordbook of the Old Testament* says this of the term *sane*:

"The verb śānē and its derivatives have the root meaning "to hate."
It expresses an emotional attitude toward persons and things
which are opposed, detested, despised and with which one wishes
to have no contact or relationship. It is therefore the opposite of
love. Whereas love draws and unites, hate separates and keeps
distant. The hated and hating persons are considered foes or
enemies and are considered odious, utterly unappealing."[1]

A biblical worldview gives a leader a clear and accurate view of the world in which he or she leads. Such a leader sees the world as society really exists, not how one wishes the world to exist. David used God's Word as a lamp to his feet. God's Word illuminated every step he took in life. Just as headlights provide light for the driver of a car, so also God's Word lights the path ahead of a leader so he or she can navigate the road of leading others.

David followed God's righteous laws without reservation. God's words guided his every decision and action as a leader. David took an oath before the Lord to live by a biblical worldview. The attitudes and actions of David's life confirmed his commitment to this oath. David made a conscious decision to form and follow a view of the world based on God's Word. A leader who desires to follow Christ must lead from the sure foundation of a biblical worldview. To see clearly the world in which one leads, a follower of Christ must allow God's Word to transform his or her mind. In Romans 12:2, the Apostle Paul challenges Christ followers to resist conformity to the world and to be transformed by a renewed mind:

> [2] *Do not conform any longer to the pattern of this world,*
> *but be transformed by the renewing of your mind.*
> *Then you will be able to test and approve what God's will*
> *is—his good, pleasing and perfect will. (Rom. 12:2)*

The Apostle Paul encourages followers of Christ to resist the world's efforts to mold their lives to the secular patterns of culture. Paul knows that before knowing Christ, a person invariably behaves in a manner consistent with the norms of society. A lost person really has no choice but to follow and obey the principles for living propagated by the world's system. For a leader, conformity to the pattern of the world involves adopting the core values and practices that worldly leaders use instead of biblical core values and practices. A follower of Christ should leave the teachings of the secular world behind. A follower of Christ should embrace the truths of the faith laid out in the first eleven chapters of Romans and form a new worldview based on God's Word. A "transformed" life provides visible results of embracing a biblical worldview. Paul describes a life transformed by God's Word in Romans 12–16.

The leader who conforms to the pattern of the world will embrace a view of the world consistent with secular thinking. Conformity to the world will never lead a person to a biblical worldview. The leader who claims to follow Christ but embraces the pattern of the world will never become the type of leader God desires. The impact on one's worldview when based on secular culture points 180 degrees in the opposite direction of a biblical worldview.

By nature, everyone possesses a secular worldview. Living with a biblical worldview requires transformation. The Greek term for "transformation" used by Paul in Romans 12:2 is *metamorphoo*. Strong defines *metamorphoo* as follows: ". . . to change into another form, to transform. . . ."[2] Swanson adds: ". . . change, transform the essential nature of something. . . ."[3] Based on a follower of Christ's justification by faith, Paul states that a corresponding change in attitude and actions should become evident in the life of a true believer. Salvation instantaneously and permanently changes a person's essential nature. Consequently, the saved should begin to live differently than those who continue to be controlled and conformed by the world. Sadly in today's culture, too many leaders who claim to follow Christ still conform to the world and lead others in a manner no different from leaders who still embrace the world's system. Does how you lead demonstrate a life that has been radically transformed by Christ?

The Apostle Paul states that the process of transformation begins by "the renewing of your mind." The Greek term for "renewing" is *anakainosis*. Strong defines this word as follows: ". . . a renewal, renovation, complete change for the better. . . ."[4] Paul states in no uncertain terms that salvation should be evidenced by a change in behavior that starts with a complete change in how a person thinks about the world in which he or she lives. Paul expected the worldview of a follower of Christ to change from secular to biblical. This renewing of the mind presupposes an intake of God's Word that the Holy Spirit then uses to transform one's life. The only way you will experience the life transformation Paul describes in Romans is to commit yourself to developing and living out a worldview based exclusively on the Bible. To become the leader God desires you to be requires a biblical worldview.

The Entrusted Leader's core value number one is: *A HEART willing to do all God asks.* Two key factors come into play that determine if a person will lead with a heart willing to do all God asks. The first is a decision on the part of a leader that he or she is willing to do all God asks. The second is a commitment to know and understand what it is that God is asking a leader to do. A leader must know what God's will entails if he or she intends to do it. God has revealed His will in His Word.

Paul reveals in Romans 12:2 a benefit of a transformed and renewed mind in regard to discerning God's will: ". . . you will be able to test and approve what God's will is—his good, pleasing and perfect will." A biblical worldview is the lens through which a leader perceives God's will, His "good, pleasing and perfect will." No other path for the development of a heart willing to do all God asks exists. Paul tells the follower of Christ that renewing one's mind with God's Word fuels the Holy Spirit's transformation of one's life and orients one's heart in line with God's will.

A secular worldview is not capable of transforming a leader's heart. A view of the world based on human culture and society will never produce the attitudes and actions God desires for leaders who claim to follow Christ. Only a biblical worldview can transform a person's mind and heart, which in turn produces the character and compassion required to lead as God desires.

The leader who desires to follow Christ must view the world from a biblical perspective. Every attitude and action must spring from a biblical worldview. Consider the temptation of Jesus by the Evil One in Matthew 4:1–11. All of Jesus' responses to the Devil were quotes from God's Word—the book of Deuteronomy. Jesus viewed life through the lens of God's Word and responded accordingly. As a leader who claims to follow Christ, it is essential that you adopt a biblical worldview.

Two broad steps will start this transformation of your mind. The first step requires a decision and commitment to lead from a biblical view of the world. Knowledge of the Bible provides little or no value to a leader if no commitment exists to let biblical truth and an understanding of God's will impact one's attitudes and actions. Be aware that a decision to lead from a biblical worldview will often run counter to secular culture and conflict with the desires of the flesh. The first step in leading with a worldview based on God's Word is one you can take right now. If you have not already done so, I encourage you to commit to God your intention to lead others based on the Bible. In your reader's journal, write a note to God that articulates your commitment to a biblical worldview, whether you have just made this decision or have done so in the past.

The second step in transforming your mind involves creating a disciplined effort to take God's Word into your mind. This is not to suggest a leader must become an expert in theology. Simply reading and meditating on God's Word releases the power of the Holy Spirit to transform one's thinking and leadership. The Holy Spirit does the transformation, but the follower of Christ must do his or her part first, which involves feeding God's Word into one's mind. Paul encouraged "the holy and faithful brothers in Christ at Colosse" to "Let the word of Christ dwell in you richly . . ." (Col. 1:2, 3:16). As you become a leader who desires to follow Christ, I highly encourage you to adopt a routine of feeding God's Word into your mind daily. Many good "how to" books exist that address the topic of studying God's Word. I recommend you secure a copy of Dr. Howard Hendricks and William Hendricks' book *Living By the Book*. Their approach is simple and practical, yet will help you develop a disciplined approach to studying God's Word that will lead you into a deeper understanding of God's Word and create in you the basis for a biblical worldview.

A person's worldview formulates the basis for all the attitudes and actions that shape one's life. For a leader, one's view of the world provides a foundation for one's motives, drive, priorities, and actions. Sadly, few Christians today have heeded Paul's advice. The worldview of the average Christian living in America today is more influenced by secular culture than the truths of the faith. Very few followers of Christ actually possess a worldview shaped by God's Word.

Christ followers lead in a world where secular philosophy has replaced the Judeo-Christian (biblical) view of the world. Historically, a biblical worldview dominated western civilization thinking, even for most non-Christians. This is no longer true, especially for the post-baby boomer generations. For a leader who desires to follow Christ, leading from a biblical worldview is becoming a less popular and more treacherous proposition. This biblical view of leadership, however, is the basis from which God desires followers of Christ to lead others.

God intends for you to develop and use a worldview founded on absolute truth and the words of Jesus Christ. Only a biblical worldview illuminates the path of God's will and transforms a leader's thinking in a manner consistent with God's Word. A leader who desires to follow Christ should commit to developing a biblical worldview through a disciplined routine of studying God's Word.

Discussion Questions based on "A Biblical Worldview"

1. In Psalm 119: 98–100, David proclaimed that God's Word made him wiser than his enemies, gave him more insight than his teachers, and more understanding than his elders. Describe some ways that you can apply the wisdom, insight, and understanding of God's Word where you lead others.

2. In Psalm 119:105, David said that God's Word served to illuminate his path as he traveled through life. Describe how God's Word might provide a light for the path of leadership you have chosen to follow.

3. What source(s) of information form the foundation of your worldview? How did you develop what you believe to be absolutely true about the world in which you live?

4. What do you think it means to conform to the pattern of this world? How might conforming to one's secular culture impact one's worldview?

5. What comes from a transformed life and renewed mind? How might seeing God's will clearly impact a leader's view of the world and how he or she leads others?

Ever leader possesses a worldview.

A biblical worldview illuminates the path to discovering God's will and ways.

Internalizing God's Word will transform how a person looks at leading others.

Seeing others through God's eyes will change how you approach every leader-to-follower relationship.

PERSONAL APPLICATION EXERCISE

Describe one discipline you can commit to today that will increase your intake of God's Word such as reading a passage of Scripture every morning, joining a weekly Bible study group, or reading the entire Bible in one year.

A Foundation for Leadership
Luke 6:46–49

The Bible provides reliable materials for constructing a strong foundation for leadership. The words of Jesus Christ paint an accurate picture of the world in which you lead others. The basis upon which you view the world will dramatically impact how you engage in a leader-to-follower relationship.

A person's worldview provides the raw material from which one constructs a foundation for leadership. A secular/human worldview supplies unreliable materials. A biblical worldview supplies reliable materials. A person's view of the world determines what materials he or she will have at his or her disposal for constructing the foundation upon which one's framework for leading will rest. Only the words of Jesus Christ provide reliable material for a biblical worldview and a sure foundation for leadership.

A sturdy building rests on a foundation of reliable materials (concrete and steel) attached to bedrock. The foundation must be well constructed and attached to bedrock so that shifting soil, rain, and wind won't cause the framing or outer skin to crack or become unbalanced. A solid base protects a building from outside pressures that seek to compromise the integrity of the structure. Bedrock naturally exists as part of creation. The key to constructing a sure foundation involves using reliable materials and digging deep enough to attach one's substructure to the immovable footing of bedrock. The same can be said of constructing a sure foundation for leadership.

For the leader, God's Word provides an immovable footing of bedrock and a reliable resource of materials for the construction of a sure foundation. David said of God's Word: "All your commands are trustworthy . . ." and "Your word, O LORD, is eternal; it stands firm in the heavens" (Ps. 119:86, 89). A leader can confidently attach his or her foundation for leading to God's Word because Scripture stands eternal, firm, and trustworthy.

God's Word contains an unlimited resource of reliable materials from which a leader can confidently construct a foundation for leadership. David also said of God's Word: "Open my eyes that I may see wonderful things in your law" and "Turn my eyes away from worthless things; preserve my life according to your word" (Ps. 119:18, 37). The person who opens his or her eyes to the storehouse of God's Word will truly find wonderful building blocks from which to construct a foundation. A foundation for leading built using God's Word serves to protect a leader from outside pressures that seek to compromise his or her structural integrity.

In Luke 6:46–49, Jesus taught His followers the importance of constructing a solid foundation for one's life and attaching it to bedrock. The Lord communicated this lesson in the form of a parable titled The Wise and Foolish Builders.

> [46] "Why do you call me, 'Lord, Lord,' and do not do what I say?
> [47] I will show you what he is like who comes to me and hears my
> words and puts them into practice. [48] He is like a man building
> a house, who dug down deep and laid the foundation on rock.

When a flood came, the torrent struck that house but could not shake it, because it was well built. [49] But the one who hears my words and does not put them into practice is like a man who built a house on the ground without a foundation. The moment the torrent struck that house, it collapsed and its destruction was complete." (Luke 6:46–49)

The Entrusted Leader: Seven Core Values

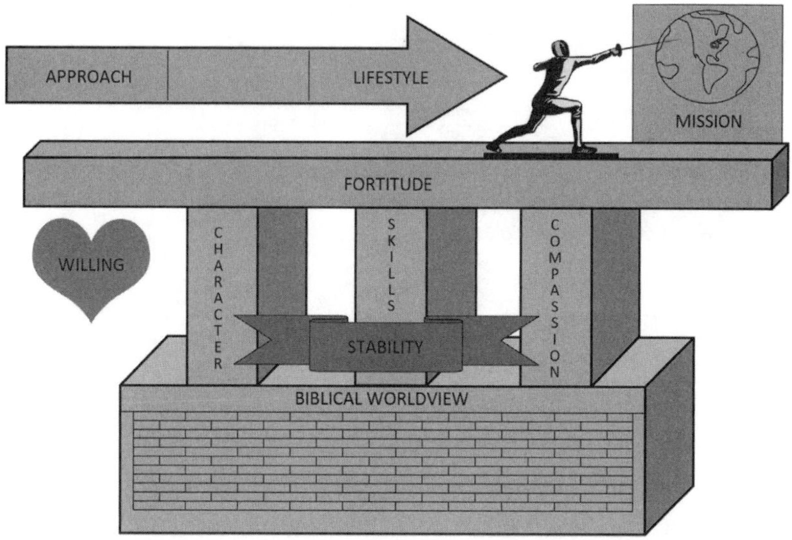

Figure 11.1: The Entrusted Leader

An Entrusted Leader resembles the wise builder spoken of by Jesus in this parable. This leader laid a foundation for leading others constructed from God's Word.

All the core values of an Entrusted Leader are anchored to and rest securely on the foundation of a biblical worldview. This foundation and framework for leading cannot be shaken by the storms of life that are sure to come every leader's way at some time. Inside the Entrusted Leader beats a heart willing to do all God asks. This leader finds inspiration in a calling to God's eternal mission that supersedes one's own temporal goals. He or she voluntarily denies self in order to approach leading as a servant. The Entrusted Leader engages in every leader-to-follower relationship with a lifestyle beyond reproach that extends faith, hope, and love to all. A proper balance of skills, character, and compassion provide added stability for the Entrusted Leader. Faith in the love and sovereignty of God bolster this leader with the fortitude to lead others in the face of great adversity. Practicing God's Word makes all this possible for a leader.

The "Foolish" Leader: Seven Core Values

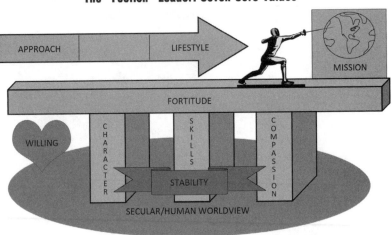

Figure 11.2: The Foolish Leader

The foolish leader resembles the foolish builder Jesus spoke of in this parable. This leader laid no foundation for leading. Secular and human philosophies shape this leader's view of the world and provide the basis for his or her core values. Initially the fool's visible framework of leadership may resemble that of a wise leader. The core values of a foolish leader, however, are anchored to nothing. This leadership framework will be shaken by the storms of life. Inside the foolish leader beats a heart unwilling to do all God asks. A mission to satisfy one's earthly desire to climb a ladder to fame, fortune, and power drives this leader. He or she actively promotes self in order to approach leading as an authority. Followers see the hypocrisy of a lifestyle that speaks one way but acts another. Stability evaporates because of an overreliance on skills and underdeveloped character and compassion. Faith in self alone leaves this leader paralyzed with fear and doubt when facing great adversity. Not putting God's Word into practice makes this leadership house of cards a reality in the life a foolish leader.

The "Foolish" Leader: Seven Core Values

Figure 11.3: The Foolish Leader

The ground under the fool's leadership framework washes away when exposed to the storms of life. Because this leader laid no foundation for leading, his or her house of cards collapses, and the destruction is complete. When put to the test of leadership pressure, secular and human philosophies will melt away like sand on the banks of a flooding river. The fool's core values, which were shaped by a secular/human view of the world, will be exposed as something less than the outward image falsely propagated on an unsuspecting group of followers. When the pressure of leading gets intense enough, the heart unwilling to do all God asks will generate outward actions and attitudes contrary to God's will. A foolish leader's mission, approach to leading, lifestyle, overreliance on skills at the expense of character and compassion, and lack of real faith in God will all be exposed as self-centered when the storms of leading blow. Once the collapse of the foolish leader becomes complete, the contrast to the Entrusted Leader becomes visible to all.

Jesus' story of the wise and foolish builders takes the form of a parable. A parable contains an obvious, simple story arranged to communicate a more subtle and deeper spiritual truth. Many hearers of a parable never think past the obvious story. The wise listener, however, reflects on the obvious to understand the deeper spiritual truth.

Luke places this parable within the context of Jesus describing for the twelve Apostles what characterizes a true follower of Christ. Read Luke 6:12–49 and you will find the following sequence of events that set this context of defining real discipleship.

- Jesus calls the twelve apostles from the masses (12–16).
- Jesus characterizes a true follower of Christ (20–49).
  a. Treat enemies with love and mercy (27–36).
  b. Extend forgiveness without judging or condemning others (37–38).
  c. Think truthfully about self and others, and avoid hypocrisy (39–42).
  d. Display good fruit (43–45).
  e. Put Jesus' words into practice (46–49).

The parable of the wise and foolish builders stands as a contrast between two men: one who puts Jesus' words into practice and one who does not. On the outside, these two men look identical. The structure of the foolish man with no foundation may actually rise above ground first because the wise man takes time to dig deep and lay a solid substructure on rock before building. When trouble comes, however, the structural difference becomes clear. The wise man weathers the storms of life unshaken, while the foolish man collapses and is swept away.

Jesus uses a rhetorical question to identify the subject of this parable: people who call Him "Lord, Lord" but choose to ignore His words. To call someone Lord essentially involves a loud and public pronouncement that a person has chosen to voluntarily submit one's will to another. The Greek term for "Lord" is *kurios*. Strong defines the term as follows: ". . . he to whom a person or thing belongs, about which he has power of deciding; master, lord . . . the possessor and disposer of a thing . . . the owner; one who has control of the person, the master."[5] Claiming to follow Jesus as one's "Lord" can only be viewed as a voluntary act. Jesus neither claimed nor sought to exercise authority over His followers. Jesus simply notes the hypocrisy of making such a vocal and voluntary statement of loyalty without a corresponding visual display of obedience. Jesus calls into question the sincerity of those who claim to be His followers but fail to obey what He says. To publicly pronounce Jesus as one's master but not do what He says dishonors God and brings humiliation upon oneself. Jesus clarifies that obedience to and application of His words is required of His true followers. Does how you lead others reflect a commitment to put Jesus' words into practice?

Jesus expects His followers to give more than lip service to His teachings. Jesus expects believers to go beyond proclaiming publicly a relationship with Him and to privately practice His words in all situations. Transformed lives provide evidence of obedience to His words. True followers of Christ conform their will to God's will, and they sacrificially serve God's interests in the world rather than their own.

Instead of harshly criticizing these hypocritical disciples, Jesus warns foolish builders that they have hastily built a house of cards that will inevitably collapse under the pressures of life. Jesus makes His point by contrasting two men who both have heard Jesus speak, but only one listener puts Jesus' words into practice. Knowledge without obedience leads to pride, pseudo-spirituality, a Pharisee complex, a holier-than-thou attitude, and a false sense of security. Practically applying Jesus' words results in life transformation and a public lifestyle that glorifies God and brings stability in times of trouble.

The foolish builder laid no foundation. He immediately began constructing a house anchored to no substructure but the ground. This builder did not invest the time and energy required to lay a solid foundation. Surely the outer shell looked stable, and construction proceeded quickly for all to see. When the floods came, however, this deception was exposed for all to see.

The wise builder performed three actions the foolish builder did not. This man excavated the ground below the intended location of his house, digging deep to expose the natural bedrock of creation. The second step this man took involved building a solid foundation using reliable materials. Finally, he attached the solid foundation to the exposed bedrock. All this was done prior to construction of the house's framework, outer shell, and roof.

Constructing a foundation for leadership comprises actions similar to laying a building's foundation. Building a biblical worldview to lead from requires digging below the surface, constructing a foundation from reliable materials, and attaching the foundation to an immovable object. Developing a biblical worldview requires the spadework of digging into God's Word with an open mind and obedient heart. You cannot view the world through the lens of the Bible if you don't take the time to routinely study the Scriptures. One must, however, go beyond digging into God's Word and put what Jesus says into practice. The only sure foundation for leadership is constructed from the reliable material of applying God's Word to every facet of a leader's life. Lastly, God and His Word stand eternal, absolute, and fixed. Faith in God and a commitment to follow His word provide the immovable objects of heaven and earth to which one's foundation must be attached.

The best time to lay a solid foundation precedes the construction of the house. Repairing, shoring up, or trying to lay a foundation after the fact constitutes a losing battle. Laying a foundation for a house must take place prior to constructing the framework. You cannot go back and lay a foundation when the torrent strikes and cracks begin to appear. Note that a correlation exists between the size and strength of a foundation and the size and height of the building. A large, tall building requires a deep and sturdy foundation. The same correlation exists for leadership. The more lofty and difficult the leadership position a person holds, the deeper and stronger the person's foundation needs to be.

Listeners of God's Word glean another key insight from the story of the wise and foolish builders. The simple story evokes torrential rain that produces a flood of water. The resulting torrent erodes the ground under the houses, causing the one without a foundation to collapse. We all have seen pictures of the destructive power of flooding waters.

Every leader will face pressures that will test the presence and strength of the foundation upon which one has erected his or her leadership framework. Every leader can count on having to face potentially destructive forces that the average follower will never understand. The wider one's span of responsibility grows, the greater the leadership pressures one will face. The leader with no real foundation for life will eventually crack under the pressure, and his or her destruction will be complete.

The crumbling of one's effectiveness as a leader may show up in a variety of ways. *The ENTRUSTED Leader* is designed around seven core values of an Entrusted Leader. One of the key motivations for this design stems from a conviction that many leaders who fail falter because they give in to the pressures of leading and compromise one or a combination of these core values. Observation of leaders who fail suggests that the compromising of one's core values results in a leader's demise more frequently than a deficiency of skills. A commitment to put Jesus' words into practice lays a foundation for leadership that protects a leader from the temptation to give in to pressure and compromise his or her core values.

The words of Jesus Christ provide reliable material for a biblical worldview and a sure foundation for leadership. Claiming to be a follower of Jesus Christ must be evidenced by a commitment to put the words of Jesus into practice everywhere you lead others. Building the framework of your leadership upon the foundation of God's Word (biblical worldview) will protect you from the pressures of leading others that can potentially bring about your downfall.

Discussion Questions based on "A Foundation for Leadership"

1. Relate in your own words the discipline you must exercise in your life in order to put Jesus' words into practice in such a way that they protect you from destructive forces you might encounter as a leader.

2. Relate in your own words the potential risks of collapse associated with hearing but not practicing Jesus' words in the midst of destructive forces swirling around you.

3. What destructive forces and temptations can you think of that have the potential to cause a catastrophic collapse of a person's effectiveness as a leader? How does a well-built foundation constructed from God's Word keep a leader unshaken when struck by the torrent of pressures associated with leading others?

4. What hypocrisy do you see in calling Jesus "Lord, Lord" and not applying His words? What evidence might one expect to see in the life of a leader who does what Jesus says?

A person's worldview provides the raw material from which one constructs a foundation for leadership.

A secular/human worldview supplies unreliable materials. A biblical worldview supplies reliable materials.

The basis upon which you view the world will dramatically impact how you engage in a leader-to-follower relationship.

PERSONAL APPLICATION EXERCISE

Using Figure 11.1 as a guide, draw a picture of your foundation for leadership and how this foundation supports the other six core values of an Entrusted Leader.

Truth: A Navigation System for Leadership
John 17:17 and Psalm 119:24

God's Word stands the test of time as absolute truth.

The words of Scripture remain consistent with the facts and reality of this world.

What God has spoken and revealed in His Word applies universally to all peoples in every generation. What is true today was true yesterday and will be true tomorrow.

Consequently God's Word serves as a fixed reference point for a leader's view of the world and his or her navigation of the turbulent waters of leading others. A wise leader develops a thorough understanding of God's Word and allows absolute biblical truth to counsel and guide one's choices and decisions.

Every navigation system depends on a fixed point of reference that does not move or change. A compass utilizes the earth's magnetic field. Since the creation of the universe, travelers in the northern hemisphere have relied on a simple viewing of the North Star to direct their way. More recently, complex Global Positioning Systems can calculate a person's location, speed, and direction by receiving data from satellites. Whether simple or complex, accurate navigation requires a fixed point of reference that does not move or change.

Just as a compass directs travelers, so also truth provides a reliable navigation system for a follower of Christ who leads others. The landscape traversed by a leader is not so much geographical as it is relational. Every organization exists as a complex web of human relationships. Wise leaders understand that functional human relationships and healthy organizations only exist when the truth that governs human relationships is respected by all. Truth helps a leader navigate the complex web of human relationships with which he or she has been entrusted.

Truth serves more as a compass which points out the right direction than a GPS device that provides detailed turn-by-turn data. The needle of a compass aligns with the earth's magnetic field and points to either the North Pole or South Pole of the globe. From these fixed points of reference that do not move or change, a traveler can get his or her bearings and decide which way to proceed. The compass will not provide data for every twist in the path or every rock to step over or every pothole to avoid, but a compass will keep a traveler headed generally in the right direction.

Truth helps a leader navigate relationships in a similar manner. No relational GPS device exists that will exhaustively cover every detailed circumstance a leader may encounter when relating to followers. The compass of truth, however, does apply to every situation and will provide adequate direction for how a leader should proceed. For example, it is universally true that all people want to be treated with dignity and respect, regardless of one's station in an organization. This truth stands as a fixed point of reference from the mail room to the boardroom. Any leader who ignores the compass heading of this reality of human existence will most assuredly pursue a path of relating to others that results in less than healthy relationships.

The leader-to-follower relationship exists as the primary context within which principles and practices of leadership come alive, find meaning, and receive practical application. The long-term health and strength of an organization depends on these relationships. Wise leaders foster healthy relationships with followers. Certain truths foster healthy relationships when respected by a leader. Conversely, human relationships deteriorate rapidly when a leader violates these truths.

We consider something to be "true" when its essence agrees with the objective reality of existence. Consider the following definition of the word "true" from *Merriam-Webster's Collegiate Dictionary*: ". . . being in accordance with the actual state of affairs . . . conformable to an essential reality."[6] Furthermore, *Merriam-Webster's Collegiate Dictionary* defines the word "truth" as follows: ". . . the state of being the case . . . the body of real things, events, and facts . . . a transcendent fundamental or spiritual reality . . . judgment, proposition, or idea that is true or accepted as true . . . the body of true statements and propositions . . . the property (as of a statement) of being in accord with fact or reality."[7] When people deem a reality as "true" or "truth," this absolute fact serves as a fixed point of reference that one can count on as they navigate this journey called life.

The idea of some truth being "absolute" can have many nuances. Pertinent to this lesson becomes the idea of a truth or reality being universal or applicable to all creatures and the truth being eternal and unchanging over time. *Merriam-Webster's Collegiate Dictionary* defines "absolute" as follows: ". . . having no restriction, exception, or qualification . . . perfectly embodying the nature of a thing . . . being self-sufficient and free of external references or relationships."[8] A truth called absolute stands alone as self-evident to all. Such a reality is not influenced by any outside pressures to change or conform over time. The influence of an absolute truth comes to bear on all who come in contact, regardless of time in history or geographic location or social/cultural bent. The most obvious such "truth" is the law of gravity. The pull of the earth's gravity always has and always will hold a person's feet firmly to the ground. Many such absolute laws of nature exist that rule the universe. Violate one and the consequences can be tragic.

Absolute truths also exist in the world which serve to govern a person's relationship with God and his or her relationship with other people. These are fixed points of reference that do not change over time and are universally applicable to all mankind. Wise leaders internalize these truths and let them guide how one relates to others. Consider the following passages of Scripture from the Bible.

The God of truth—accurate, reliable, and trustworthy

> [5] Into your hands I commit my spirit;
>> redeem me, O LORD, the God of truth. (Ps. 31:5)

> [16] Whoever invokes a blessing in the land
>> will do so by the God of truth;
>> he who takes an oath in the land
>> will swear by the God of truth. (Isa. 65:16)

God's truth revealed by His Spirit, Son, and Word

> [6] This is the one who came by water and blood—Jesus Christ. He did not come by water only, but by water and blood. And it is the Spirit who testifies, because the Spirit is the truth. (1 John 5:6)

> [6] Jesus answered, "I am the way and the truth and the life. No one comes to the Father except through me. [7] If you really knew me, you would know my Father as well. From now on, you do know him and have seen him. (John 14:6–7)

> [17] Sanctify them by the truth; your word is truth. (John 17:17)

The Holy Spirit's role in regard to truth

> [13] But when he, the Spirit of truth, comes, he will guide you into all truth. He will not speak on his own; he will speak only what he hears, and he will tell you what is yet to come. [14] He will bring glory to me by taking from what is mine and making it known to you. [15] All that belongs to the Father is mine. That is why I said the Spirit will take from what is mine and make it known to you. (John 16:13–15)

12 We have not received the spirit of the world but the Spirit who is from God, that we may understand what God has freely given us. 13 This is what we speak, not in words taught us by human wisdom but in words taught by the Spirit, expressing spiritual truths in spiritual words. 14 The man without the Spirit does not accept the things that come from the Spirit of God, for they are foolishness to him, and he cannot understand them, because they are spiritually discerned. (1 Cor. 2:12–14)

Truth as guide and counselor

24 Your statutes are my delight;
they are my counselors. (Ps. 119:24)

59 I have considered my ways
and have turned my steps to your statutes. (Ps. 119:59)

Not only is God's existence a truth, a fact, a reality, but also the essence of His existence can be said to be truth. God remains a "God of truth." Since truth resides at the core of God's being, every word He speaks and every act He performs remains true, accurate, and consistent with reality. No "untrue" property resides in God's being. By definition, God never speaks a word or performs an act inconsistent with the reality of His creation. God is 100 percent reliable and trustworthy. God is not just a conceptual idea created in one's own mind, but He exists as an authentic being with whom one can have a personal relationship, a relationship based on all that is true about the world in which we live and lead.

Your view of God's truthfulness has an enormous implication on your view of the world. If you accept God's being as truth, then to the extent that you view the world through His revelation of Himself, you view the world accurately and truthfully. Conversely if you choose to view the world through a lens that contains a measure of "untruth," such as human philosophy, a false religious system, or "Hollywood," then your view of the world will be unreliable and inaccurate. When you look at the circumstances of where you lead through the eyes of the "God of truth," you can count on your worldview being reliable and trustworthy.

The God of truth has revealed His truth in at least three ways. The Holy Spirit is truth. Jesus is truth. The Word of God is truth. The more you interact with Jesus, the Holy Spirit, and God's Word, the deeper your understanding of truth becomes. This interaction can take many forms such as praise and worship, prayers of petition, thanksgiving, fellowship with other followers of Jesus, service, quiet time and devotions alone with God, and Bible study.

One of the primary ministries of the Holy Spirit concerns guiding followers of Jesus to what is true. The Holy Spirit helps Christians understand God's truth. God wants you to know what He has said and provides the Holy Spirit in the life of the believer to aid in this process of understanding.

Understanding God's truth requires spiritual discernment. Natural man (anyone not born again) cannot fully grasp God's truth, because such a person is void of the Holy Spirit. God's truth may even appear as foolishness to the lost. Those without the aid of the Holy Spirit often question or even reject the truthfulness of God's Word. Correspondingly the person who tries to lead others without the benefit of God's Word and the Holy Spirit does so blinded to what is really true.

The Apostle John proclaimed the Word of God to be truth: ". . . your word is truth" (John 17:17). The Greek term for "truth" is *aletheia*. Strong defines this term as follows: "objectively . . . what is true in any matter under consideration . . . in truth, according to truth . . . of a truth, in reality, in fact, certainly . . . what is true in things appertaining to God and the duties of man, moral and religious truth."[9] Swanson adds additional insight into the nature of *aletheia* when he states: "truth, *i.e.*, that which is in accord with what really happens, facts that correspond to a reality, whether historical (in the time/space continuum) . . . or an eternal reality not limited to historical fact."[10] From these definitions we can conclude that the words of God recorded in the Bible correspond perfectly to reality. Consequently Scripture provides a reliable source of guidance for making choices and decisions for one's life. The Bible is a fixed point of reference on which a leader can count as he or she navigates all that comes with leading others.

David understood the value of God's Word as a basis for his view of the world. David considered the unreliability of his own judgment and ordered the steps of his life according to God's Word. The wise follow the path of God's Word even when His truth appears to be contrary to or at odds with one's human perception of reality. David delighted in God's Word. He allowed biblical truth to saturate his mind and heart. In Psalm 119:24, David refers to God's Word as his counselors: "Your statutes are my delight; they are my counselors." The Hebrew term for "counselors" is *etsah*. Swanson defines this term as follows: ". . . advice, counsel, i.e., the act of telling someone what they should do based on a plan or scheme. . . ."[11] David relied on the truth of God's Word to give him advice and counsel as he led others. David's worldview was shaped by what he understood to be true from God's Word because he believed God's Word to be absolutely true for all people and all generations.

You lead in a culture where the predominant view of truth is relative. Most people accept the myth that truth changes based on circumstances and time elapsed. People who base their view of the world on such fallacy lead others blindly without the benefit of understanding what is real. The leader who claims to follow Jesus can gain a more accurate perception of the world by allowing the Holy Spirit to guide him or her to a deeper understanding of God's truth.

God's Word constitutes absolute truth that serves as a fixed reference point for a leader. The truth found in God's Word never changes over time. God's truth applies in equal measure to all circumstances. For a leader, God's truth provides an accurate and reliable view of the world. A leader can count on God's Word to help guide decisions and choices because the Word remains true. A wise leader develops a thorough understanding of God's Word and allows biblical truth to counsel and guide one's actions as a leader. Only the absolute truth of God's Word provides a leader with a navigation system that he or she can trust as one journeys to lead others.

Discussion Questions based on "Truth: A Navigation System for Leadership"

1. Given that God is a "God of truth," discuss some implications (reliability, trustworthiness, accuracy) of basing one's worldview and leadership on His Word.

2. List three ways in which God has revealed His truth to mankind. Discuss some things you can do to gain a more comprehensive understanding of truth given these sources.

3. Discuss what role the Holy Spirit plays in gaining an understanding of God's truth. Explain how vital this role is.

4. What hope does a leader have to lead according to God's truth apart from the ministry of the Holy Spirit in one's life?

God's Word stands the test of time as absolute truth.

The words of Scripture remain consistent with the facts and reality of this world.

What God has spoken and revealed in his Word applies universally to all peoples in every generation. What is true today was true yesterday and will be true tomorrow.

God's Word serves as a fixed reference point for a leader's view of the world and his or her navigation of the turbulent waters of leading others.

A wise leader develops a thorough understanding of God's Word and allows absolute biblical truth to counsel and guide one's choices and decisions.

PERSONAL APPLICATION EXERCISE

Write a short plan of action that will increase your understanding of truth based on God's Word. Include in this plan how God's truth will impact how you lead others.

Conclusion
What a Faithful Entrusted Leader Looks Like

An Entrusted Leader is a person of vision who faithfully serves the investment God has "entrusted" in one's life by using skills, character, and compassion to encourage others toward a common goal while upholding an Entrusted Leader's core values.

How would you like to follow a leader who consistently adhered to the seven core values presented in this book? Would following an Entrusted Leader, whose influence emanates from core values forged by biblical truth, encourage your heart? Imagine in your mind for a moment what such a leader looks like.

Think about a leader who makes choices and decisions based on a HEART oriented toward God's will instead of his or her self-will. Contemplate the benefits of being led by a person openly seeking God's will in every circumstance. How awesome might it be to follow a leader who possesses a heart truly willing to do all God asks?

Can you envision the rewards of following the leader whose life stands conjoined first and foremost to an eternal MISSION and not just short-term temporal goals? Visualize the positive impact a leader can have on others when pursuing an agenda that involves encouraging their spiritual growth as opposed to using them for personal gain. Picture a leader faithfully committed to the mission of Jesus Christ that supersedes all other endeavors.

Comprehend, if you can, the healthy leader-to-follower relationships that could be forged by a leader whose APPROACH toward others is based on a willingness to forego power, deny self-interests, and serve his or her followers' needs first. How refreshing would it be to see a person heed Jesus' call to lead by serving instead of by exercising authority. Conjure in your brain a person whose leadership is characterized by denial of self and serving others.

As hard as it might be to conceive, it is possible for a person to face the pressures of leading with unshakable STABILITY. Such leadership dependability comes from relying on a combination of skill, character, and compassion. Consider the sense of calm and security followers can have in the face of adversity and chaos when being led by a skilled leader who also has an impeccable character and a sense of compassion for others. Stability for leading others can be created by applying a balance of skills, character, and compassion.

Fancy a mental picture of a leader with a LIFESTYLE that is above reproach. Can you conceive of the confidence created by a manner of living that confirms the presence of self-discipline and self-control? How wonderful would it be to follow a leader with a public image that coincides with an impeccable private way of life. Followers are naturally attracted to a lifestyle that is beyond reproach and publicly demonstrates faith, hope, and love.

Imagine a leader whose FORTITUDE stems from an inner confidence that God cares and is in control. Others take note of the leader who prays to a higher power. Followers feel a sense of security when a leader faces adversity with a courage based on God's love and sovereignty that is forged by prayer. Real fortitude for leading others comes from faith in the love and sovereignty of God and the discipline of prayer.

Envision the impact of a leader with a WORLDVIEW based on the limitless expanse of God's perspective. Followers take comfort in the knowledge that their leader makes decisions from the vantage point of God's infinite view of the world, as opposed to mankind's finite view. A leader can stand firmly during the storms of life when anchored to the foundation of a biblical worldview based on absolute truth and the words of Jesus Christ.

The ENTRUSTED Leader seeks to help a leader establish a positive relational influence on followers. This book addresses every skilled leader's need to transform one's heart and develop biblically sound core values. Developing these core values naturally produces leadership behaviors that in turn encourage the hearts of others and promote healthy leader-to-follower relationships.

The Entrusted Leader's approach to leading strives to promote healthy and functional leader-to-follower relationships. The role of the Entrusted Leader in any leader-to-follower relationship includes encouraging the hearts of others. Through encouragement followers receive inspiration to become all God intended and to form a bond of unity based on love.

> [2] My purpose is that they may be encouraged in heart and united in love, so that they may have the full riches of complete understanding, in order that they may know the mystery of God, namely, Christ, [3] in whom are hidden all the treasures of wisdom and knowledge. (Col. 2:2–3)

From a single parent to a chief executive officer, the question remains the same: How can I influence and relate to those I lead in a more positive and meaningful way? God has purposely entrusted every follower of Jesus Christ with all the assets required to serve as a leader. God expects His Entrusted Leaders to heed a calling higher than "self" and to invest His assets in a manner that encourages the hearts of others. The development of a positive voice of influence among followers begins with a leader's core values.

The ENTRUSTED Leader presents a biblical perspective of seven core values that impact every leader-to-follower relationship. The choices a leader makes in respect to heart, mission, approach, stability, lifestyle, fortitude, and worldview ultimately determine how one relates to those who choose to follow and help forge a meaningful sense of unity.

The lessons contained in *The ENTRUSTED Leader* center on teaching a leader seven core values that can help a leader encourage the hearts of others.

The lessons contained in *The ENTRUSTED Leader* center on teaching a leader seven core values that can help a leader encourage the hearts of others. The goal of this book is for a leader to take ownership of these core values and apply them to his or her life. Once these core values are adopted and applied, a leader is well on the way toward leading in manner worthy of the calling of Christ and faithfully serving what God has entrusted. The core values of a leader taught in *The ENTRUSTED Leader* are:

1. A HEART willing to do all God asks.
2. A MISSION for leading characterized by a faithful commitment to multiplying followers of Jesus Christ that supersedes all other endeavors.
3. An APPROACH to leadership characterized by denial of self and serving others.
4. The STABILITY for leading created by applying a balance of skills, character, and compassion.
5. A LIFESTYLE that is beyond reproach and publicly demonstrates faith, hope and love.
6. The FORTITUDE for leading built on faith in the love and sovereignty of God and the discipline of prayer.
7. A WORLDVIEW founded on absolute truth and the words of Jesus Christ.

God will entrust all you need to lead according to His desires and intentions. I use the term "entrusted" to define a leader because I truly believe each follower of Jesus Christ who leads has been entrusted by God with everything he or she needs to fulfill God's purpose for one's life. Becoming the type of leader God desires and intends you to be requires faithful service to God's investment in your life.

Each leader must stop and ask questions such as: Am I using opportunities associated with my position of leadership as God intended? Am I faithfully serving God's desires and intentions? What am I investing my life in? God allows each of us to decide where, when, and how we invest the valuable assets He entrusts to us.

May every follower of Christ who leads be motivated to:

Invest faithfully in others

*And the things you have heard me say in the presence
of many witnesses entrust to reliable men who will also be
qualified to teach others (2 Tim. 2:2).*

and

Hear Jesus Christ say:

*[23]"His master replied, 'Well done, good and faithful
servant! You have been faithful with a few things; I will put
you in charge of many things. Come and share
your master's happiness!'"
(Matt. 25:23)*

Who wouldn't want to follower a leader committed to these seven core values? You may not be able to change the leader(s) you follow; however, you can change the way you lead and influence others. You can be the kind of leader described above. You can positively influence and encourage the hearts of others. You can start the journey whenever you want of becoming a source of encouragement to those who follow. You can develop healthier and more functional relationships with those who follow.

Notes

Chapter 2

1. *Merriam-Webster's Collegiate Dictionary.*

Chapter 3

1. James Strong, *The Exhaustive Concordance of the Bible*, G3860.

Chapter 5

1. Dallas Theological Seminary, Howard G. Hendricks Center for Christian Leadership, brochure.
2. James Strong, *The Exhaustive Concordance of the Bible*, H3824.
3. R. Laird Harris, *Theological Wordbook of the Old Testament*, 466.
4. Ibid.
5. James Strong, *The Exhaustive Concordance of the Bible*, G2588.
6. Gerhard Kittel, *Theological Dictionary of the New Testament (abridged)*, 416.
7. James Strong, *The Exhaustive Concordance of the Bible*, G2307.

Chapter 6

1. James Strong, *The Exhaustive Concordance of the Bible*, G1849.
2. Ibid., G3101.
3. Ibid., G4103.
4. Ibid., G2425.
5. Ibid., G1321.

Chapter 7

1. Dallas Theological Seminary, Dynamics of Leadership class notes, fall 1999.
2. James Strong, *The Exhaustive Concordance of the Bible*, G2634.

3. Gerhard Kittel, *Theological Dictionary of the New Testament*, 3:1098.

4. James Strong, *The Exhaustive Concordance of the Bible*, G2715.

5. Gerhard Kittel, *Theological Dictionary of the New Testament*, 2:575.

6. James Strong, *The Exhaustive Concordance of the Bible*, G1249.

7. Ibid., G1401.

8. C. Gene Wilkes, *Jesus on Leadership*, 18.

9. Ibid.

10. James Strong, *The Exhaustive Concordance of the Bible*, G2008.

11. Ibid., G533.

Chapter 8

1. *Merriam-Webster's Collegiate Dictionary.*

2. Ibid.

3. R. Laird Harris, *Theological Wordbook of the Old Testament*, 103.

4. James Swanson, DBLH, 9312, #2.

5. James Strong, *The Exhaustive Concordance of the Bible*, G5486.

6. James Swanson, DBLH, 9448, #1.

7. *Merriam-Webster's Collegiate Dictionary.*

8. James Strong, *The Exhaustive Concordance of the Bible*, H2889.

9. Ibid., H3559.

10. Ibid., H7462.

11. *Merriam-Webster's Collegiate Dictionary.*

12. John F. Walvoord, *The Bible Knowledge Commentary*, 2:73.

13. James Strong, *The Exhaustive Concordance of the Bible*, G4139.

Chapter 9

1. James Strong, *The Exhaustive Concordance of the Bible*, G1985.

2. *Merriam-Webster's Collegiate Dictionary.*

3. Ibid.

4. James Swanson, DBLG, 1178, #7.

5. James Strong, *The Exhaustive Concordance of the Bible*, G2889.

6. Gerhard Kittel, *Theological Dictionary of the New Testament*, 1:37.

7. James Strong, *The Exhaustive Concordance of the Bible*, G4102.

8. Ibid., G1680.

Chapter 10

1. *Merriam-Webster's Collegiate Dictionary.*
2. Ibid.
3. James Strong, *The Exhaustive Concordance of the Bible*, G1933.
4. Ibid., G3309.
5. Ibid., G5432.
6. Ibid., H6186.
7. Ibid., H6822.

Chapter 11

1. R. Laird Harris, *Theological Wordbook of the Old Testament*, 880.
2. James Strong, *The Exhaustive Concordance of the Bible*, G3339.
3. James Swanson, DBLG, 3565, #2.
4. James Strong, *The Exhaustive Concordance of the Bible*, G342.
5. Ibid., G2962.
6. *Merriam-Webster's Collegiate Dictionary.*
7. Ibid.
8. Ibid.
9. James Strong, *The Exhaustive Concordance of the Bible*, G225.
10. James Swanson, DBLG, 237.
11. James Swanson, DBLH, 6783, #2.

Works Cited

Dallas Theological Seminary. Dynamics of Leadership class notes. Fall 1999.

Dallas Theological Seminary. Howard G. Hendricks Center for Christian Leadership. Brochure (undated).

Harris, R. Laird, Gleason L. Archer Jr., and Bruce K. Waltke. *Theological Wordbook of the Old Testament* (electronic edition). Chicago: Moody Press, 1980.

Holy Bible, New American Standard Bible. La Habra, Calif.: The Lockman Foundation, 1960, 1962, 1963, 1968, 1971, 1972, 1973, 1975, 1977, 1995.

Holy Bible, New International Version. Grand Rapids, Mich.: Zondervan, 1973, 1978, 1984.

Kittel, Gerhard and Gerhard Friedrich, eds. *Theological Dictionary of the New Testament,* (electronic edition; abridged), Vols. 5–9. Vol. 10 compiled by Ronald Pitkin., ed. Gerhard Kittel, Geoffrey William Bromiley and Gerhard Friedrich. Grand Rapids, Mich.: W.B. Eerdmans, 1964-c1976).

Kittel, Gerhard and Gerhard Friedrich, eds. *Theological Dictionary of the New Testament.* Translated by Geoffrey William Bromiley. Grand Rapids, Mich.: W.B. Eerdmans, 1964. Originally published as *Theologisches Wörterbuch zum Neuen Testament* (Stuttgart: W. Kohlhammer, 1978).

Merriam-Webster's Collegiate Dictionary, 10th edition, includes index. Springfield, Mass.: Merriam-Webster, 1993.

Strong, James. *The Exhaustive Concordance of the Bible: Showing Every Word of the Text of the Common English Version of the Canonical Books, and Every Occurrence of Each Word in Regular Order* (electronic edition). Ontario: Woodside Bible Fellowship, 1996.

Swanson, James. *Dictionary of Biblical Languages With Semantic Domains: Greek* (electronic edition). Oak Harbor, Wash.: Logos Research Systems, Inc., 1997.

Swanson, James. *Dictionary of Biblical Languages With Semantic Domains: Hebrew* (electronic edition). Oak Harbor, Wash.: Logos Research Systems, Inc., 1997.

Walvoord, John F., Roy B. Zuck and Dallas Theological Seminary, *The Bible Knowledge Commentary: An Exposition of the Scriptures.* Wheaton, Ill.: Victor Books, 1983-c1985.

Wilkes, C. Gene. *Jesus on Leadership*. Wheaton, Ill.: Tyndale House Publishing, 1998.

About the Author

L. Hollis Jones, DMin, has held numerous corporate executive management positions, and is currently an investment manager, and the founder and CEO of The Center for Entrusted Leadership, an organization dedicated to leadership development for all walks of life.

Dr. Jones received a BSBA in administrative management, and an MBA from the University of Arkansas. He also holds a Master of Arts in Biblical Studies and a Doctorate of Ministry from Dallas Theological Seminary. His doctoral research and dissertation focused on the question of how to train the heart of a leader.

Dr. Jones is a teacher of God's Word, and has spoken and written extensively on the subject of leadership development. His mission focuses on mobilizing a generation of skilled leaders who adhere to rock solid core values, apply Biblical principles of leadership, and see the leader-to-follower relationship as an opportunity to encourage and unite others.

Dr. Jones has been married to his wife, Dawn, since 1981. They have two adult children and reside in Dallas.